LINES OF LIGHT & SHADE

Edited by Angela Fairbrace

First published in Great Britain in 2009 by:
Forward Press
Remus House
Coltsfoot Drive
Peterborough
PE2 9JX
Telephone: 01733 890099
Website: www.forwardpress.co.uk

FOREWORD

Poetry Rivals 2009 was one of the biggest and most prestigious poetry competitions ever held by Forward Press, and a talent contest like no other.

Poets of all ages and from all corners of the globe were invited to write a poem that stood out from the rest - a poem that showed true creative talent.

This vast collection, chosen by the Forward Press editors, is the result. I'm sure you'll agree that the diversity and richness of the poetry included is unique - and a reflection of the inspiration to be found in modern day poetry.

As well as providing an exciting opportunity for poets to showcase their creativity, Poetry Rivals has given today's poetry a public platform to be showcased and rewarded, as it deserves.

CONTENTS

THE POEMS

JEALOUS OR FOOLISH?

It seems that you have everything
money, fame, a fast car too
while I, it seems, have nothing
oh why can't I be more like you?
Your suits are cut at Savile Row
my threads are always off the peg
you're like a magnet to success
while I am left to scrape and beg.
The sparkling diamond on your hand
reflects the twinkle in your eye
if you can live a wealthy life
then surely somehow, so can I.
In depths of wanting and despair
consumed by greed and jealousy
I realise I've been a fool
and chide the envy deep in me.
I've tasted love and happiness
for a while I had your heart to hold
my riches are worth so much more
than any money, jewels or gold.

Linda Hughes

YOU AND I

So long we lived our lives apart,
Just friends, nothing more.
Our lives took us on our separate journeys,
Apart we embarked on our different life stories,
Neither one knowing what lay ahead.
Then one day our paths met once more,
Fate? Destiny? Who knows?
But now we live our lives as one,
No more you and I, just us.
I see my dreams reflected in yours,
Your love, an image of mine.
I live now for you, and you for I,
There's no more you and I, just us.

Victoria Abbott

PLEA OF A BROKEN HEART

Parting from you is not such sweet sorrow,
The anguish inside makes me wish for no tomorrow,
I yearn for one chance to correct my mistakes,
I'd make you the happiest person alive, whatever it takes.

The intense love I have for you is undying,
I believed I gave you the life you deserved without trying,
Arrived in the real world now and it doesn't work that way,
Given hindsight I'd never have had to beg you to stay.

So angry with myself for assuming I'd grow old with you,
When I was too blind to see I had to grow up with you too,
I'd give anything for a way of going back to give myself warning,
My world wouldn't have collapsed when I woke in our bed alone this morning.

I realise that without a lot of effort this nightmare cannot end,
And this destroyed heart I currently possess will never mend,
This realisation means my new life starts now,
I pray it can be 'our' perfect life and you'll forgive me somehow.

Steven Bloy

DISCOVER

Look closely.
No, closer.
Why is there precious water streaming down her face?
How can a big success feel like a failure?
I don't know.
Then look closer.
How can she feel ugly, when she doesn't know what pretty is?
How is she compared to a diamond, when she hasn't got
                                    a penny to her name?
I don't know.
Then listen carefully.
How can you question her misery, when you don't realise
                                    your own happiness?
How can you look at someone, without discovering yourself?
Look at you.
Look closer.

Shenin Anowar

LOVE IS . . .

(For William)

Love is a delirious madness,
a somersault backwards
into a dreamless night.

Love is a song without words
a tango of soft caresses.

Love scatters the days like leaves
and feeds your dreams
with peppermint sparkle.

Love embraces certainty
and makes millions sigh
with its rapture.

Love is like an actor in a play
without a script, masquerading
as an ignorance of monkeys.

Love does not ask for charity,
but should you offer your soul
in exchange for ecstasy,
Love will not refuse your request.

Do not play games with Love, for you
could disturb a basket full of funky trickery,
unleashing unthinkable revenge.

Love is a quantum leap into the unknown.
Love is not for the fickle or faint-hearted.

Emelie Buckner

A MOTHER'S LOVE

She bears down to give birth
To a son that takes her heart.
A new life is born on Earth
And a love you cannot part.

She's as proud as she could be.
As she sings a lullaby song,
Her love's for all to see,
Her bond so incredibly strong.

Caring for him through his infant years
And protecting him with all her might,
Wiping away his innocent tears
And keeping him safe at night.

She tolerates his cantankerous ways
And wipes his dirty nose,
Lapping up his childhood days,
While his curiosity grows.

Then comes the teenager from Hell,
With his temper ever flaring,
But she won't give up as she can tell
He still needs her caring.

Her little boy is now a man
And he's ready to fly the nest,
She knows she's done the best she can,
But still her heart won't rest.

She whispers the words, 'I love you'
As she watches her young man leave,
She knows it's what he now must do,
But still she can't help but grieve.

A new beginning, a new life
As he moves on to pastures new.
A first job, a beautiful wife,
But a mother who'll always love him too!

Diane Beamish

DIMENSIONAL TEMPLE

What were we?
The faith that I was gathering
Was scattered among the few.
Dreams were shadow-play stories
And someday to come true.

The magic of nature, futile,
The Ancients daubed with scorn.
The Earth is timed revolving
With day and dark and dawn.

I saw with given insight,
Celebrated with the clever,
But cannot reach across the universe,
And I cannot live forever.

I will ask and ask, for then -
Ah, the joy of knowing!

What are we?
The temple dwellers come to speak,
They hail the soul who dares to seek.

What will we be?
The wisdom that we will scatter
Will gather us to the few.
The shadow-play of gifted lies
Could never, ever come true.

Nature will await the brave
To tell her truth again,
But the world is slow evolving,
Secrets will secret remain.

We will see with given insight,
Have reward for each endeavour.
We can reach across the universe
And we can live forever.

We have been told, told, and now -
Ah, the burden of knowing!

Art Sloan

A DAY TO REMEMBER

Was it all those years ago?
We were amongst the throng,
Laughing and cheering for joy
As a young queen
On the way to her coronation
Passed by in a golden coach.

Throughout the night
We sat, we stood, we tried to lie down,
Not feeling the hardness of the pavement.
As the crowds grew
Our territory narrowed.
There was talking, joking and mocked groans
As strangers' feet encroached our space.
And yet -
We might have been friends for years.

At the first sign of dawn
A cheer was heard
Had we missed her?
Had we dozed off?
Oh no, just Londoners' wit,
As a road sweeper with barrow
Swept the road for the procession.

Then suddenly, a voice announced
Edmund Hilary's conquest of Everest.
For a moment my bones suggested
I had been with him.
Discomfort was soon forgotten.
Remember, it was all those years ago.
Breakfast packed the night before
Made a welcome interlude, with
A stretch in the park in turns -
We couldn't risk losing that prestigious spot.
Now, was it Green Park or Hyde Park?
I can't remember.
An atmosphere of fun and good will
Filled the waiting hours.
Suddenly - a rush of cheers from afar
The coach must be nearing.
Through a curtain of rain I saw Her Majesty and
I declare she saw me.

Was she on her way to the Abbey
Or on her return?
It doesn't matter now,
We were there!

Then as a bonus
The Queen of Tonga in open carriage.
She seemed unaware of the rain.
Perhaps the warmth of welcome
Replaced the sunshine she had left in her homeland.

At last it was over,
After all those hours of waiting.
Was it worth it?
Of course it was.
Would I do it all again?

Well here I am,
A comfy chair replaces the pavement,
The television avoids the rain.
The pomp and ceremony repeated
For the anniversary.
Whilst thousands of loyal subjects
Re-enact the scene;
Cheering and singing - 'God Save Our Queen!'

Sheila Marson

TECHNOLOGY!

I've paddled through the packaging
And looked at all the labels;
With military strategy,
I've plugged in all the cables

And now it's smiling smugly,
As it sits on the TV:
The shiny, silvery set-top box
Is grinning back at me!

It has amazing functions
(Or so the advert said)
Though I really know I shouldn't
Fall for everything I've read.

With its ultra high-definition
It scans for all new channels
And displays them with precision
On its liquid-crystal panels.

I've read the short instruction book
On how to set it up;
The longer one's still on the floor -
I'm summoning up the pluck

To peruse its geeky pages,
Full of trite scientific terms
In a litany of languages
And esoteric words

From Spanish to Swahili
And stations in-between
And what looks like hieroglyphics
In a hideous shade of green!

This whizz-bang new technology
Is really state-of-the-art
And it makes my fading living room
Begin to look quite smart.

I'm keen to see what things it does;
I'm dying to discover
If, instead of Big Brother watching us,
That we can watch Big Brother!

I've triggered all the switches
And twiddled all the knobs;
I've wiggled all the widgets
And tried to check the cogs,

But still the thing is leering
And refuses to come on
And now I've started peering
To see if the fuse has gone.

I check rainbow-coloured wiring
In spaghetti-like formation;
I've read, re-read and read again
To check the information.

But sullenly it simpers
As it sits upon the set
And declines each imprecation
To start: I'm now quite vexed.

I hit it and I thump it;
I try to use a spanner;
I shake it and tap it;
I'll resort to that big hammer!

As you have guessed, my patience now
Is wearing very thin:
If it won't work, I'll pick it up
And chuck it in the bin!

So now I yell and swear and curse,
(I'm sure my language has been worse)
But now it's getting very terse,
As you can see, penned in this verse!

So I go and fetch my neighbour,
Who's quite a clever chap:
He once drove down to Cornwall
And never used a map.

It takes him just one second
To make it come to life.
He spotted it in an instant,
Didn't have to ask the wife.

And so, in brief conclusion,
I've found out, to my chagrin,
That, as with all technology:
It works best if you plug it in!

C Richard Miles

AN EMPTY LOVE

Love like gold is precious but cold
The greatest story waiting to unfold -
Or maybe it's a diamond bought with time
Its appearance breathtaking, sublime
Its authenticity not easy to tell
At first sight, all looks well
The weight pulls true enough
The exterior appears to be quite tough
All the small and narrow sections
Shine through a million minute reflections
The seven colours shine on through
A rainbow you think is just for you -
But test the jewel under the strong light of day
The surface will slowly start to decay
Reflections fade, as colours deceive
The moment of truth. Stop. Breathe.
A lie uncovered, a truth to face
A silent soul, an empty place
Nothing gained, your time is lost
You check once more, aware of the cost -
The diamond is a phoney one . . .
Nothing but cheap zirconium.

James Carney

THE OLD CEMETERY

The sky it is trembling and I must follow the call
'cause summer rain makes better times too distant to recall.
The sky's lost its pigment and the clouds are far too low
and they are starting to flood … so I must go.

The night comes screaming! Alas, I cannot sleep!
I must follow the light or else stay here and weep
as now the cigarettes that once reminded her of me
conjure up such a different image in her memory.

Darling, please take me to the old cemetery,
I want to find a place where we can get married.
So, please take me to that old cemetery,
to just wander through, to think of the buried.

Explain to me in science, for I cannot understand,
what it is that makes me feel that I'm failing as a man.
Please be my cane, for it seems I cannot see,
maybe it's getting dark . . . but then again, it might be me.

Don't judge me on my failures! You cannot understand
what it is I've had to overcome to become this man.

Father, despite my failures now,
please promise me that you'll never stop being proud.
Mother, it was out of your control,
there was nothing you could have done to prevent me from growing old.

So, darling, please take me to the old cemetery,
I want to find a place where you and I can get married.
So, please, please take me to that old cemetery.
Or just wander through, and forget the buried.

Max Horberry

POETRY NIGHTS (UPON THE DEATH OF MY FATHER)

Remember, Dad, those dreamy nights,
We sat across the oak
Of Mum's old dining table -
And of poetry we spoke?

We burned the oil of midnight bright
As all the household slept,
And freely passed the whisky
As imagination leapt

From Keats and Blake to Wilde and Yeats,
Each stanza was suffused
With tears of rage and tenderness,
No passion was refused.

We lingered under Milkwood oaks,
And 'neath the apple boughs,
We wandered home as Hardy's folk
Were counting in the cows;

We listened to the nightingale,
Beheld The Grecian urn,
We gazed as Autumn's mellow fruit
To florid russet turned.

A waterfall of images,
I hung on ev'ry word;
And deep inside the switchback ride
Of strange new feelings stirred.

Your voice could shake the very walls
Interpreting a line,
Your operatic tenor sent
A tingle down the spine.

But in a trice your tone would fall,
You'd hunker closer in -
And then a sound one could discern
From a falling pin.

And as the sweet, soft summer night
Slipped slowly into morn,
And 'ere the lonely piper
Piped the gates of dawn,

We made a vow to ever let
The fire of passion burn,
And to these words of men long dead
For inspiration turn.

And so, dear Dad, I'll say goodbye,
But I shall ever wander -
Among the dreams you wove for me,
Into the brightness yonder.

John Brodrick

MOM

You said you would buy me the moon, Mom
That was if you could
And you've always looked after me
Like every good mother should

It's just one of the many reasons
Why you're the very best
Like the way you make me feel special
And that I'm capable of any test

What we've got is more than most, Mom
And I know this to be true
Because no one has the love that's here
Between us, me and you

So thanks for all the songs you've sung
And the stories that you've told
Thanks for checking my breathing
Even now I'm 18 years old

And for all the things I'll do in my life
I'd like to thank you for them now
For without your love and support along the way
I wouldn't even know how
Happy Mother's Day, Mom.

Daniel Pountney

COBWEBS

If I could rummage in your brain
And I could blow away the pain
Fill bin bags with your fears
And buckets with your tears
Throw them in the gutter
If I could just de-clutter
Your soul - hose away the stress
Replace with fonts of happiness

If I could spring-clean your brain
And buff up the parts that remain
Obliterate the thoughts that torment you
Hoover away the thoughts that prevent you
From reaching what it is you seek
Come in, in a pinny, maybe once a week?
If I could polish your self-esteem
Until I made it sparkle and gleam

If I could sandblast your defences
Place gold cushions around your senses
If I could compost the weeds of pessimism
Nurture and water the seeds of optimism
If I could tuck your inner child into a cosy bed,
Safe in the clutching of a favourite ted
Employ bouncers to keep your demons at bay
If I could, what would you say?

Would you let me help you to be free?
Oh . . . and . . . would you do the same for me?

Fran Isherwood

LOVE UNSPOKEN

They walk, hands held to silent night
One kiss beneath a dim street light
Without surrender, fear or grace
Their pounding heartbeats quick with pace.

Their entwined fingers lock grip-tight
A love hard broken without hard fight
Their anxious glances filled with thought
A chance, at least, they might be caught.

They part, embrace, then part once more
A secret love unknown to all
Without compassion, thought or care
A lie unspoken, a love affair.

Debbie Langham

CRY

Don't look down on me like I'm a failure,
I have given my best in life for sure,
I tried to be the best, day and night,
Nothing would ever work out right.

Don't look down on me like I'm a failure,
I already feel like my heart has a puncture,
I cry inside, hiding it well,
I was always a youth, never came out of my shell.

Don't look down on me like I'm a failure,
I've already seen a life full of torture,
Laugh all you want, laugh at all this,
It's my life you just won't miss.

Don't look down on me like I'm a failure,
I won't be missed by him or her,
In fact don't look down on me at all,
I can never answer your call.

Darran Ganter

THE PRICE OF FAME

He found success whilst still in his teens
but it could sometimes be annoying.
The lack of privacy was a burden,
life in the spotlight proved to be cloying.

He did his best to cope with stardom
whilst journalists exaggerated and cameras flashed,
but he steadily skidded off the rails
and on every front page, the news was splashed.

He clawed his way back, found some control,
continued singing, doing what he loves best,
but it can be lonely when you're at the top
if mistrust and confusion can't be suppressed.

Annabelle Tipper

INSOMNIA

I was lying in bed trying to sleep
When upon me inspiration did creep
Seems I have my best ideas at two in the morn
No matter how I try I can't help but be drawn
To the pad, pen and book
As words dangle like bait on a hook
In front of my mind and torment me so
They are my greatest joy and deepest woe
I scribble them down as they float on past
Just wishing they would let me rest at last
Frustration, relief and corrections abound
As onto the page the verses are wound
All my thoughts are on the paper vent
Then I collapse, at last I am spent.

Louise Venning

WHAT A SHOCKER!

I went to the doctor with this lump
that had appeared on my breast,
had I hurt it - was it a bump?
I'll go to the doctor's - this is best.

'Don't think it's anything to worry about,'
that was his answer to me,
'can refer you if there's any doubt,'
but his answer I accepted happily.

Six months later, again I went
to the doctor with the lump in my breast,
referral to the hospital this time he sent
to get examined and have some tests.

I was poked and prodded most of the day
scans and X-rays they also took,
biopsies taken and sent away
then the doctor had another look.

I asked the question, 'What is it?
Do you have the answer?'
To the floor and back I hit
when she said, 'Breast cancer.'

Elaine Murdoch

KAREN

You had such vibrance, rhythm and control
You held others in rapture with the purity of your soul.
You were the sun in a world of dark
And in your hands you held my heart.

Though your body has left this place
Gone from the world and its hectic pace
Your light shines on and your rainbow flies
Strong in memories, hearts and minds.

Helen Woods

THE HEARTBROKEN

She wakes up in the morning praying how life is . . . isn't a dream,
She feels like she's found happiness, life and love working
                                        together as a team,

He's the only thing she thinks of day and night,
She believes he's the one for her, he's the Mr Right,
She claims they fell in love at first sight,
Reality is what she must face and take a bite!

While she sits there praising how he treats her,
She knows not that he plans to cheat her,
Playing the player's game, it's like a curse,
He treats all his women like a nurse,
One-night stands, heartbreaks and tears, what could be worse?

She's up next on his victim list,
She's another girl that will soon be heartbroken,
Played like a doll, thrown away like a token,
It's like a game console filled with emotion!

Come next day she hears a rumour,
He's cheating on you, he thinks it's humour,
But the confusion starts to take over her like a tumour!

She decides to find out, clear her heart full of doubt,
She doesn't know if she wants him or whether to kick him out!

She follows him the very next day,
As he takes a different turn, meets a girl and begins to say,
'She's a fool and thinks I've gone to work, see the game I play!'

She realises she's been played and then admits
To being heartbroken and used! Her heart begins to split!
She tells him it's over, shut up player, save it!

She walks away in tears, heart full of pain
After being stabbed with spears!
I loved him so, why me? How could this be?
Her mind speaks as her heart hears!

She sits there now heartbroken,
Her eyes filled with tears and her heart full of emotion.

Sageer Khan

WHY?

Because when the ancestors came, backs whipped raw
They were very, very tired

Because when the grandparents' trialled hands blistered sore,
They too were so tired.

Because Mother deserves to retire in luxury, South of France.
Sacrifices need to count
Don't they?
She's so, so very tired.

So my children can be proud
Their beauty and talents shine.
But, I need to be the light that illuminates the path they take,
Make damned sure it's informed choices they make.
So my skin can feel the sun and I am finally home,

The failure and dysfunction I see, can finally cease to be.
So in the end,
Finally,
We get to pull up a chair,
Sit at table,
And finally feel
Just a little less tired.

Pauline Tomlin

KNOWING

I know I love but how can I
Believe in you before I die?
Their hearts were young, they lived for life,
and may I see a world, not strife,
I hope, I pray
I know how much we cry today.

Georgia Dickin

ARE WE STRANGERS?

I see your face
But I do not know you
I hear your voice
But it seems so strange
I feel your touch
But it feels so new
Is this all down to a simple change?

The way you once were seems so different to me now
Like the world has flipped upside down.
Is this a good thing
Or something to fear?
All I want is for you to be near

I want you to hold me and tell me you care
Tell me you need me
And that you'll always be there
But you are not you anymore
You have become something new
Is this the way that you will help me through?

Become something more than you once were
You are showing me the paths to choose
I thought I once knew you
But maybe this is the real you.

Eran McPike

MOTHER EARTH WATCHES US

When Mother Earth watches us, she starts to lose her temper
she'll blow a fuse eventually at the way we humans treat her
she'll build up such a swipe at the foolish things called 'Men'
she's capable of catastrophe, and she will if we do it again . . .
But we still push our luck, so she simmers and she bubbles
until she loses her once strong patience with our self-inflicted troubles
and since we showed such disregard she will, with one volcanic roar,
take us all down to the Gates of Hell where she'll dump us at the door!

Kathryn Swainson

DEPRESSED? NO, NOT I!

Depressed?
No, not I!
I just break down and cry sometimes.
But depressed?
No, not I!
Life just seems pointless at times.
But depressed?
No, not I!
I get numb with emotional pain sometimes.
But depressed?
No, not I!
I forget how to smile at times.
But depressed?
No, not I!
I shed tears without reason sometimes.
But depressed?
No, not I!
There's no reason to live at times.
But depressed?
No, not I!

Rahela Begum

NUMB

When we spoke last, I had no feeling,
Love had passed, yet remained,
Words were not at hand, nor my pain,
A house I once shared with you, stained,
Try as I might to feel again, all in vain.

Mark Chadwick

BLUE

Through the thick skins
I take a quick peep,
Rapid palpitations and then
My face turns green.

I sit on a bench
And gaze at the sky,
It's shimmery
And times fly.
Almost as if it attempts
To connect with me,
My soul now dry,
I seek inspiration from the sky.

As times move on
And so do we,
With skies the limit
We set foot forward,
We yearn,
We earn,
We fall and learn,
We establish, we demolish,
The journey, now its last leg,
Is blue, a deep blue.

Ridhi Parekh

TWIN

A womb with a view
A view of my twin
Sucking your toes
And kicking your head
Holding your hand
As I feel your heartbeat
Never questioning the nearness of another

There in our pram
Sucking your toes
Feeling your moods change
Loving our closeness
Feeling the bond
Part of another
Never questioning the strength of your love

So where did it go?
Lost in the years
Hidden by grief
And knowing
Blocked by the pain
Of not sharing
Never questioning there'd be another chance

To love you again
Like we did at the start
When our hearts beat together
And I sucked on your toes
And felt our bond
Part of another
I pick up the phone and feel the strength of your love.

Sarah Wilson

CEASE AND DESIST

Once again, the generations are dying
In the wrong order,
It's happened enough times before,
War always sends the young to die before the old.

Every time we were fighting for something,
But, now we can't remember
What, why, or even who to some degree.
Liberty gets a lot of airtime
But what's that to the dead?
Mothers' sons all safely tucked up
In the nation's flowerbed.

Danny Shaw

IS IT A SPARK?

Tearing families apart, the rockets start.
Widows, craters, orphans - these their mark.
No love, just debt, a world losing its heart.

The reds, the blacks, a gruesome work of art,
Depicting a dump that once was a park.
Tearing families apart, the rockets start.

The round Earth once whole, now cracked every part.
Lamp lost its light, lone dog lost its bark.
No love, just debt, a world losing its heart.

Child without mother and horse without cart.
Shrouded and lost, humanity dark.
Tearing families apart, the rockets start.

The sky all ablaze - gunfire a dart.
But far away, is it a spark?
No love, just debt, a world losing its heart.

Reporter's comments sound so tart.
But a rainbow-filled sky; hope in the ark?
Tearing families apart, the rockets start.
No love, just debt, a world losing its heart.

Morvern Tomison

DRIVING TEST

Just heard the good news today
You passed your driving test - hooray!
Throw your L plates away
Cos now you're on the way
To road rage, when you're stuck in a queue
Cursing and turning the air blue
Filling up with petrol isn't cheap
Each time you fill up it will make you weep
When you see the price
You have to pay for fuel
Just to get you on your way
And insurance costs are really cruel
Don't forget to pay your car tax too
Otherwise the boys in blue will be after you
Happy motoring.

Denise Peach

THE REVIEW

They say that when you die you live your life again,
If I was to review mine, what would I feel?
Regrets, sadness surely?

At my time to pass what advice would I pass?
'You're a fool! Now be strong and never hesitate,'
Or
'Have one ambition and never give up,'
And
'Life is like lightning, over in a flash.'

But how much of the night will mine alight
I want to see past the shadows, but with lighting,
I have only a few moments to capture full illumination

They say that when you die you live your life again . . .
All I can hope for . . . is when the time comes . . .
I will be more than happy to live mine again.

Jason Briggs

THE CHILD HAS CUT HIS HAND

The child has cut his hand
On a broken glass,
The blood is crimson
And like water
It spills onto the carpet.

'Why do you break
Everything?' she shouts.
'Why do you ruin my carpet?'
The child cries. The mother cries.
They both go to their rooms.

In her room,
The mother wipes her eyes,
Touches her lips, her skin,
Reapplies her make-up,
Lies on the bed, shuts her eyes
And rests.

In his room,
The child plays.
Blood on his toys. Oh dear.
More blood on the carpet. Oh well.
He feels a bit tired, a bit sick,
He lies on the bed, shuts his eyes
And rests.

In her room,
The mother wakes up.
Gets up. Make-up on the pillow.
Oh no.
Where is he? she thinks.
Soon it will be time for dinner.
She leaves her room.

In his room, the mother walks in.
Blood on his toys. Blood on the carpet.
Blood on his bed. Why me?
'Wake up,' she says.
He does. 'Look, Mummy,'
He says and points to his hand.
'I know,' she says.

Downstairs they go.
Plaster on his hand. All better.
She cleans. Upstairs, downstairs.
All the blood is gone. It's OK now.

Sarah Wright

ONE YEAR ON . . .

One year on, my daughter is 12 months old!
And yet through all those sleepless nights,
My love for her has not gone cold.
During those 41 weeks of pregnancy
I grew, she grew inside of me
That time of awesome mother-baby connection
Within my protection she grew perfectly
She came into this world pretty fast
She was a beautiful miracle in my arms at last!
How she has grown day by day, what a mystery
How she has blossomed hour by hour is a joy to me
Each smile, each breath, each cry
Has made my big heart sigh
She has been relentless in her desire to crawl and now walk
She is quickly developing an ability to talk
My daughter has stretched my heart to love her unconditionally
Her tenacity has surely inspired the hero in me
My hope for life has hugely grown
My faith in God has been reborn
My daughter, a gift from above, full of love, 12 months old
Delightful, honest, beautiful and bold . . . one year on.

Samantha Hlambelo

THE ONLY ONE WE'VE GOT

Look at our lovely Planet Earth
(Though it should be called Planet Water).
How will it look for your children
Or your great grandson or daughter?

Ask yourself, 'Am I bothered?'
Ask yourself, 'Do I care?'
Ask yourself, 'Can we make a change
Or are we simply full of hot air?'

Are we prepared to make a switch
From burning coal and oil
Or will we sit, like the frog in water,
And slowly heat up and boil?

Will we step out of our vehicles
Or is this all just talk?
Will we cycle, catch a bus
Or sometimes even walk?

Are we prepared to pay a little more
For wind, solar, wave
Or is it your pocket, not Mother Earth
That you think of when you save?

The problems are plain for all to see
And the problems are on the plane
As people board Flight 304
For Portugal or Spain.

It's difficult for us to avoid
Because it must be true
That Mother Earth is being drugged
With tonnes of CO_2.

Doing your bit for the planet
Might seem an effort (or a pain)
But ask yourself, is this a pace
That we can possibly maintain?

Has this made you worried?
Under the collar are you hot?
Let's hope so, as Mother Earth
Is the only one we've got.

Mark Cowan

THANK YOU

Thank you for giving me a chance
When no one else would take me on.

Thank you for believing in me
When everyone thought I would fail.

Thank you for listening to me
When no one else even cared.

Thank you for helping me
When others turned away.

Thank you for loving me
When I found no love elsewhere.

Thank you for getting me through
When others had given up.

Thank you for your patience
When everyone else had lost it.

Thank you for everything
When I really needed you most.

You are truly special
And thank you is not enough.

Love, Claire.

Claire Diane

GRANNY'S HANDS

There you lie.
Your hands
crossed above your chest.
So still.
So white.
So smooth.

You cut bread
with your hands.
And you spread butter and jam
a thousand times.
Forever you darned the
holes in the socks
of your family.
You carried water
from the well to the wash house
and you scrubbed the linen
with a brush and a board.
All this with your hands.

You chopped logs
for the hob and
you dug up potatoes
with your hands.
You mended the nets
and knitted socks for your men.
You stirred porridge
and plucked chickens.
And you raised pigs
and shelled peas and beans
for the Sunday roast.
All this with your hands.

You wiped away tears
and caressed rosy cheeks
with your hands.
You scolded and reprimanded
and you put the children to bed.
You prayed in desperation and in hope
and clapped with overflowing joy.
You stuck plasters on broken knees
and combed the tangles out
of your daughters' hair and

you decorated the house at Christmas.
All this with your hands.

In winter you chopped ice from the lake
and fed hay to the deer
with your hands.
You cooked stews full of strength
and baked cakes with raisins and apples.
You gathered wild garlic in spring and
planted a garden full of vegetables and flowers.
Each summer you carried picnics to the beach
and rubbed our sunburns with soothing witch hazel.
By autumn you roamed the woods for mushrooms and nuts
and filled the larder with jams and jellies and cheese.
And in the evenings you'd leaf through a book
telling us stories of a long time ago.
All this with your hands.

How often have we sat
with you in your kitchen
around the hearth, listening to your voice.
Talking, singing and watching
your hands.
These fingers so gnarled and bony from a lifetime of work.
These hands so reliable and strong, so rough and yet so gentle.
Your hands
that I have never seen idle nor still.
Your hands
that were forever moving, forever busy,
never resting.

And now,
there you lie.
Your hands
crossed above your chest.
So still.
So white.
So smooth.

Assja Baumgartner

POPPY

Why is this life in which we care
Devoid of time to stand and stare?
When surging through this living stem
Flows blood and hearts of mighty men

Beneath these roots and petals red
I feed upon the bones of dead
Where boots once slipped in muddy slime
Their souls and laces left behind
Prints of life from father, son
Dreams of freedom just begun

Here you are, your smile so light
A sea of poppies glowing bright
Petals bending in the breeze
I hold my head for you to please
I'm not the flower you espy
I'm every hero that's gone by
I wave at you so you might see
How bloody war has painted me

I shade the virgin stones that weep
I hide the trenches dug so deep
I shield the sound of screaming soil
I cradle souls of blood that boil
But in my heart I have a place
For each and every soldier's face

When next you see a poppy red
Please honour all our heroes dead
Make me proud to see your smile
Take some time to think awhile

Please pray and fight for evermore
To rid the stench of bloody war
What if this world was full of care?
There'd be no time to stand and stare.

Patti Savage

DANCE IS LIFE

I am a dancer,
I move and glide,
I'm dancing through life,
The future that only I can decide.

I remember my first dance class,
I was four and a half years old,
I didn't know my future,
The future that would unfold.

I remember my first competition,
I know I didn't lose,
I didn't know the future,
The one the spirit of the dance would choose.

I remember my first pointe shoes,
The way you stand upon your toes,
I didn't know my future,
Because nobody really knows.

I remember my first big achievement,
A little girl of ten,
It was then I knew my future,
I just wondered where and when?

From then I wondered when it would happen,
When I'd glide along the stage,
My future is to come,
And it comes at every age.

Only you can choose your future,
It could be smart but by chance,
I already know my future,
My future is to dance.

One day it will happen,
But first I have to go through strife,
But I will make it happen,
Because dance means life!

You see, I am a dancer,
And one day I'll be free,
Because I am a dancer,
And that's all I'll ever be.

Olivia Roach

HOME HELPS HEALING

Are you sick of things being hectic?
Does life in the fast lane make you moan?
Then you need a sense of well-being,
in a perfect world called home!
To help what's needed is a chill-out zone,
a room to call your own space.
Somewhere that's quite, calm and secluded,
away from the busy rat race.
Our pad is private and habitual;
it keeps us feeling safe and secure,
we can quietly hide away -
behind our own front door.
Life at home will always be there,
for us to go back to day or night.
Away from the hustle and bustle,
somewhere that feels just right.
We all have separate agendas,
often away from our humble abode,
in the know that home still stands
down the same familiar road.
Pets and animals can also share
With us, making it a joint habitat.
Any type - whatever our preference,
be it a goldfish, lizard or cat!
It can be just a retreat for sleep,
when it gets lonely, late and dark.
A place to stay - in a shop doorway
or even a bench in the park!
Everyone needs a resting place,
whether it's a flat, house or castle.
As long as it's peaceful, tranquil,
stress-free without any hassle.
There's time for meeting family and friends
around the dining table.
We should not take our homes for granted
if we are willingly able.

Clear clutter, keep in control -
and you won't get yourself in a tizz.
Your life at home should be amazing,
because it's where the healing is!

Trav (Sharon Caradice)

SUPERHERO

I went on a date,
blind. Restaurant.
He wasn't there,
I sat down to wait,
he turned up late,
of course. He wore a suit
and glasses,
his tie didn't match
his shirt.
I drank a bottle
while he waffled
and droned.
I got drunk.
I heard alarm bells
and he jumped up,
muttered an excuse,
he went to 'crime fight'.
Yeah right.
I paid the bill.

Lara Brown

THE DRIP

You were born as just another leaf of aural scenery -
I never even noticed when you plopped.
Nothing more than quaint and dainty blips -
Blending in the background; there and not.

But over time the fracture in the washer
Crawled a little further, to elongate the fissure.
The leak began to bulge with greater eagerness
In splitting the film that tried to hold the sac of water.

And now my inner mind was picking up a rhythmic tone
Emerging from the background - worthy of perception.
Nonetheless, the gap between the plips
Was evidently tolerable; bearable, if you like:

For after registration of the casual bleeding,
I forgot. But time wore on -
As the washer split a little more,
The drip became a conscious bearer.

You spoke again - but now with volume:
My brain had found a nidus for my consciousness;
A challenge for my psyche: tolerance.
After all, a drip is like a baby's cry: there's a threshold!

And now the gap between the drips had further lessened!
Nerves began to coil, and sinews tautened.
I gazed robotically at the tap -
If I could have a telemetric channel

Directly to the drip, to tell it, 'Stop!'
Otherwise I'll have to haul my lazy body
Up and out into the shed
And find some tools to fix the bloody thing!

I want to stay all stretched
And fuzzy,
And comfy
In my lazy chair - I beg you, please!

But as the baby has its way,
So your dripping reached the point of
Critical threshold, and I was bound to fate.
I couldn't stand it anymore.

I tried resisting one more time, but in the end
The manic screaming in my stormy head
Had hit the peak. I had to kill the tyrant beast!
I had to fix the drip for peace!

Mark R Slaughter

LAST WORDS SPOKEN

If you could choose your last words spoken
Would they be the type to leave hearts broken?
You know, the type that cause you pain
When you realise you can't take them back again
But as it's all been left too late
You fear you're riddled with only hate
Always asking yourself and questioning why
You left on bad terms and made them cry
Thinking all the time it was for the best
Never realising things would get in this mess
Now you're only left with an almighty regret
Feeling you'll never be forgiven, you'll never forget
The last words spoken just play on your mind
Wishing you could replace them with something kind
The type you always used to choose
Never realising they'd be someone you'd lose
You should always try and be the bigger man
By biting your lip, doing the best you can
Is it really worth the hurt in the long run
Knowing now there's nothing that can be done?
So what is the moral at the end of all this?
You should never leave without one final kiss.

James Williams

THE PRINCE'S RAPUNZEL

Once when a poor man's wife conceived
Her first child she did believe,
That to feed the family of three
A wish must be made to the sacred tree.

But the sacred tree did stand
On an evil witch's land
So she made the terrified husband go
To wish and wish their money would grow.

The wish worked and the family became rich,
But the witch saw their trick
And made them pay a terrible price
By taking their child from their life!

The child, Rapunzel, was placed in a tall tower
Deep in the woods and surrounded by flowers.
Rapunzel remained till 16 years of age,
Until a prince learned of the child's cage.

The prince happily believed the rumour
Of a delicate female creature.
He set out to seek the beauty
And marry her out of duty!

He spied the witch's way in;
Rapunzel's hair gleaming like a golden ring,
From the only window to the forest floor
As the witch descended once more.

Ready to save an innocent young girl,
Straightening up the prince did yell,
'Rapunzel, Rapunzel, let down your hair!'
So what a surprise when he saw a boy was there!

'And what do you want?' a sour face snapped.
No! thinks the prince. It must be a trap!
However no enemies spring to sight,
Just the prince standing, with a look of fright.

'Oh not again,' Rapunzel moaned,
'You came expecting to take a girl home!
How am I ever going to escape
When everyone who comes has the IQ of an ape?'

'They said you were female!' the prince protested,
Trying in vain to look uninterested.
'Well, I guess it's the witch who did that,
She's completely hopeless, blind as a bat.

But if you would help me escape,
I won't even hold you to a date.'
Quickly deciding, the prince yelled, 'All right!
Stand back; I'll throw you my knife!'

So Rapunzel climbed down;
Using his own golden hair
And turned to the eager-looking prince
Still standing there.

Smirking, Rapunzel leaned into the prince
And on his lips, he placed a kiss.
'I'm not letting you off that easy,
A marriage to a prince is too good to miss!'

So three days and one marriage later
On honeymoon, the prince had to confess,
Despite having no choice at all,
Rapunzel was better than any princess!

Natasha Wraight

SUNLIGHT

I laid upon the silky sand
And let the grains run through my hand
I closed my eyes, lay there awhile
And felt the sun beam his big smile.
The rays were warm, it filled my soul
And then at that point I felt whole.
For all I could hear were the birds in the sky
I breathed in the sea air and let out a sigh.
I knew the sun was smiling for me
And I smiled back as I looked at the sea.

Janet Jakubovic

PHOTOS IN TIME

Time rolls by
Dark clouds across a twilight sky
a long-lost photo of black and white,
faces from a sunken word
Drowned in quiet but eyes alight
eyes which sparkle through the night
eyes which look out over time
eyes that burn in foreign climes
Their gaze - the gleam of stars expired
a hope to echo each ghost's desire
And somewhere in the distance brews
though hidden behind those faded hues
A storm - the dread black vapours churn
time's blaze where in black fire does burn
But first the now is wreathed in shadow
as cool dusk looks set to flee
And through the storm - it's night pallor hallowed
still starlight falls pristine.

Tony McKenna

BEREAVEMENT

(To my late wife)

Now, now! Lord Jesus, make me now believe
since You have humbled me and taught me love
that, though I die of grief, I shall not grieve
when I shall see Your face and my lost dove.
Though Death persuade me mortal life is vain,
and though my darling in my arms lay cold,
yet may I know from Your example plain
Death shall release her, and her arms enfold
me once again, body and mind perfected.
Teach me, Lord, in my remaining years
to cleanse myself lest I should be rejected
by so pure a soul and left in tears.
Then, she in Heaven twice lost to me in Hell,
I in this sorrow must forever dwell.

Bernard Brown

TOO MUCH

The land of bread and butter,
That's what I heard you utter.
It should be the land of
Milk and honey,
I really need some money.

It should be paved with gold,
Or so I've been told.
It's not supposed to be old
And grey,
It should be light and gay.

I don't need bread and butter,
I don't need to stutter.
I don't want milk and honey.
I don't need too much money.
I've got my life and health,
That's all I need in wealth.

Rita Joel

FOR ALL WE OWN AND ARE

For all we own and are
days narrow into night;
for all we note, compare
the light and the half-light
we'll sniff the evening air
and still fall cowed, contrite.

For all we love and like
foul seasons follow fair -
monsoon and earthquake strike
for all we do and dare . . .
and time ticks up the stair
for all we owe, and are.

Kevin Saving

MIDDLE AGE

Middle-aged?
Don't make me laugh
I've only just started
The adventure of my life!

Earlier I was younger
It was all mapped out
I turned around today
And didn't recognise much

Suddenly I realised
I'm halfway through
And very soon
I'll be considered old -
Already am, to some so young

I don't think there is
A middle age
I was just young
Now I'm getting old.

Colin Galbraith

STIR OF ECHOES

I can see sometimes in my mind's eye
Things that will happen and I wonder why
Have I been here before, is it just unrest?
As I fight with the crowd and strive for my best
People who have come and gone for all time
Create a stir of echoes in a soul so fine
As I awake from the darkness, I am still a child
With my stir of echoes so comforting and mild
Is it two worlds, two hearts or two minds
That tell me my future is my past far behind?
I call for an easement to understand how
I can understand people as before and now
My stir of echoes is all I can be
My beginning, my end and my present to see.

Lee Cassidy

THE WORLD'S END

You do not know me or I you,
and each of us care not for the things we have or do.
Hopefully we share together one common goal,
to make this life a better place for everyone we love and know.
We know no one has much time in this fast-paced time of life,
all rushing to make material gains and achieve status in its own right.
After we reach our target of success, an emptiness takes over
as we look for something else.
Now is the time to listen to our inner voice, is the world we live in fair?
Do we all have the same conscious choice?
Do we say we love each other?
Do we really care?
How many of us really want to share?
So I know you don't know me,
and I don't really care.
The important thing that really matters is the world will
                              soon no longer be there.

Catherine Keepin

LIFE

Life?
Who knows what it's all about?
You are born to laugh and you are born to cry
You are born to wonder and you are born to die.

Life, it's a miracle!
You mustn't waste one day
Wondering what it will be like . . .
Lots of ifs and buts come and go away

Life is for living
That is what you must say
Life is good and life is bad, don't let it worry you
Sometime a day will come and then
You will know the meaning of life!

Ana-Marie McKeever

NOTTINGHAM LACE

A much younger man she met that day
He made her feel so bright
Took her out of the darkness she'd been living in
And once more back into the light

She loved him so deeply that she didn't care
What others would do or say
She just wanted him to be there
Every night and every day
But he left her with nothing, just tears on her face
And memories wrapped up in Nottingham lace

He took all her possessions, her silver, her gold
It all disappeared without trace
Just left the battered tin box that she'd hold
Full of memories wrapped in Nottingham lace

He didn't know what love was, only material gain could he see
Didn't understand her feelings because he just wanted to be free
All he left was an old tin box that she held to her face
Full of memories she'd treasured, wrapped in Nottingham lace

She'd remember what it was like before he came along
No smile, no laughter and in her heart was no song
The one thing he showed her was how to stand tall once again
Even through suffering, heartache and pain
The opening lid of the box reflected tears on her face
When she looked at her memories wrapped in Nottingham lace

She could not feel anger or hatred inside
Even though she'd lost her possessions and he'd dented her pride
He didn't know it but he left more than he took
The poems, the letters, the photograph book
These things brought a saddened smile to her face
In her old tin box wrapped in Nottingham lace.

Fred Gates

ON THE EDGE

Thinking, thinking, thinking.
Thoughts tumbling in my head
Like pieces of a jigsaw.

Walking, walking, walking.
Anxiety sets the pace,
Eating at my brain.

Talking, talking, talking.
Truth and lies entwined
Confuse my troubled soul.

Running, running, running.
Towards the finishing line
Of the never-ending race.

Falling, falling, falling.
Down a funnel of despair,
Clawing frantically to survive.

Drowning, drowning, drowning.
No one sees or hears as
I spiral out of control.

Margaret Rowe

WAGS

Hair extensions and silicone boobs
Designer shoes and bags
Chit-chat and gossip columns
Who are all these wags?

Hanging on an arm of a football legend
Flashing a pearly-white smile
Wearing a two-grand frock
While popping to the local shop!

What is all the fuss about?
And please tell me, what is a wag?

Rebecca Nicholls

TRADING PLACES

There was a time when one
Only needed to have one skill
Throughout your working life,
Well maybe two.
Overall, when you'd done your time,
Served your apprenticeship,
Traineeship, you were made.
Unions gave you help within all sorts of ways too.
In today's world, how many of us can say
They never lost their job? A few.

In today's world there's little
Which we can touch that's
Not somehow run by a computer chip,
So it doesn't need winding up anymore,
It does not click.
Whatever happened to using
Ring and open-ended spanners?
Remember famous brands,
Snail Brand, King Dick.

During my much younger days
Most mums did their main wash on Mondays.
If your kitchen had a microwave for
Cooking treats like scrambled egg
Or jacket potatoes you were lucky.

As for one-man buses,
Prior to them arriving, fellas,
When in your teens you might
Have fancied the female clippie,
Wearing her seamed stockings free of ladders.
What was your maths like
Prior to electronic adders?

Remember when there were no
Plastic front or rear house doors,
And due to retail trading laws
Barriers had to be put inside stores
To secure beers and spirits
From the public purse?

Rikki Makers

MORNING IN HEAVEN

I wandered in the garden, one morning warm and bright,
When dewdrops sparkled in the grass in brilliant gold sunlight,
The birds were singing happily, and the cuckoo, loud and clear,
Was calling out across the fields, a sound that brings spring cheer.
The woodpecker called, high above my head, from a willow tree,
And if he exists, I'm sure that God smiled down benevolently.

A small voice called out, 'Grandad,' much to my delight,
A little girl came running to me through the dewdrops bright.
Her lovely face surrounded by a frame of golden hair,
And I could only stand transfixed as I saw her there.
So innocent and so beautiful, a vision of delight,
And I felt overwhelmed with joy at this lovely sight.

Then, with her tiny hand in mine, we walked in Heaven's light,
Scattering dewdrops far and wide, like coloured diamonds bright.
She chatted to me constantly in her angelic way
And I wished that I could stay with her throughout that sunny day.
The most beautiful things in life are free, there isn't any price,
And in those precious moments of my life I dwelt in paradise.

In the future years to come, when I am old and grey,
I will remember, with great joy, the magic of that day.
And hope one day the creator will forgive my every sin,
Transport me up to paradise and call me from within.
I hope that He will welcome me through Heaven's open door,
And I will then say, 'Thank you Lord, but I've been here before.'

Philip Brown

THIS OTHER EDEN

The world outside sounds a wondrous place,
Great British Isles, you have far more grace.

Start where I dwell, the Essex coastline,
With seaside resorts to spend summertime.

Then quiet, gentle Suffolk just up the coast,
Peace and tranquillity will relax me the most.

We must go inland so we cannot miss
Great towering colleges standing sun-kissed.

Oxford and Cambridge lurk alongside lofty trees,
Clever academics are taught, learn and pass degrees.

A nearby visit to the homes of the grand,
And marvel after years they magnificently stand.

Move onward to Stratford, the home of Shakespeare,
Who wrote 'Hamlet', 'The Tempest', 'Macbeth' and 'King Lear'.

Norfolk next call, the delights of the sea,
Crab, mussels and oysters all ready for tea.

And you must see the villages down by the shore,
Glistening sea like a mill pond, you are bound to want more.

Up! Up! I must go to the counties much higher,
Industry and more fishing ports if you desire.

Now on to Scotland we must pay a call,
Lowland and Highland mountains, ascend but don't fall.

Have I got time to search for 'Nessie' so old,
Who is in the loch, bluey-green and dead cold?

Boat trips to the Orkneys, Shetlands and Skye,
Then a visit to Glasgow; Scotland, goodbye.

Yorkshire moors, heather-covered, grouse ready for flight,
Quick, here come the guns! Fly! Fly out of sight!

Green, green grass of home, we are now into Wales,
Daffodil and leek in my buttonhole, and fine-singing males.

One of the world's greatest writers born and lived here,
'Under Milkwood' and poems, I just love them so dear.

Dylan Thomas was so young when he prematurely died,
We are the poorer for this, and the whole world sighed.

Sea crashing against the rocks of Lands End,
Seagulls screeching they have much time to spend.

South coast resorts for holiday trippers,
Isle of Wight boat trips in the hands of good skippers.

Travel to France by ferry or train,
'Oh God! I'm so seasick . . . never again!'

The orchards of Kent, cherries, apples and hops,
Don't drink that much beer or look out for the cops.

Now I have reached London, the great capital city,
Impossible to view in a day, more's the pity.

Bright red buses and cars fly on through the street,
Watched by Nelson so tall, with lions at his feet.

Back now to Essex, my journey now done,
It's all in my head, maybe it's the sun.

One day I'll do it - well some, that's for sure,
'This blessed plot', this earth, I want no more.

Frances Pitt

A TRUE FRIEND

A friend to me is hard to find
Who treats you as if you were divine,
And greets you with a smile sincere
Whene'er you meet throughout the year.

A friend to me is willing and strong
They're close by when things go wrong,
With a supporting hand and a word of cheer
To help you wipe away your tears.

A friend to me is honest and true
With a heart of gold to carry him through,
Who looks on life as a joy to behold
A friend to have and a friend to hold.

A friend to me can never fail
To do their utmost for a pal;
In sickness and in health alike
As always, a friend for life.

Brian Russ

READ ALL ABOUT IT

Headlines are vital to papers
They rely on sales to exist
Quite often they are misleading
Body blows by pens, not fists.

There's smut and sleaze in plenty
About people in public view
No privacy if you're famous
They're watching whatever you do

Always there's saints and villains
Amongst those wealthy or poor
The wealthy can pay smart lawyers
To keep the police from their doors

Reporters harass everyone
Trying to be first with the news
Ignoring the grief and suffering
I'd not like to be in their shoes

We often read that 'dog bites man'
Or the crash of a real road hog
Publishers would sell millions
With the headline 'Man Bites Dog!'

So when I read news of sadness or pain
About people I'll never know
I wish all the newsprint to stop
Thus leaving the trees to grow.

Moira Hodgkinson

YES

We want people to be healthy and feel extremely fit,
hospital patients to get better very fast and quick.
Children to enjoy learning every day in schools,
listening to their teachers and respecting them and the school rules.
Places to be safer, more police to walk the streets,
so people can feel secure when they see them on their beats.
Roads to be updated, more lanes on motorways
to keep the traffic moving instead of endless queues, delays.
Maybe replace some speed cameras with flashing 'Slow Down' signs,
give some cameras the chop.
However let the ones stay that are on a dangerous black spot.
Look after our wildlife, we must do our best,
we have such beautiful trees where our birds can make their nests.
Keep our countryside spick and span, we should not be careless,
for it does not take to long for it to get in a state, a mess.
When we are sorted we can have a rest,
knowing that for the next generation we have done our best.

Sue Koert

OUR FAVOURITE UNCLE COLIN POEM

We will have fond memories of you
of all the shared moments with laughter
and tears and fancy dress through the years.

The happiness we have loved of camping trips
to dancing country and western video clips.
You loved to watch the football and cheer your local team
with your lucky bear sitting beside you.
How your luck will shimmer and gleam.
You were a fighter to the end
and you were everybody's friend.
For in the stars at night, tuck up nice and tight
When they scored a goal you used to make a din
and every time I looked at you, I saw your cheeky grin.

Amanda Renyard

TEENAGE DILEMMA

We don't believe in sin these days, yet I've slipped up somehow;
I didn't stop to think, back then; what mattered was the 'now'.
A moment's grasp for happiness and peer group pressure strong
Now I've a mega problem. Was I right or was I wrong?

Well, everyone I've spoken to says there's no problem here,
What happened was quite normal and your conscience can be clear;
So simple to get rid of 'it' and get a life once more,
But I'm not sure that they are right; my heart is very sore.

I've heard somewhere of centres, and they welcome people there;
A pregnant girl can safely go and find someone to care;
They give advice and friendship, yet they let you choose your way,
They'll stand by you - when you decide - and help you come what may.

One thing they do make clear to you, and with concern that's real,
You have a tiny life inside; for that they would appeal.
No foetus, quite impersonal, on life's scrapheap to throw;
Think well before you send it there: give it a chance to grow.

If you're not able to take care of the precious child within,
There are so many childless homes who'd long to take it in,
So give to one, their heart's desire, a little girl or boy;
Your courage will place in their hands the peak of human joy.

Ray Silvester

SUNDAY LUNCH

Sitting in the garden in the morning sun,
Sunday lunch 'prep' has just begun,
Who's that gorgeous blonde at the kitchen sink?
Perhaps she'll top my beer up if I give her a wink!

This is paradise, I couldn't want for more,
Now, 'Who the *##**!!?? is that knocking at the door?'
These are our days to enjoy undisturbed,
A moment in time in my own peaceful world.

If the family arrive it adds to my joy,
We got it 'just right' with a girl and a boy,
Happy with partners (both names the same), and
Well, you know how proud I am Bethanie Jane.

The 'toilet bell' announces 'food cooked with love',
By a woman whose name proves she was sent from above.
A joke or two later and all the plates clean,
'Where do they put it? It's completely obscene!'

Don't be sad, I have cherished it more than you'll know,
But I told you I loved you from the 'get go',
Where I may have travelled, no one really knows,
But you can bet . . . I'm sleeping off all those roast potatoes!

Chris Foden Davies

THE WINGS THAT FLY US HOME

Wayside poppies toss their heads
In the dance of a foreign breeze,
Fathers, brothers, lovers, sons,
We've left to lie with these.
Their song is sung, their lives are done,
Their spirits long have flown,
But I'm sure they'd say a prayer
For the wings that fly us home.

Over deserts where we may
Have perished in the sun,
Over oceans where our ships
In toil and peril run,
Over icy mountains, where men
Must fear but roam,
And in our hearts we say a prayer
For the wings that fly us home.

Like an eagle up she soars
To the air above the clouds,
Battle-torn with troubled minds
We sing or cry out loud,
For loving arms and tiny hands
That are ours and ours alone,
And eyes that wait and watch the skies
For the wings that fly us home.

Jean Jones

A BIRTHDAY

It was my niece's birthday
We booked a soft play for her first birthday
We had 19 kids in the soft play area
They were so happy to be there
We had to finish the birthday party before 6 o'clock
Because another party was booked in at 6
It was a dressing-up party we had
And she ate too much sugar beforehand
Then we did the cake - Princess cake
After all that sugar she was sick all over her mum!
She and her mum went home and got changed
And then we went to McDonald's
At the end of the day she was tired
She had looked gorgeous!

Shelley Batchelor

IN THE LIGHT OF THE NIGHT

When the clouds draw their curtains,
And the lands relieve a sigh,
And the seas adorn a blanket for all that lie nigh.

When the lover receives the apple of his endurance,
And the secret, escapes the day, is clear,
And the immoral live in no fear.

In that moment, in that time,
When slumber cannot meet the eye,
When chores cannot distract the mind.

Let me know the fate of souls.
Let me know where I lie.
Let me, for one last time, cry.

Cry for you, cry for me and cry for those who cannot see,
See the wonder which keeps the stars apart,
See that I only love a little.

Omara Nawab

SINGING BIRD

Singing bird, my silence about the way
I feel for you is making my whole world
Suddenly dark. I love to love you. Could
I be your soul food, singing bird, today?
What can I do to be your sweet lover?
Because my obsession for you is strong,
Like smoking cigarettes, although it's wrong.
My soul is cold and I need your cover.
Singing bird, I need a sign or a word.
If I could fly away and sing with you
Up in the clouds, I'd promise to be true
To the love you'd show me, my singing bird.

I've fallen in an instant, just like night,
And need you, singing bird, to bring the light.

Nike Ademuyiwa

REFLECTIONS

Once upon a time,
There were things that brought me down.

The first was love,
That sly, seductive clown.

The second, bereavement,
A wounding so profound.

The third, a bullying vulture,
Tearing at my carrion of grief -

(Behaviour beyond belief).

A trinity of suffering
When I was vulnerable or ill.

Still, leavened by life's tough school,
I have survived them all.

Vivienne Blanchard

ICONOCLAST

A professional poet! Don't make me laugh.
Many artists just play the same game.
Rearranging scrap, then calling it art,
The two things just aren't the same.

Honest toil is what you are short of.
You've conned us far too often, you know.
Get out there; use some muscle or brain,
Learn a trade or a skill you can show.

Ever thought of being a plumber?
Forty hours a week will leave you time
To play with the words of your language
And just maybe come up with a rhyme.

At least justify your time on Earth.
Don't pretend you're some kind of muse
Or imagine you're going to be famous.
You'll probably end up on the booze.

Mankind has to strive for existence,
Get out there and earn a crust.
If we rely on your type for survival,
We'll be grovelling about in the dust.

Come down from your ivory tower.
Hone your skills and with luck you'll be fine.
You might even write magic poetry
When experience has tempered the rhyme.

John Troughton

TO BE FAMOUS

I want to be famous
That's what I long
Be a famous songwriter
And write great songs
The most beautiful words
So all over the world
They can be sung and heard.

I want to be famous
Sing or dance on stage
Or be a top actress
And act in a play.

I was born to be famous
In a soap on TV
Be a famous movie star
It's what I want to be.

I want to be famous
In the spotlight
I know what I want
As it feels so right.

I want to be famous
A well-known writer
Even a great dancer
Write the best poetry
Or be a famous pop singer
That's what I want to be
To be famous - yes, me.

Lindy Roberts

YOU THINK YOU KNOW ME

You think you know me, what do you know?
What makes my heart beat fast or slow?
Do you know my mind, my every thought?
What makes me laugh or be distraught?
Do you know my likes, is it rain or shine?
Is my choice water or a glass of wine?

You think you know me, well here's a test
Do I like to be host or be a guest?
What makes me laugh, what makes me cry?
What makes me stay or say goodbye?
What makes me shudder and turn away?
What makes me tingle, goosebumps display?

What makes me love, what makes me hate?
Do I like to listen or debate?
Do I rise early or lie in bed?
Would I prefer to talk or leave things unsaid?
What colour do I like, what clothes, what shoes?
If it's silver or gold, what would I choose?

You think you know me, think, that's all
What gives me pleasure, do you recall?
Do I take the lead or want to follow?
Do I rush headlong into tomorrow?
Do I like the feel of winter's chill,
Or to the sun readily thrill?

You think you know me, that's a joke
I laugh so much I almost choke
You've never known me, you've never tried
You've never held me when I've cried
Doubts of love is all you sow
You think you know me, what do you know?

Barbara Lambie

COME ON, OLD SOLDIER

Come on, old soldier
Though you carry those wounds
You can still travel further
By the light of the moon
You feel battle-weary
And I understand why
But if you stay close to me
We both then can try

So rouse up your spirit
For the gunfire has ceased
Let's continue our journey
In hope and in peace
Come on, old soldier
We can treat all those wounds
Don't now be weary
For we'll be home by noon.

Stuart Delvin

DEATH

Death stands close to me,
His breath on my cheek like a lover's.
He is not pale,
His grip is firm,
His warm hand on my shoulder.

'Come,' he whispers, soft as a rose petal,
'Just a step, a mere step,
Across the bridge and all is done.
The fight is over, the battle won.

Just a step and you will sleep
A sleep of dreams, of peace, of bliss.'
He touches me, I see his face,
One kiss, my love, one last embrace.

Trevor Bentley

THE CYCLE MASTER

John's Bike Shop stood in a prominent position
To sell as much as possible was his ambition,
With cycles and spares plus accessories galore
Repairs executed, who could ask for anything more?

With greasy hands being part of his appearance
He soon presided over all manner of problems' disappearance,
The till bell rang out with monotonous regularity
All boded well for the future with clarity.

But no, what is this appearing on the distant horizon?
'Ben's Bikes' was the name and it's hardly surprising,
Competition got tough so it called for ingenuity
John put on his thinking cap to deal with this incredulity.

His window bore the sign 'Big Enough To Cope, Small Enough
                                            To Care',
Then on Ben's window appeared 'Coping and caring is not so rare
In nature we see it all through the year'.
John, not to be outdone, displayed 'Bike It You'll Like, It's Not So Dear'.

Now the competition has gone, John can breathe again more freely,
Ben's shop has changed hands to become a tanning studio by Keeley,
It is said, 'If you can't stand the heat get out of the kitchen'
And it's a well-known saying 'Truth is stranger than fiction'.

John Waby

THE POET'S TRUTH

The poet's truth, an open door
Releases thoughts, allowed to soar

The inner eye absorbs events
Simmer slowly left to ferment

Then pen and paper painfully blend
To tell the story, explain the end

My words will never turn the tide
Change the world, challenge pride

But someone, somewhere might relate
To my experiences, quirks of fate

Read on my friend and let's just see
The similarity between you and me.

Catherine Hislop

THE SPARK OF LIFE

The lightning comes crashing down all around me.
I am lost forever in this maze.
Electricity is shooting through my body,
As I stumble through the haze.

A loud crackle of thunder fills my eardrums,
I feel shaky and all alone.
I put out my arms in front of me to feel my way,
As I move aimlessly, deafened by the loud drone.

My mind screams to let me out,
The haze is starting to clear, but my legs feel weak.
My eyes open wide, with yet a new spark,
I am lost in the wonderment from which I seek.

As suddenly as it comes it stops.
There is excitement and anticipation in the air.
Then the heavens open up and I am singing.
I am soaked like a leaf, but all I can do is stare.

Kimberly Harries

DREAM BY THE STREAM

At the stream by the mill
He fishes there still
In the glorious September sun
As the leaves turn to brown
And carpet the ground
He fishes as he always has done

As he sits by the stream
He has time to dream
Of all the wonders he sees
From the first flowers of spring
And the first birds that sing
In the beautiful, leafy green trees

Now he knows at first hand
That it's all God's to command
As he's only a memory to me
For I picture him there still
At the stream by the mill
And that's where I'd rather him be.

Daphne Cornell

WHAT BLOWS AROUND COMES AROUND

Primitive man; he has to make fire
And primitive man's all around us.
We'll tell him the dangers, but it's his heart's desire.
He won't be denied; he'll confound us.

We may have washing out on the line,
Or be taking afternoon tea in the garden,
But he'll ignore our pleas; 'Please not when it's fine.'
He'll shout abuse and his resolve will just harden.

But one fine day, if neighbours' wishes prevail,
The wind'll change and he'll lose all his bombast.
The bonfire smoke he is making, he will inhale
And his ashes will make some great compost.

Edward Lyon

THE ROCK THAT WEPT

I watched the saline droplets well up into his eyes
Spill over and run freely to my great surprise.
He was my hero, my rock, my friend
And to my daily needs he'd tend
What disaster could cause such grief?
His face was a mask of disbelief
I later learned to my dismay
His final visit was to be today.

My health prognosis was never good
The medics had done all they could
I'd lived my life in a metal shroud
He was my dad and I was proud
That he called me son and stroked my head
He held my hand and sat by my bed
Alas those tears never before seen
Were there when they turned off my machine.

Fear not, dear friend 'tis but a poem
A darkened verse as my mind did roam
Inspired by a care-worn sigh
When someone asked if a man could cry.

Men are beings wherein emotions dwell
And experience life in every cell
To control one's feelings does not mean
That one is bereft, because they're not seen
A weakness is ascribed to tears
So Man has learned to hide his fears
Instead he cries within his being
And grieves without the whole world seeing.

L Burt

A FAIRY STORY

The old man is a character who has a tale to tell,
And when he has an audience he tells it very well.
It happened on a moonlit night (is how his story goes)
Admiring his vegetables, growing in neat rows.

The field by his allotment was prepared for harvesting,
But that night something caught his eye - a perfect fairy ring.
A circle patterned in the grass, shadowy and white,
Where fairy folk were said to meet, silently at night.
There and then, to his surprise, small figures could be seen,
In hats of red, with silver shoes and mantles of dark green.
Quietly and daintily they gathered in the ring,
And in the centre, holding court, was Oberon their king.

Alongside him the fairy queen was looking to one side.
She'd seen the old man standing there (he hadn't time to hide).
She spoke to him directly in a voice so crystal clear,
And in a daze he listened as he struggled with his fear.
'We never should be seen,' she said, 'we must not form a bond.
But as a sign of goodwill I shall wave my magic wand.
I'll sprinkle stardust on your land and fruitful it will be.'
With that they disappeared and there was nothing left to see.

And now his vegetables grow to quite enormous sizes,
And at the annual village show he wins most of the prizes.
Whenever he's persuaded his secret to regale,
He never mentions horse manure - he tells his fairy tale.

F Jensen

IT TAKES ALL SORTS

You don't need to be up with the lark
to take a smiling stroll through our park
see the birds glide on their soundless wings
hear the glee of the kids on squeaky swings,
I sit and muse, watching the rhythm of the shoes.
Vinnie jogs past, muscular, tattooed
he believes in his own press-ups
and many a damsel he has wooed
but today, alas, he has the hiccups.
On the bench Alfie enjoys a can or six
with the Dutch courage of his five previous convictions.
He shows his dog Narler new tricks
like the spilt beer he licks.
Flo knows that like the winds sway
her days are ebbing away,
all the more reason to make hay
she has been known to say.
Along the path trundles old Curly
who's long left behind the hurly-burly
the rush and the tumbles
now bread for birds he crumbles.
Bernard's writing a book
about how his life unravels
he's called it 'Gullible's Travels'
but won't allow me a look.
Rumour has it Vera was in showbusiness
if asked she'll rasp, 'Mind your own'
in a far from entertaining tone.
Not much goes on without Mick knowing
from Elaine's toenails ingrowing
to the dubious plants Tommy's sowing.
Some names have been changed
to protect the innocent
for, to be sure, no harm is meant.
'Tis a park full of life, full of vigour
can you find one whose heart is bigger?

Allen Beit

PITY HIM
(For Donald Crowhurst)

Pity him who cannot keep
Away from danger as it sleeps.
But has to poke and pry to prove
That if that snoring mongrel moves
With sling and stone he'll bring it down -
Then on to glory: homeward-bound!

Pity him who cannot help
Asking questions of himself.
Questions of future, present, past;
Which accumulate and at last
Burst like a bludgeon to a brain
So ill-equipped to take the strain.

Pity her who couldn't hear
The silent screams of someone dear.
Who never sensed the hidden wrong
Or kept at bay the madding throng.
But joined them in their cheers and shouts
Without a thought to say, 'Look out!'

Pity them with spirits high
Watching sun and sea and sky.
Separate; then coalesce.
(Unlike the mind that paced the deck)
Hoarse with 'Hurrahs!' and 'Hurry homes!'
Their words less ballast, more millstones.

But pity him, finally,
Cast adrift on stormy sea.
Vainly steering with rudder awry;
Log-book false, but conscience nigh.
Losing the fight for sanity
Walks the plank to eternity.

Bernard Doogan

A PICTURE OF AGE

I glanced at a picture
That was hanging on a wall,
A portrait of an old man
Standing wearily and small.

I stopped a while to study
That man's familiar stare.
The ageing features of his face,
His thinning, greyish hair.

His skin looks kind of lived in,
Revealing the effects of time.
The tribulations of his life
Are etched in every line.

Unforgiving shadows gather
Around his tired eyes.
He looks a bit like me,
In an elderly disguise.

The picture that had stopped me
Is not a portrait at all.
In fact it's my reflection
In a mirror on the wall.

I realise it really is me,
That fact I cannot deny.
I guess I'll grow old gracefully
As the years sneak by.

Mark Ainslie

THE RIGHT TO CHILDHOOD

When we think of how we spent our days,
Running through fields of golden rays,
We skipped, we jumped, we ran with glee,
Our hearts like seeds on winds of spree,
Now children watch everything with fear,
They look for danger, they sense it's near,
Childhood for them is different today,
Mothers tell them, 'Don't stray away,'
Our children today stay locked inside,
Videos, computers, they are their pride,
How safe the world was for us then,
To build a den down in the glen,
Is childhood for our children gone?
They have the right to have some fun,
To play outside without fear of harm,
To run through golden wheat of calm.

Winnie Curran

UNTITLED

I was a banker
Very poor
Couldn't afford
A new back door
To get a pension
Beyond my dreams
Not to mention
One of my schemes
Lend bank money
Every day, willy nilly
I know what you think
That sounds silly
The more I lend
With interest returned
Or maybe not
My pension improves
A great big lot.

Frank Oldfield

HOME

Home started in Dundee where I grew up
And played and learned and ventured out to school.
I think of family, high jinks and fun,
And making music round the piano stool.

Friends called at home and asked me out to play.
I'd have them round for cake on my birthday.
We'd huddle round the fire and change our clothes
And toast our bread on forks and warm our toes.

I'd skip and jump and bounce a rubber ball,
While playing 'one a leary' 'gainst the wall.
My teenage years were scary - bigger house
And mortgage, stress and monumental rows.

I moved from 'family home' and friends and kirk,
And graduated to the world of work.
And then went overseas where I felt sad
Cos 'home' felt far away with Mum and Dad

Until I married; then we moved around
And home was where my husband was. We found
Where'er we were, we'd make new friends and then
Have open house, serve Indian food to them.

Eventually we bought a spacious flat -
Full circle to Dundee. Now fancy that!
With central heating, laptop and TV -
A corner of a jute mill in Lochee!

At home I can 'chill out', feel safe, share love.
A happy home's a blessing from above.
But sad to say, for some, home's a disgrace -
A shack, or hut, or cell - a lonely place.

I pause . . . and think . . . when Jesus came to Earth
He had no fixed address or home. His birth
Was in a smelly stable. Yet 'tis He
Who says to weary trav'lers, 'Come to Me.'

'I'm going home,' was what my grandma said,
As peacefully she joined the faithful dead.
I realise, and breathe a grateful sigh,
True 'Home' is where I'm going when I die.

Lynda Samuel

GRANDFATHER WILFRED THOMAS

(A man I never knew. 1902 - 1960)

Grandad Wilfred, this man I never knew, who passed away before
I came into this world in the June of nineteen sixty-four
Who was the stationmaster at Stoke Golding until he passed away
Aged fifty-eight, he now rests in peace in the village cemetery

Wilfred came from Carmarthen with his wife Marie Hannah Francis
Marie passed away around nineteen-forty,
then came Elizabeth Gwladys
Elizabeth passed away three years before Wilfred,
his heart full of sadness
From what I've been told, he was a big man, gentle but stern
This is what Wilfred passed to me through the family gene

With help from local records, I have now found his grave
With my sister and my son we'll visit, a moment to save
The feelings I have are so many yet so few
For Wilfred was my grandfather, a man I never knew

There are so many people in the family who have passed on
To find any of them still living is why I carry on
My heart is in Wales, of where my roots belong
Wilfred, my grandfather, will help me sing this song

On this coming Saturday, 14th of February, 2009
I will visit my grandfather, Wilfred for the very first time
The emotions will build up during the morning drive
For when we walk towards Wilfred we will go back in time

Wilfred was stationmaster at Stoke Golding in Leicestershire
Working on the railway as he had done for many a year
Wilfred was my grandfather, a man that I never knew
However, thanks to local records, his grave I will now view.

Dylan Swann

FORBIDDEN TIME

Quiet time . . . waiting
All prepared, and just . . . waiting.
Timelines silently slipping by . . . uncounted.
Waiting for the first guests.
Pulse rate 68.
Anonymous pairs and single strangers.
A friend, a colleague, a somebody new.
But where are you?
Introduce Peter, say, 'How are you, Paul?
This is Penelope, had a great fall.'
I'm bored.

The sound of your voice!
Warm, melted butter starts to flow into hollows within my heart.
A void expands within my chest,
Echoing to the sound of faltering heartbeats.
Stay calm. Exterior normal; interior alive!
Pulse is hammering. Now 85.
There you are, laughing, talking with friends.
God, you're lovely!

Look this way, start moving across.
Bit by bit . . . bit by bit . . .
You see me and smile.
Those eyes I have surfed forever and
swum in their wonderful depths.
Tonight is no exception; they engulf me.
Pulse 97 and rising.

You are next to me, I feel your warmth.
You are beautiful.
Can't you taste my lips on yours?
Can't you feel my arms around you?
Can't you imagine that you do?
But no, being you, all that is taboo.
I shouldn't love you.
Signed; Me.
End transmission.

I cannot quell this passion, nor quench this inner fire.
I must not taste forbidden fruits . . . the sweetness of desire.
How do I know it's sweet?
I must not attempt to taste.

The creed is repeated and the evening moves on;
More boring people with evening dress on.

The room is full of shadows.
We are fireflies in a room of grey moths.
We pass, touch and two rainbows briefly blossom,
Then fade as we part.
Flicker, flicker, moment irretrievable.
So near, so far is hard to endure.
Remove the pain . . . provide a cure.
So go!
Goodbye
Goodbye
Stay, stay!
Goodbye
Goodbye
I just want to be with you!
Goodbye
Goodbye
Nooo!

Johnnie Atherton

THE LOOM

A loom sat in a lonely room
A loom craved the sound of its flowing tune
A loom was empty and missed its woven thread
A loom yearned for the hand through which its life fed.

A hand was crooked and sat broken on her knee
A hand could no longer conduct the loom's symphony
A hand that could deftly weft and weave
Now lay warped upon her lonesome knee.

A weaver sat within her lonely shed
A weaver would no longer create a tapestry with thread
A weaver's hand had flax and fibre interlaced with pain
A loom sat empty and held a pictureless frame.

Deborah Burton

A PRICE TOO HIGH (CARERS' RAP)

When the price demanded by love is too high,
Long days, short days, years passing by,
Carers holdfast: taking up the slack,
Sleeves rolled up, they're on their Jack.

Unqualified nurses' demanded sacrifice.
'Try more tea, dear. Come on, be nice!'
Teetering on the edge of personal abyss,
Wailing inside, keening for what they miss.

With no let up on the morrow,
Just another day of toil and sorrow.
Slogging hard from early light,
At every frustration and another fight.

Carers always die first, statistics show,
Worn out, defeated, always on the go.
While unburdened, the 'cared for one'
Happily lives on and on and on and on.

Not 'voluntary' work! Just unpaid.
Bowed and broken; nerves shot and frayed.
Shattered, living on a different planet,
Every sacrificial hour tested to the limit.

Caring isn't a choice, it's not a 'vocation'.
There's no chance of a fat promotion,
No direct lines of communication.
No one sane signs up for tribulation.

Without respite, without let up,
Day in, day out. Over-spilling cup,
Losing their own life's inner beauty,
Caught in a spiral of love and duty.

Stephanie Spiers

THE MERCENARY

Jack had hated his miserable wife
for all twenty years of their sad married life,
and now, he was sat in a pub drinking beer,
discussing with a stranger their chosen career.

The stranger, called Arthur (but Arty, for short),
killed folk for money, but never got caught.
And Jack found that he became quite fascinated
in ridding himself of the wife that he hated.

He asked Arty how much he'd charge for the killing
and Arty replied that he would be quite willing
to strangle Jack's wife for only a pound,
but he'd need to know where the wife could be found.

Jack told Arty his wife always went
on Friday afternoons to Safeway in Gwent,
and wore, every time, a red anorak.
So Arty agreed, and shook hands with Jack.

In Safeway that Friday, Arty was waiting
for the anoraked-wife that Jack had been hating.
And soon, he spotted the lady in red
selecting a bloomer of wholemeal bread.

Arty went over, and took off his tie,
which he yanked round her throat and left her to die.
But on his way out through check-out four
he spotted another red coat by the door.

So, just to be certain, he choked this one too
and made his escape, while the lady turned blue,
only to see in the cark park out there
another poor victim in anorak-wear.

So he choked this one also, just to be sure
(though captured on film by the closed-circuit viewer).
And the newspaper headlines which appeared the next day?
'Arty Chokes Three For A Pound In Safeway'!

Margaret Sanderson

THE CLEANER

A cinema, a dark old place
Where kids can go to feed their face
And watch a film or maybe two
But something's there, it's watching you.

And when you're munching on your sweets
Sitting with your bag of treats
And you have chocolate round your chops
Some ice cream, a can of fizzy pops,
Have you ever wondered where
The rubbish goes beneath your chair
And who cleans up when you're not there?

The film, it ends, you leave your seat
The cinema does not look neat
It's full of bags and sticky things
It's gross, it smells of onion rings.
Then who pops out and takes a sniff?
A 'cleaner' who just loves the whiff
But does he clean? Oh no, not likely
He eats the mess so fast and sprightly.

The 'cleaner' runs around the aisles
Just like a goblin, he never smiles
He's short; he's fat and smells of wee
He's really not my cup of tea.
His face is red from all the food
He's eaten, he is very rude
But is there more than just this one?
There is too much food for just one tum.

No, many more come crawling out
They run around, they scream and shout
They munch, they crunch, and they gorge their face
They think they're in an eating race
And in the blink of just one eye
The cinema is eaten dry
It's clean again, and smells no more
And there is no rubbish left on the floor.

So next time when you're in the chair
Of a cinema, think who is there.
The 'cleaner' waits with face so red
And while you're sleeping in your bed
He is eating all the food left there,
The food you left beneath your chair.

Andy Wheeler

PLEASE LET ME HELP YOU!

Please let me help you, my friend
Because I know that I can lend
A happy hand, a happy smile
Have a coffee for a while

Please let me help you, my friend
I will send you a card, oh it's bent
Never mind, send me one if you like
You can post it on your bike

Oh please let me help you, my friend
Because I know that I can lend
A helping hand, a happy smile
Have a cup of tea in style

Please let me help you, my friend
Got a problem that I can mend
It's a few odds and ends
A friend is a friend to the end

So please let me help you, my friend
Because I know that I can lend
A helping hand, a happy smile
Is a friend to the end
Yes a friend is a friend
Till the end.

Susan E Penfold

THE HOUSE

The landscape was white as driven snow
A shrouded figure walked with nowhere to go
Hunched and stricken the woman's face told a morbid tale
The moonlight on her face made her seem so pale

Up the winding path she gingerly trod
Hoping that this way would lead her to God
Hesitating and terrified she opened the door
Immediately sensing the warmth arising from the floor

In the darkened room a tall man stood up
A hot tea simmering was offered in a cup
She knew instinctively that he was gentle and kind
Not like the husband tied to like a bind

Here she felt safe, warm and swell
Never wanting to return to the living hell
Never having a real home for many years
Her eyes started streaming with torrential tears

The door slammed shut with a loud bang
A nearby church bell rang, rang and rang
She knew now that she would never leave
Lying softly at peace with a rose on her sleeve.

Catriona

RED RIDING HOOD

The fear returned
And I remained awake
A knot deep inside
And I began to shake.
These deep feelings
That were buried
From a long time before
Had begun to surface
And they began to roar.
Why had they come back
These feelings of hate?
The words of this man
Had rekindled a spate
And they rolled from my mouth
As a river in flood
He had made the words form
And they curdled my blood.
I couldn't believe
I could utter these words
But he'd unlocked a gate
And it seemed absurd
But I knew, to remain
Would be too much to bear
So I opened the door
And I ran like a hare
To a place of safety
From this monstrous wolf
Who would have gobbled me up
Under my very own roof.

Moira Whittley

CRUISE

'I've booked a cruise this year,' he said,
'I know you don't like flying,
No heights this year for you, my love,
Just sun and rest and dining.'

We boarded in Southampton
And we headed for the Med,
But when he asked, 'Where is our room?'
'The tenth floor is your bed.

And dining's on the fourteenth floor
And bathing next floor up,
And if you join in all the games
May even win a cup.'

And every dock we stopped at
The coach drove near the edge,
We went up every mountain
And hung over every ledge.

Next year I'll book the holiday,
I think we'll go to Spain.
I'll pack the bags, get in the car
And get on the first plane.

Julie Anderton

HUMUS

I bought a tub of humus today
Took it away
Looked forward to eating it
Got home
It had escaped
All over my plastic bag.
I licked off as much as
I could
Then I stopped and thought
This is my life
I find something special
Something I want
And it escapes from me
I can't win
I'm fighting a losing battle
Next time
I'll keep the lid on.

Ornella Bushell

POSTCARD MESSAGE

Poem you must travel
Go now into this world
Poem you cannot be mine alone
From that dream you are hurled

Poem go out and cheer
Travel around this Earth
Stay free and wander as is your role
Now I've given you birth

Poem return when your
Mission is completed
When you have touched all hearts
Your magic secreted

Poem only then when
On all shores you're scattered
Have you conquered, if so,
A whole world you have mastered.

Barbara Sherlow

LONDON TUBE

I board the train, it's half-crowded.
A tramp sitting further up the carriage.
An old grey shirt and holey, dirty jeans,
Chewing gum and looking mean.

A pretty teenage girl sitting opposite me.
A smart black fur coat, mid-skirt and white boots,
Applying bright pink lipstick in a mirror.
Jog here, jog there,
It's no wonder it goes on her.

It stops at Camden.
Oh no, a thirty-ish hippy man gets on.
Long hair, baggy get up.
Playing a guitar.
Bob Dylan 'Blowing in the Wind', it's a dream.

I'm quite skint,
But I search for a pound.
He thanks me -
Gives me a cheery grin.

A few stops more, a lady in red gets on -
Looking down and singing to herself she is.
Can't stop staring at her.
So much red.
Little Red Riding Hood is she!
Then she gets up and sits with me.
A little tipsy she is.
A teacher, she says.
So friendly.
No babies she has.
She momentarily seems sad.
She mentions you could film
All different characters on the Tube.
I say, 'I'll write a poem on the Tube.
About tonight -
Goodnight!'

Stella Robinson

THE CHAINSAW

There was an old bachelor
Who lived next door,
I was often awoken by his snore
Although he was very wealthy
He was not very healthy
And just as dirty
As an old boar,
He was so mean
He would not part with a thing
But hoarded things up by galore.
A tree surgeon by trade
He would often parade
Around the village
With his old chainsaw
Felling trees and bushes
He would oblige
Just to earn a few bob
On the side.
He was an old miser
With age he grew tighter
And banks were a thing of the past.
He placed all his notes
Under his floorboards
In a bag that was tatty and torn.
A pregnant mouse by the name of Molly
Spotted the bag and
Ripped out all his lolly
But would not rest
Until she made her nest
For her young ones
Who were yet to be born.

Doreen Brialey

BENNY'S BOOTS

Benny Hive
Took a drive
Inside his motor car,
He had fun
In the sun
Till it got stuck in tar.

Feeling hot
Out he got
The car was stuck like glue,
Ben cried out,
Gave a shout,
His boots were stuck fast too!

All was still -
On a hill
Benny saw cows grazing,
They had heard
Every word,
Wasn't that amazing!

With a moo
They came through
From the hill of clover,
In a line
In no time
The cows had all come over.

Then a cow
Pulled a bough
Down from a big oak tree,
Ben climbed on
Whereupon
A swing soon set him free.

But his boots
Just like roots
Had stuck fast to the street,
He sat up there
Feeling bare
In his stockinged feet.

From that height
He took fright,
'Oh, how can I get down?'
But a bird
Overheard
And then flew off to town.

From a steeple
She told people
All about Ben's plight,
Soon they knew
Said, 'Thank you,'
And the bird took off in flight.

All was well
For a bell
Told Ben not to fear,
He could see
From the tree
A red fire engine near.

In a while
With a smile
Ben climbed down the ladder,
Before long
Things went wrong
He was feeling sadder.

Boots and car
In the tar
Could not be pulled away.
Back, front, side,
Firemen tried
But there they had to stay.

Then bad luck!
Feet got stuck
No one could get free,
Till the cow
Pulled the bough
And they all got up the tree.

So once more
Benny saw
That things were looking black.
The firemen
Numbered ten
But none could get him back.

Then a man
In a van
Said, 'Hey, what can I do?'
He stepped down
On the ground
And he got stuck there too!

So the cow
Pulled the bough,
The van man climbed the tree.
All the town
Came around
To see what they could see.

Doctor Snow,
Baker Joe,
The blacksmith and the cook,
Policeman Stan,
Grocer man,
They came to have a look.

One by one
In the sun
All had to climb the bough.
Ninety-three
Up the tree,
How'd they get down now?

'It is four,'
Said Jack Moore,
'Milking time's at five.
Just an hour
In this bower
Then the cowman will arrive.'

'What a pity,'
Said Miss Kitty,
'The fire ladder was put away.
Up the tree
Are all of we,
Lost in every way.'

'We'll get down,
Farmer Brown
Won't step on all that tar.
For he will
Come by hill
And meadow, not by car.'

Right on five
Benny Hive
Heard the voice of Farmer Brown.
'Do not worry,
I will hurry,
I'll soon have you down.'

Soon with hope
The farmer's rope
Came from the field below.
'All take hold,
They were told,
'Don't rush it. Take it slow.'

The whole town
Then got down,
They laughed on the grass,
For they saw
Things galore
To the roadway sticking fast.

The next day
It was grey -
Not sunny, there's no doubt.
From the tar
Every car
And shoe was pulled right out.

But Ben's boots
Just like roots
Would never come away.
Deepest blue
They're on view
Till this very day.

This is true,
So if you
Along that roadway drive,
You will see
By the tree
The boots of Benny Hive.

But be sure
On your tour
That it's not too sunny,
For a car
Sticks to tar
And then things get rather funny!

Clive Melville Beeks

TEDDY

I have a little teddy
And really, I'm not a child
Why do I feel I need him
With his face so meek and mild?

He sits there in the armchair
I pick him up sometimes
And stroke his furry body
And finger his silky nose.

I should give him to some little girl
But the thought to me occurs
I should hate to see him lie
Quite forgotten out-of-doors.

So I'm keeping him around me
As a small companion
And his beady eyes will watch me
And be glad that he is mine.

Mavis Downey

MY CHOICE

Don't tell me what I must, or mustn't do.
I'm old enough to buckle up my shoe
And old enough to be let out alone
It's been some years since I was fully grown.
You seem to think that I can't manage on my own.

Just because I've always toed the line,
And until now we've both thought that was fine
And just because I've never answered back
You seem to think it's brain cells that I lack.
So now I'm telling you to please get off my back.

I may want to be a mouse, or make a noise.
God blessed me with free will. I'll make the choice.

Joyce Walker

AGE-OLD PHILOSOPHY

Spring sun shyly sends a single shaft
Of summer light to lift a silent heart,
A heart that longs and aches for inborn laughter;
Looking skywards, can we be a part
Of light and love, of softly opening eyes?
A sight to welcome gently parting lips,
Truly a sight that is no disguise
For a near but recognised eclipse
Of the mundane, everyday routine.
The tedious pattern of the daily toil
Whose logic cannot easily be seen
But nonetheless acts as a living foil
Taking our spirit to an unknown height
Where joy replaces sorrow in full measure
And drear darkness gives its way to light,
The earthly element of human treasure.

K M Inglis-Taylor

THE PERISHERS

'Oh Cynthia, do please be quiet.
You sound just like a football riot.
Go and sit right next to Jill
Before you make us all feel ill.'

'Iris, don't pull Mabel's hair.
Do stand up and move your chair.
To the corner would be best -
Far away from all the rest!'

'We'll now do the five times table,
One at which you should be able
Without cheating, to do well.
Susannah, what's that awful smell?'

'No it isn't Mabel's sweaty feet,
(now that's a thought quite hard to beat!)
Lavinia, now I know you're 'green'
(the greenest pupil I've ever seen!)
But don't think you can go to sleep
Because your head is full of sheep!'

'What's that Olive, she's an ass?
I really cannot let that pass.
You can go without your lunch,
And Lavinia, don't attempt that punch.
Olive isn't quite your size,
You don't even reach her eyes.'

'This class surely is the worst.
Today I feel that I am cursed.
I don't think I can stand the strain
Of shouting at you once again.
I'll be glad when this day's done,
I can feel a migraine coming on.'

Florence Barnard

THE DAY I MET CHERIE BLAIR

When you have spent most of your life
Suffering from panic attacks, agoraphobia and strife,
The last thing you need to happen to you
Is for your glasses to suddenly break in two.
Only an hour before you meet Cherie Blair,
Help, what a total nightmare.
Then on the next table you spot David Blunkett,
As you sit there filling your face with junket.
There is always someone worse off than you,
Especially at this type of do.
Then she comes over, Cherie Blair, and starts to talk to us.
It feels like a dream, we are chatting to the Prime Minister's wife,
Telling her all about my broken glasses and strife,
Telling her how we can hardly see.
She is so nice, as nice as can be.
She's done her homework, she knows what we were all about,
She impressed us, without a doubt,
I just hope I didn't stare,
The day we met Cherie Blair.

Pat Dring

UNTITLED

Let me take you to the land of happiness
Come and have a peep
Come to the land of joy
To the land of sleep

Off to the land of solitude
Into darkness I creep
I'm gently drifting off
To the land of sleep.

Terry Knight

MANIC DEPRESSION

My life alas, is like a seesaw,
Sometimes up and sometimes down,
My face either wreathed in manic smiles,
Or disfigured by a frown.

I've known times high in cloud cuckoo land,
And in the depths of deep despair,
How I long for those more stable times,
When I feel normal and aware.

Mood swings may take me to Euphoria,
Or leave me frozen with apathy,
This cross I bear weighs heavy now,
Please will you pray for me?

If I could dispense with medication
And flush these tablets down the pan,
I could lead my life on an even keel,
A happy, carefree man.

W J Dovey

POETRY

Is evergreen, immortal
A tonic for the uneasy head
A medicine for the sick
A teaching for readers
A crutch for the lame and crippled
A solace for a troubled mind
A memory of your existence
A gift to all
A spice for human endeavour
A pulse to progress
A light to the shadows and darkness
                    never condemned
A step in the right direction
To the horizon you'll never meet.

Dennis Parkes

GERIATRIC? NOT ME

Please don't knock my door, old age, I'm not in
I won't consider suffering your aches and pains
Don't give me that look, don't intimidate me
I'm adamant, determined with staying lovely

My nails will be varnished, my hair blown dry
I'll wear high heels, feet can suffer like I.
My dress, it will plunge, decidedly hot
Now where am I going? I think I've forgot

The neighbours will pass me, I'll give them a 'Hi'
I know I have changed in appearance that's why
I now walk tall with shoulders well back
No sticks or Zimmers for this little chick

Leisure and pleasure is what life's about
There's so much to do, where do I start?
Ride pillion on Harley-Davidson is this year's treat
Who is the driver? I really can't think

Go worry another old age, leave me in peace
This girl's not for wrinkles or incontinence!

Freda Symonds

TEARS THAT FREE THE SOUL

I didn't weep, I shed no tears when you said goodbye.
Yes, maybe my pride was hurt, but I wouldn't cry
But as the comforting life I knew began falling apart,
I knew it must be the strain of nursing a broken heart.
But time does heal pain, and a long time has passed.
My spirit is free and I am able to move on at last.
But now my eyes moisten when I think of all those wasted years.
Yet now I can weep, and at long last I can shed my tears.

Tony Beeby

RAT AND MOUSE

They met at the bottom of gardens,
The pink-eared rat and the mouse,
They met at the bottom of gardens,
Well out of sight from the house,
They met with twitching whiskers,
The dove-grey mouse and the rat,
Well screened by rotting cabbages,
Enjoying their evening chat.

Then one night, greatly daring,
Behind the garden shed,
The pink-eared rat suggested
That they should soon be wed.
And great was the rejoicing
Down in the rodent world,
In grand, pre-nuptial dances
They leapt and waltzed and twirled.

They wed in Hedgehog's garden,
'Neath trellis swathed in vine,
The feast was slugs and toadstools
And elderberry wine.
And there, at the end of the garden,
Now joined in wedded bliss,
The pink-eared bridegroom tenderly
Gave dove-grey mouse a kiss.

How short are life's bright moments.
'Twas so for mouse and rat,
For stealthily on velvet paws
Approached the neighbour's cat!
They met at the end of the garden
To mourn, lament and wail,
For all that remained of dove-grey mouse -
Her long and slender tail.

They met at the end of the garden,
The rat and feline foe,
And how rat wreaked his vengeance,
No one will ever know.
But from that day so bloody,
No more of cat was seen,
And still at the end of the garden,
Rat mourns his dove-grey queen.

Kath Hurley

ONE LAST CHANCE

Just twenty-four hours now left to go
The world will end . . . and I'll have to go.
I've got no choice, so it's no good swearing
Just pick up my heels
And decide what I'm wearing.
I've paid the gas and electric too
I've got no debts . . . so that will do.
But what about my Auntie Flo?
She has a birthday tomorrow, you know.
Oh dear! I wish I had more time
My head's in a spin and I don't feel fine.
I wanted to go and see a friend,
I also had my coupon to send.
Now I don't know where to start
Alas the time . . . it goes so fast.
And what in the world am I thinking of
I don't do the lottery and I don't have gas.
I've dithered about and lost the time
So I'll give in and sit and waste the time.
I'll put on the kettle and make some tea
And end my days in ecstasy.

Janet Kirkland

FANTASY

Sitting reading on my couch
cosy as could be
when there came a knocking
someone visiting me.
Looking through the window
to my great surprise
there stood a strange man
trying to sell me pies.
I said, 'What are you doing
knocking on my door?
Go away, I tell you
don't come back no more.'
Just as I had settled down
there came another knock
looking through the window
I got a nasty shock.
There on my doorstep
stood two more strange men
holding out their pies to me
I said, 'Go away,' again.
Back onto my cosy chair
in I went once more
I just could not believe it
another knock at my door.
This time I was ready
to sort these fellows out
it was funny when I looked
there was nobody about.
But there on the doorstep
a bright light shining bold
standing in the corner
like a pot of shining gold.
Bending down to pick it up
this thing they'd left for me
it disappeared before my eyes
'twas all a fantasy!

D Angood

BEING OBESE!

Life has been good, I'm enjoying my food,
I am told I am over-indulging!
I admit to being rude - look away if you're prude!
I'm afraid that my belly is bulging!

It would seem such a sin, if I held myself in,
And might give me a fit of depression!
I recall there has been, once - a time I was thin,
And eating was not my obsession!

I've been told I should try it, and keep to a diet,
Of exercise, I should take plenty!
But I don't really buy it, and tend to keep quiet,
It's too hard - when my stomach is empty!

With this exercise lark, I must run round the park,
And the gym is a place I detest!
With machines that are stark, lifting weights until dark,
Working hard there - without any rest!

For they say that it's bad, and it really is sad,
That we end up in such a poor state!
In the life that we had, and I fear that we're mad,
In becoming so much overweight!

So I'll take a step back, and get on the right track,
Overeating I'll definitely cease!
Then the food that I lack, will make my belt slack
And I will then not be - obese!

Ron Bissett

SLAINS CASTLE

At Crudenbay in Buchan, not far from Peterhead
There lies a castle in ruins, the people all are dead
So picturesque the settings and views so wild and free
Film producers thought it perfect
For Bram Stoker's Dracula fantasy
The author of the novel, his imagination ran free
The story of Dracula, a creepy tale, no glee
And so they made the movie and Dracula buffs loved it so
Mystery and magic the tale it goes to show
The cliffs around the castle, fiercely steep and still
And birds they cry their hungry calls
Need some herrings for their fill
Back to the days of long ago
With servants scurrying to and fro
And the family who lived in their stone abode
With large fires burning, to keep out the cold
Horses in the courtyard
Clip, clippety-clop places to go
Spiral stairwells and sunbeams aglow
Looking out the windows, gazing out to sea
The rocky coast of Buchan much mystery
And seagulls cry their warnings
Be careful everyone,
A little boy fell over, his life not long begun
There is now some fencing and a plaque of sympathy
So take care and tread very carefully
If you care to visit, be careful when you call
Dracula may be sleeping, hiding from you all
On the coast of Buchan, winds can blow severe
Ships they lie in shelter for life is very dear
And so this tale I've told you
Imaginary and true happenings too
At Slains Castle, please visit, do
A scenic walk at any time of the year
Snow flurries or sun to cheer
But beware, is Dracula near?

The only way is to go and see
I have been and he didn't get me
But it was daylight and I had no fear
Maybe at night another story to hear.

Sheila Macdonald

POETS EVERYWHERE

Where does a love of poetry come from?
The poets of the past!
Why does it last your lifetime through?
Their offerings are vast!
They encompass all of human emotion,
They fill your mind with dreams,
And, when you grow to 'Man's estate',
There they still are, it seems!

Poetry should be contemporary,
Tell the story of the day.
A record worth reading up on
When all of these things have passed away!
There is no rivalry in poetry.
We all see things from our own point of view.
But, I can admire a good poem from anyone,
And I am sure that applies to you.

As I scribble my way through life,
Commenting on joys, commenting on strife,
I'm happy to see so many kindred souls,
Scribbling away, till the great bell tolls!

J M Jones

FOR NICOLA WITH LOVE

There she is . . . there's Nicola
she surrounds us everywhere.
In that ray of sunshine through a window
bringing warmth and light to every room.
In that gentle breeze rushing past your face
that's like a feather touching your skin.
In that drop of rain that hits your nose or cheek
in that mischievous sort of way.
In that invisible touch that brushes your hair
which you gently flick away.
In that tiny delicate snowdrop showing so much strength
as it pushes through the winter's snow.
In the fragrance of a blossom that can capture your senses
and for a moment take your breath away.
In the song of the birds as they sing their tunes
in that happy and carefree way
and the grace and elegance of their wings
as they fly gliding freely, soaring high.
In the pictures of clouds as they form and take shape
and oh so casually roll on by.
In the leaves of the trees as they rustle away
and dance to their heart's content.
In the smallest of stars in the darkest of skies
flickering brightly for the whole world to see.
In the smile on the face of the man in the moon
shedding light on you and me.
In the roar of the thunder that makes you jump
then you laugh thinking, silly me.
In that song that keeps running around your head
that you find yourself humming and singing repeatedly.
In that contagious laugh you hear in a crowd
that makes you smile, you know not why.
In the midst of that brightly-coloured rainbow
that at its end promises a pot of gold.
And in the belief that whatever befalls in our lives
in our hearts true love never dies.
There she is . . . there's Nicola.

Love

Gez.

Gez Larkin

100

A TASTE OF YESTERDAY

I am from a time where:

Saturdays full of trips to market
fruit and vegetables were still
in fashion. And pink newspaper
allowed us to check the pools.

Children played football, cricket
on grey, gravelled streets, motor
cars still so few. Jumpers used
as goalposts.

Nights full of beef and beetroot
sandwiches fresh from the oven.
Grandparents drank Guinness just
because it was 'good for you'.

'They even went to work on an egg'

Watched 'Match of the Day' with
light just from the telly.
When Billy Bremner was king and
Jackie Charlton walked on water.

Where children seldom seen had run
of open fields. Adults still held upper hand
and boy they had some clout.

But we were the lucky ones.

Julie Walker

IN DAYS OF OLD

In days of old
When knights were bold
And Guinness wasn't invented
They made a brew
From Irish stew,
With yeast, till it fermented.
They took two sips
And sunk two ships,
Then laid the maidens plenty.
Then drunk the dregs
From wooden kegs
Until they were all empty.
The clash of steel
Brought them to heel,
The enemy grew much nearer,
And they did fight
With all their might,
But wished their heads were clearer.
Their arms grew tired,
Their bosom fired,
They needed strength anew,
And straight away found
In pockets sound,
A cup of Irish stew.
So there they supped
From silver cups,
And they felt the marrow rising,
Their armour felt much lighter now,
And the smell was appetising.
To England, Ireland, Scotland too,
To Wales and its fine dragon,
If we win this bloody battle then,
We shall all go on the wagon.
But, temptation is a funny thing
And may cause an addiction,
So they found a monastery,
Just to learn the Benediction.
So many pious monks were made,
Unknown to but a few,
In those Irish monasteries
They kept brewing Irish stew.

With honey added from the bees,
So potent it became,
Till all the people flocked to them,
As the drink soon found a fame.
An aphrodisiac so rare,
It caused some men to grin,
And even seemed to restore hair
When rubbed on head and chin.
This story's true, avouched by words
Passed down throughout the ages,
When told by men, and told again,
A-noted by their sages.
Exaggeration? Heavens no,
Well perhaps a mite or two,
But a warning now what befalls the man
Who is hooked on Irish stew.

Yvonne Sparkes

MY FINAL WORD

Now I have reached three score years plus ten
It is time to lay down my brushes and pen.
I have written my life story these past few years
With pictures and poems showing laughter and tears.

Despite any setbacks, I have enjoyed the time
Spent writing my story in pictures and rhyme.
My sight is blurred and the lines are wonky,
Which makes a dog look like a donkey.

I can no longer read a book, or walk a mile
But there is plenty around to make me smile.
A garden full of flowers, a child at play
A cheery greeting on a dismal day.

So please laugh with me
Because it is difficult to see
Doesn't mean my brain is dead
There is plenty of laughter in my head.

Lynne Walden

AN ELEPHANT IN THE LIVING ROOM

The elephant in the living room,
A phrase I do not understand,
It's said with a tone laden with gloom,
About a subject that's mutually banned.
But why an elephant? I do not know
As there is always one in my lounge,
I could understand if they said 'rhino',
Those horned-nosed beasts just scrounge.
I said to Nelly, just the other day,
As she sat at the sink having a perm,
'What's so absurd about what people say
Is surely every house has a pachyderm!'
Now what I would find embarrassing to note
Would be a gorilla riding a giraffe,
Or a Swiss Alpine yodelling goat,
Or a hyena who refuses to laugh!

But an elephant? It doesn't make sense,
As our Nelly will certainly concur,
I find that I can't just sit on the fence,
This conflict I cannot defer!
I demand that you desist your elephantism,
Or ask you not to be a pachydermophile,
Don't let our living room dweller cause a schism,
They are quite trustworthy, unlike the crocodile.
Try in future 'The volcano on the table'
Or 'The aircraft carrier by the phone'
Or make up another if you feel able
But please leave our house elephant alone!

Bill Hayles

UNDER THE WEATHER

Hello! Our kid . . . how are you?
I thought I'd drop you a line
I ain't felt so good m'self
But 'the missis', 'er seems fine

My varicose veins are playin' me up
Got arthritis 'n' vertigo
Bit o' trouble with my thyroid
And my BPs bin very low

Got catarrh, cramp and insomnia
Water on the knees
I'm takin' loads o' tablets
An inhaler for when I wheeze

I take two pills every mornin'
Round about half-past seven
Then I have to take four more
Just after half-eleven

I take one after dinner
And two after my tea
A special before bedtime
That's supposed to make me sleep

I still have my Guinness though
So that's half the battle
But I'm takin' that many tablets now
It's a wonder I don't rattle
Next week I see the doc again
To have summat else injected
But apart from that, our kid
I'm as well as can be expected

See ya, our kid.

Jean Mason

I 'AD A PIMPLE

I 'ad a pimple on me bottom
And it didn't 'alf 'urt,
When along came Nurse McMuffin
In 'er crisp, white, starchy skirt.

'Pop up on the bed,' she said
'Wiv your bottom facing me.'
I 'ad to pull me drawers down
Baring all, for all to see.

'This pimple's really large,' Nurse said,
'It's like a big red dot.
I'll 'ave to squeeze it very 'ard,
It's such a massive spot.'

Well, the spot exploded and the gunge
Sort of slithered to the floor,
The poor nurse went and trod in it
And skidded straight towards the door.

Just then, a doctor pushed the door,
'It Nurse right on the 'ead.
She did a double somersault
And landed wiv me on the bed.

Whatever did we look like
Spread-eagled in that way?
I looked like I was 'mooning'
Wiv Nurse's clothes in disarray.

The doctor's eyes was out on stalks,
I fought they'd leave 'is 'ead.
'Whatever's going on in 'ere?'
In disbelief he said.

We never did explain it,
We couldn't if we tried,
Nurse said we'd 'ad an accident,
But we laughed until we cried.

So if you've got a spot or pimple,
If it's 'uge, big as a bubble,
Then my advice, leave well alone,
It could cause you a lot of trouble.

B Webber

I LIKE POEMS

I like writing poems, I like reading them as well,
They take me to another land and keep me in their spell.
They make me laugh out loud sometimes; sometimes
                              they make me weep,
But every poem I ever read, I always have to keep.

I have some favourite poets; they are all different for sure,
But some write some silly things that rhyme, and make you
                              want some more.
Some are so much more serious and make you want to ponder,
Like Wordsworth's Lonely as a Cloud that set my mind to wonder.

There are Dr Zeus' cats in hats and ham and eggs so green,
They're very strange to say the least, but not the strangest I've ever seen.
Pam Ayres she writes about no teeth, she lost them from her head,
Then there's Robert Louis Stevenson who writes about,
                              he writes about a bed?

Now T S Elliot he did write, his cats he thought so real,
That his poems have lasted all this time and not lost their appeal.
There are runcible spoons and there are owls, and the
                              light of the silvery moon,
Edward Lear his limericks he loved so much, I could read them
                              from morn to noon.

I like writing poems, I like reading them as well,
You pick up a poem book; see if you fall under its spell.
Go on, pick up that book; give it a read for yourself,
Please don't leave that poem book all lonely on the shelf.

Rebekah Storey-Young

CHARITY BEGINS AT HOME

No sooner had we had Christmas
Than the charity bags all came
There's one for your heart and one for your age,
Although they all look the same
I thought I would go all modern
So these came at just the right time
It's better than leaving things in the wardrobe,
All hanging together in line
I pulled out that dress with the brooch on it,
It really is next to new
My waistline has now expanded
So I'll put in a skirt or two
So I'll not need those beautiful blouses,
The ones with the frill at the neck
And I'll throw in this twin set and trousers
Though we're not over winter yet
Now which bag should I be packing?
They are both for a very good cause
In fact it couldn't be simpler,
They collect from your own front doors
All done now, I've made my decision,
I've chosen to give to the aged
After all I'll be joining them shortly
As the book of life turns over each page
I've always liked that blue twin set,
It always looks good with pearls
And that dress with the brooch brings back memories
Of how we danced that night and pretended
We were still just young boys and girls
I'll need a skirt for the winter,
My this season has been very cold
And trousers are always much warmer
For legs that are growing old
Oh dear, the bag's almost empty,
This time I'll have to decline
I'll just keep the bags in the cupboard
And decide what to give them next time

I'm sure to find something to give them
When I buy all that modern new stuff
Till then I'm sure other folks will give plenty
And then they'll have more than enough.

Milly Holme

OUR FRIENDS WE KEEP

The years are passing swiftly now, this happens when you age.
A simple task like reading takes me a long time each page.
My lifelong friend, Ms Sarah Brown, she worries about me.
I try to show her glories on Earth to take her mind off me.
Look Sarah, lots of tiny newts all swimming on that side
And baby ducks who've just been hatched, they love being free.
The ice cream man just pedals fast or his creamy stock will melt.
It's going soft already, his kids won't get any for tea.
A space just where his table goes now is filled with plates,
Where tasty birthdays were held here, such wonderful dates.
A king inside his castle could not wish for more,
It is so miraculous, we love counting the score.
Dad and Mum put on best clothes, we do that as well.
Mother likes us to look nice be destination Heaven or Hell.
We enjoy variety, also the way we cook.
Together people wave to us, we open the book.
The years have slowed our paces but we can look good.
Slow but surely on we go through the neighbourhood.
Everybody knows us, and we know all of them,
Never changing, keeping faithful to our friends. Pro tem.

Barbara Goode

MANSLAUGHTER

First voice
I have killed a man
With cruel words.
Destroyed,
Enjoyed
By me.

I have killed this man
He walks,
He talks,
But he is dead.

I have killed my man
Castrated,
Emasculated,
By my words.

Repressed,
Depressed
And dreary.

I cannot will him back
The word will not return
I killed his soul
And mine now burns in Hell.

Second voice
So they said, 'It's a domestic
Down the road at fifty-three.'
The neighbours heard her screeching
Somewhere round half-past three.
I know this couple well,
Been called out once or twice.
He's a pleasant sort of bloke,
She's a frumpy little mouse.
Just now and then they start up
It's a funny sort of scene
You'd think it was a drama
About a king or queen
Or Anthony and Cleopatra
Not some ordinary folk

He's no great shakes to look at
Her figure is a joke
But the rage that they exhibit
The jealousy and spite
Grade A pyrotechnics
But it isn't every night.

Most times they're quiet and peaceful
He cleans the car, she shops,
The bingo's their excitement
And then it all goes pop
Well I'd better go and call there
Cool the flames and calm the storm
Why's he sitting on the doorstep?
Has she flung him out again?

Third voice
So she said I was less than a man
No fire in my belly, no guts
Too tame like a sheep
In wolf's clothing
All talk and no action
Just struts
Around she said

A poser, a poet
All talk and no life
Wind and water
And she wants wine
I gave her wine
Intoxicating words to make her sing
Inflaming words to raise the passion in her soul
Poured out my soul at her feet
She laughed at me
And now she has her action
Blood on the kitchen floor
The knife in haste
Distaste
Thrown cannot be recalled
My nightingale sings no more.

Pat Ammundsen

TRADING PLACES

There are millions of people
trying hard to survive
from disasters and illness
needing help to stay alive.

Yet here we are complaining
when someone hurts our pride,
and broken-hearted lovers
contemplating suicide.

Some people abuse young children
not caring what damage they do,
and the seriousness only hits home
when it's somebody close to you.

Take a look inside a hospital
see the people in despair
wanting to live their normal life
but needing our loving care.

It seems our personal problems
have come to make us blind,
but trading places with one of them
would quickly change your mind.

Norman Littleford

UNTITLED

F riendship is no good on your own
R eading old messages on your phone
I t's up to you to make the move
E ach day your friendship you have to prove
N ow is the time, don't be late
D on't hang about to find your mate
S o go outside and find your buddy
H elp each other play and get muddy
I t's on each other you can rely
P lay in the sun as the day goes by.

David Marland

LONELINESS

Loneliness is an unhappy state
Like staring at an empty plate
In a crowd you can be quite alone
The sad feeling of being on your own
Looking out of your window at people passing by
Wishing you were part of them, in your heart you cry
Hoping someone will give you a ring
Or maybe a letter the postman will bring
Where are all the people you knew?
They now seem to be a very few
It's hard if you have just lost your husband or mate
You sometimes think, what will be your fate?
Promises of, 'I will give you a call'
Or, 'We'll go out and have a ball'
True friends are precious to everyone
I wonder where they have all gone.

Jennifer Parker

THE SPOKEN WORD

Words should be used sparingly
dialogue concise
nattering ad nauseum
simply isn't nice.

Sentences should be minimal
keep them clipped and clear
waffling infuriates
and wears away the ear.

So take with you this wise advice
live it like I do
my point now fully realised
I bid you all, adieu!

Keith Miller

WHAT WILL BE WILL BE

A boy or a girl,
What would be nice?
It's just a bump
That twinges at night.
I can't lay on my front,
The heartburn is a pain,
And here I go -
Off to the loo again.

A boy would be lovely,
My own little man,
Oh, he'd want to play football,
I don't know if I can!
Rough and tumble,
Play in the mud,
Clothes all a jumble,
Hate baths in the tub.
A right little handful
But a bundle of joy,
I think I would like
A cute little boy.

A girl would be lovely,
All pretty in pink,
With dollies and teddies
And ribbons and things,
Pretend tea parties
And play dressing up,
Love foamy bubble baths
And my make-up!
A right little lady,
All sweetness and light
And looks like an angel
When she's sleeping at night.

Oh what it will be
I just don't know,
Thought I'd have feelings,
Shouldn't a mother know?
A baby's a baby,
With fingers and toes,
What it will be,
Nobody knows.

A new little life,
Healthy and happy,
They all look the same
When they're wearing a nappy!

Clair Hooker

THE PHOTO BOOTH AT THE CARNIVAL

Roll up! Roll up! Now don't be shy,
Draw back my curtain and step inside,
Don't miss your chance to be immortalised,
And all for a very attractive price.

Well hello, Sir! Please do come in,
There's a stool for you here; just give it a spin,
Almost, try another turn to the right?
Spot on, Sir! You've got the perfect height.

Now, if you'd be kind enough to pay,
We'll begin your shoot without delay,
A mere four pounds please, in the slot,
One . . . two . . . three . . . four! Thanks a lot.

Feel free to make yourself at home,
Straighten your tie, whip out your comb,
Gosh, I must say, Sir, you're looking smart!
So if you're ready, shall we start?

You see the oval on the screen?
Simply line your face up in-between,
Then press the button and strike a pose,
Oh! A cheeky wink, Sir, you charming rogue!

Wonderful! That's a splendid snap!
Sure to please the ladies that,
I think now, Sir, that we are finished,
Collect your photos outside, in just one minute!

Matt Worthington

INGLEWOOD

Each morning now for many years
I've at my window stood
And watched the birds and squirrels play
In the trees in Inglewood

I've watched them every season
From spring's buds to autumn's fall
And many hours of pleasure had
Watching the trees so tall

From dawn chorus every sunrise
To evening's last refrain
It made the days feel brighter
In sunshine and in rain

But now that scene exists no more
The trees are all cut down
And from my window now I see
A ragged patch of brown

They're going to build ten houses
Where once the squirrels played
And what was once a pleasant view
Will be with concrete laid

They talk of conservation
How our heritage is treasured
But to line a builder's pocket
Is how its value's measured

What took a hundred years to grow
Was torn down in a day
What gave the people pleasure
Was so easily cast away

It is left to legal vandals
And we don't kick up a fuss
What will we say when our successors say
'What have you left to us?'

If we tell them we stood meekly by
As their heritage was destroyed
I'm sure that with our stewardship
They will really be annoyed

So let our angry voice be heard
And be well understood
That we won't stand for the destruction
Of another Inglewood.

Ian Russell

MY WORLD

It is peaceful; it is quiet except for happy sounds,
I hear the birds singing, I hear leaves fall to the ground.
I see the happy faces of people who pass by,
everyone always happy, day and night, just joyful sounds.

There is no awful shouting, no arguments or fights,
people smiling, also talking, helping each other out.
Children playing happily, always being fair,
no teasing, no bullying, no one giving threatening stares.

Couples always happy, spending time together,
no arguments, no quarrels, no working all hours.
Looking in each other's eyes and saying, 'I love you,'
is something said every day with meaning through and through.

Every day is special and every day's the same,
a place where just good happens and evil stays away.
The air, the atmosphere, a pleasant place to be,
a place where only love reigns for all eternity.

I long to share this place, I do, but who has the time?
Who believes this place can exist? It all starts in the mind.
It is my place of retreat and I long to share it,
this place can be this world; all we need to do is care it.

Barbara Hamilton

WATCH MY PLAN UNFOLD

I have a plan
Watch . . . wait and take note
Pleasure is the key to my mentality
Spiritual conversation opens up my gate
The key to my lifelong mate

Watch this unfold
His heart has been torn, battered and bruised
My arms will heal the stabbing pain
My kisses will protect his tears from the rain
He will be in awe of my love
He will watch me with a passion of obsession
Drugged and high every time I run across his mind
Don't leave him alone too long
A man's need for love and respect is great
One little opening and my plan will unfold
I will be in complete control
Don't think he won't stray

Take not of this
This is not a game
You could lose the best thing that has graced your being
Like precious stones he will enrich my life
Not yours
He might miss you at first
But his focus will soon disappear
And his spirit will merge with mine
Entwined so immensely with my energy
Hooked into my gaze
The thought of you will become a distant faze

All I have to do is wait . . .
When you let him go without positive reception
Then this man will not escape
Watch as my breasts become his pillow
A comfort to his psyche
In all completeness I will show him true appreciation
My lips will speak all that constructs and strengthens his essence
All I have to do is wait . . .

Patience will reward my efforts
This man deserves to have the best
To be fed with first-class beverages and provisions

The riches of millionaires and nothing less

All I have to do is wait . . .
As he stares into my eyes, all outside our world will be a compliment
As in me his world will seem complete
All that the world has stored as rewards will throw down a performance
My sexual . . . intellectual . . . spiritual . . . and tranquility of my heart
Will draw in his complete existence
And your heart will ache for this genius
But then it will be too late
As he will be devoted to me
Captured in my desire to sketch his obsessions
Content in knowing that I won't run away
Satisfied in knowing that my love don't play
Unlike you, who let him down the other day

Then you will see me step in and remove you from his lifestyle
Be uncomfortable as your skin will crawl with regret
As he moves in with my way of thinking
Life's lessons I have learnt
A superior man will never get away
His superior intelligence will allow him to recognise the queen in my frame
So together we will create our hall of distinction
With precision and a little sensation
Sprinkled with re-procreation
And saturated with our total satisfaction.

Kyra Simone

LOVE BEING A MUM

I never knew that I could ever become a mum
I never knew my dreams, my goals, my life would change
My children are the key to my heart
They always unlock my fear, my pain
I watch them sleep
I laugh at their mistakes
I feel a deep sadness that I never felt before
My children are joyful, full of love
They constantly do things that are humorously funny
Being a mum is overwhelming
My children are God's gift
A smile from my children gives me an unknown inspiration
As well as happiness . . .

Josephine Ayala

SHAOLIN

A thousand voices scream my shame
Telling me they see my pain
Every muscle turns to lead
The worldwide population inside my head
Look at you! Fool! Trying to be great!
My self-esteem fails to commiserate
I'm sweating, I'm stuck, my legs glued to the floor
I pin my eyes to the open door
The rest, they see and snigger too
Look at her, what she's trying to do!
Not do, prove! I can be great!
Just give me a chance and I'll show my weight!
Fall on the floor, harder, yet again
Bruise my arms, my body, be like a man
Act like I can kill, injure, defend
And all the while I pretend,
I pretend.

Michelle Clancy

THE GREAT WORKS OF MEN

What would Mr Shakespeare say
If he saw what we did with his plays?
How we analyse every small syllable
As we're taught from that early age.
What did he mean by his phrasing?
Why did he choose that word there?
Maybe he'd tell us the reason
Or maybe there isn't one there.

What would Mr Mozart say?
As we pick at his melody
Trying to understand dreams
From notes in his symphony.
Why did he use that minor third?
Why play E flat just twice?
Maybe to tell us a story
Or maybe it just sounded nice.

And what about Van Gogh and Monet
With all their colours so fine
Trying to see through the painting
For just a simple line.
And what about Mona Lisa?
What is she trying to say?
Does she have some hidden secret
Or just Da Vinci's thought of the day?

So do they have meaning behind them
All these great works of men
Or are they just idle pleasures
Practiced again and again?
Will we ever find meaning behind them?
Will we ever find out what they hide?
Because maybe the only thing in them
Is the beauty on the outside?

Natalie Stafford

PETAL

This poem is not about an ordinary cat
This poem is about my cat
My cat called Petal
Or the nickname my dad gave her, Garfield
'Cause she ate so much
And had similar markings
Even though she was a tabby cat

This was no ordinary cat
This cat could stare at you
Until you gave her what she wanted
This cat knew what she wanted
She wanted that mince beef
And she knew you would give it her
In the end

This was no ordinary cat
This cat would have been in her cat litter tray
For twenty minutes
We all thought she was digging her way to Australia
She never made it there mind you
I found her laying in there once
She was afraid of my hair dryer

This was no ordinary cat
This cat was a cool cat, a rocker cat
She would be sleeping
I would be listening to loud music, like Nickelback
She wouldn't even move
My mum thought she might be deaf
But she could hear me calling her name to give her food pretty well

This cat is no ordinary cat
This cat knew how to have fun
Even if it meant keeping me awake at night
Throwing her toy around like it was a piece of meat
Or even her running around my room after her ball
Like a footballer on the pitch
She could give them footballers a run for their money

This cat was no ordinary cat
This cat was my cat called Petal
The one my mum called Bonsai Tree
The one my dad called Garfield
Well, all I know is she was my cat, Petal
And we will all miss her dearly.

Nadia Williams (18)

THE MULE AND THE PEA

'Fool!' said the mule as he sat on his stool,
'What me?' asked the pea. 'How dare you call me!'
The mule stared at the pea and with a fork in his hand,
Sprinkled sand on the pea and called for his band.
'You sit on your plate, not knowing your fate,
If I were you I would turn into a shoe
And flee from my life as a pea.'
Said the pea in dismay, 'Oh nay, oh nay,
I cannot turn into footwear today,
Nor can I be eaten; I'm here to play.
You'll have to choose something else from the tray!'
The mule then gasped and really quite fast
He dived his fork at the pea at last,
For he wished to dine on peas and wine
And it was after all dinner time.
But seeing the mule with weapon in hand
The pea rolled off the plate onto safe land.
He fell off the table, but to his surprise,
A chicken approached with hungry eyes
And viewing the pea as a wonderful prize
It pecked him up with some mouldy fries.
So the pea was no more, an as for the mule,
He hate all the sand, and the chicken! How cruel!

Janet Catherine Nevison

PERFECT HAPPINESS

Glossy pages, TV screen,
Bronzed Adonis, beauty queen.
Free of worries, free of cares,
Happiness is surely theirs.

Perfect bodies, perfect faces,
Lying in exotic places.
You too can have this perfect look,
Just buy our newest slimming book.

A nip and tuck, some pouting lips,
Smooth, taut face and slender hips.
Oh, how perfect you will be,
If you can only pay our fee.

Perfect mother, perfect dad,
Perfect children, never bad.
You could make your life complete,
Just buy our latest three-piece suite.

Had a trip, had a fall,
We're here to help, give us a call.
We can take away your cares
We can make you millionaires.

Got no money, working hard,
Never fear, pay by card.
Think it will be much too dear,
Have it now and pay next year.

It's funny that I always thought,
Real happiness could not be bought.
True perfection's just a dream,
You cannot buy your self-esteem.

Don't feel you have to have the lot,
Just thank the Lord for what you've got.
Don't listen to that selling pitch,
Don't make those advertisers rich.

I haven't got that perfect style,
I don't need much to make me smile.
A few grey hairs are showing through,
Some exercise is overdue.

There is one thing I can't resist,
Just add it to your shopping list.
It will not stretch your budget far,
It's that gorgeous, perfect chocolate bar.

Ann Cochrane

FINGERPRINT MEMORIES

Blinds black and red moon dots
Diamond stars upon your back
Glimmering eyes and happy smiles
Every moment is worthwhile.

Heavy clouds and falling skies
No need to seek shelter now
Laughing trees which no one can see
Capture the second before it flees.

Grass green and lakes glistening
Now I know what I have been missing
Butterfly kisses and hands held tight
Everything feels so right.

Raspberry blows and crumbs in my hair
Loving every silly minute that we share
Beer balancing acts upon my face
Nothing about you I would replace.

Total darkness but seeing light
Spoon close cuddles throughout each night
Fingertip kisses that can't be erased
Fingerprint memories that last
Always.

Donna Coles

DREAM

Stars shining brightly, widening my eyes,
Take me to another place, let me rise
Excel my potential, share my soul
Respect myself, because I am whole
The view is amazing, I shiver inside,
I am almost aware to acknowledge my pride
I inhale quickly and smile at the thought,
One day I will succeed in what my life has brought,
Standing up, I feel so alert
No longer fearful, feeling no hurt
I walk away with grace, a brand new me,
A bright light shining is what I do see,
Everything fading, loss of direction
Blurry eyed, I feel no exception
Somehow I am back, or so it may seem,
Smiles, no frowns, as it was just a dream . . .

Mel Whitechurch

THE FLOWERS OF THE MORNING

The flowers of the morning, remind me so of you
They have so many colours and their beauty is on view
With each bloom and every petal turning gently towards the sun
The flowers of the morning says that a brand new day has just begun.

By midday every morning each flower has been visited by a bee
They fly along so busily, a truly wondrous sight to see
As they visit every flower seeking nectar for their queen
The flowers of the morning are so glad that they've been seen.

You are so like a flower to me as each day you start to bloom
All darkness that was night-time has been banished from your room
You remind me of a busy little bee as you take on your daily tasks so fast
You are the flower of my every morning, oh how I wish that this day could
forever last.

Philip Anthony Amphlett

SPACES

Water flowing down dry stones,
trickles turning into streams,
hillside flowers of many tones,
pinks and blues and luscious greens.

The dazzling sun causes half-closed eyes
to peer through azure, shimmering haze,
a heavenly scene of cloudless skies.
Reflecting quietly, I sit and laze.

Alone and happy in my solitude,
I ponder my life. Contained in spaces
of different import and magnitude.
Most are known and seen by many faces.

Some into which only few can go,
who will discover all they wish to see.
However, certain spaces are so
hidden they only shall be known to me.

When brooks are shallow, rocks and stones abound,
weeds and earth clear to naked eye.
Tiny fish skim the surface, dart around,
viewed by all when walking by.

Brook becomes stream as down the hill it goes,
water deeper, bed is not so bright,
babbling less distinct. The earth no longer shows.
Fish still there, all but hidden from sight.

After many miles streams to river flows
where great ships sail slowly down towards the sea.
Like those spaces of my mind which no one knows
the brook, the stream, the river resemble me.

John Willmott

IMAGINE

Imagine having nothing but the clothes you wear
Imagine being dirty and having matted hair -
Imagine everything you touch and everything you eat
Is sullied by your filthy hands from dirt upon the street.
Some think we choose to live like this and look the other way -
Offended by our scruffiness as they pass by each day.
We all had different tragedies to put us in this plight
There's nowhere left for us to go - we can't keep out of sight.
Imagine, in a perfect world, if we all had enough . . .
Imagine no more scavenging and no more sleeping rough
All humans, with a basic right
To love and understanding and shelter from the night.
Imagine.

Margy Pagram

RECESSION

Grown men fill with fright
As recession starts to bite
The news is full of doom
As financial crisis looms
Is all to turn to gloom?

Interest rates are in a state
The pound is down as travellers frown
Inflation not so great, may even deflate
Underneath the crushing weight as
Stock markets begin to break.

Redundancies are high
We're all left to wonder why
We didn't heed the warnings
As debt just went on soaring.

And now we're full of woe
As we haven't any dough
Materialistic wealth not
So good for the health.

Rory Wilson

MY PLACE

Only when the clouds cover the stars
And when the moon is far apart,
Only when a stagnant sense of air
And a sharp tension arrives as a pair,
Only when voices raise like thunder
And arguments begin to get louder,
Is when I sit wonder . . .
Only that place is where I go
To be, to be whatever I want to be . . .
This is where I go to be alone,
No one knows me there.

They don't know about my past,
Or why I ran there so fast.
They don't know my name at all,
Or why I won't answer anyone's call.

I can be whoever I want to be,
For I am a stranger when I'm there,
They don't know who I am,
Or what my dried tears are about.
They take me as I am - no questions asked
I like it this way, I don't have to lie.

This is my place, my space . . . mine, mine!
Voices here are so quiet, it's nothing but a mere whisper,
The fine air I breathe is sharper than crystal and a lot clearer.
Excitement and the feeling of freedom drag nearer!

I can't spend long in this place
Otherwise they will recognise my face
They will ask why I keep returning
And wonder why I keep running.

When the stars appear bright
And when the moon doesn't give me a fright.
When the air and tension are nothing but a breeze
And when the voices begin to ease,
Is only when I return . . . back to reality
And leave behind this stupid fantasy.

Shamiala Amin

REFLECTIONS OF MY LIGHT

(Dedicated to the person who 'touched my soul' and helped me on my journey)

Beautiful rainbows everywhere - what and who do they remind me of?
I smile deeply inside when I see them, as their beauty lift my heart and spirit …
They are even more beautiful than ever this day - what makes them so?
Is it my mood - or the pureness of my heart?
Or perhaps I'm feeling closer to God today …
It is hard to say and know quite why; though something has changed!
Inspired by starlight; a deep sense of wonder - the rainbows …
Are they my thoughts, my feelings, my spirit?
Are they part of my dreams, my love or my peace?
So then, they must also be a part of you …
As you are part of my life, my light and my learning …
You are there!

Marie Carr

THE VAMPIRE'S KISS

A strangeness in this place she found where beautiful people danced around
With porcelain skin hypnotic eyes entranced by this to her surprise
He gazed at her he caught her eye she bowed her head now feeling shy
He crossed the floor and took her hand now mesmerized by his command
He held her close as they moved slow to the haunting music with a gentle flow
He kissed her lips of ruby-red it weakened her no words were said
Her heart beats faster he feels her heat yet from his heart she feels no beat
His skin feels cold to the touch his haunting eyes they hold so much
He has a hunger he needs to feed he craves the veins of life to bleed
His lips now search her soft warm throat in a slow dance as if they float
As she gives herself to him he hesitates just scratches her skin
He can't taste her blood that trickles slow he never wants to let her go
There is something special he feels for her not now he whispers in her ear
As he disappears into the night to quench his thirst before it's light
A heavy ache is in her heart as of him she wants to be a part
Come back to me it is you I miss I am ready to embrace the vampire's kiss

Anita Wakeham

BLACKBIRD

Morning has broken like the first morning
These are the words as day is dawning
Blackbird has spoken like the first bird
Is the tune that I first heard
Praise for the morning
I smile though I'm yawning
Dad is going out to work

I remember him singing in a deep baritone
Looking back I recall Mum used to moan
'Why are you singing so early?' she'd say
And Dad would smile, it was just his way

A farmer is Dad, a gentleman proud
A good-looking chap, he stands out from the crowd
He's worked hard all his life
Wind and rain, snow and hail
Trudging through the fiercest gale
To tend the flocks and feed the cows
Where his strengths come from I do not know

His home and family mean a lot
And on good manners he was hot
Dad is a good Christian gent
Church on Sundays we always went

I remember many things about growing up
But what I remember most, was the love
Shown to us kids by Mum and Dad
Don't get me wrong, they both got mad
I just wanted to tell them before it's too late
Hey guys, you made our childhood great
When I hear a song in the morning
It means that a fantastic day is dawning.

Kim Evans

NOT THE TIN MAN

I poured out my heart till the cup
overflowed,

she watched it spill over and said she
just didn't know.

Seemed to me she just didn't
care,

I felt so naked with my soul laid
bare.

The woman I love can be cruel and
unfair.

My heart like my jeans, is fading with
wear.

Paranoia and distrust poison the
air,

The love in her eyes now an unfamiliar
glare.

Long silences and arguments seem all
we share,

Shrugging her shoulders that ice-cold
stare,

Moments of tenderness becoming so
Rare,

My heart like my T-shirt, is starting
to tear.

I want us to go back to the
sunlight, fleeing this dank, dark lair.

I want us to untangle the knotted
wire, of our self-made snare.

I want us both to return to being,
that perfect love-struck pair.

I want to feel my heart race once
again, like the mad March hare.

But my heart unlike the tin
man's.

is beyond the wizard's
repair.

Mick Smith

WOULD YOU LIKE TO HAVE SOME TEA?

The little plump bear slowly sat down,
With his wicker picnic basket.
He would like to know if you will have tea with him,
But, the question, he dare not ask it.

'Oh, little bear, please do not be shy,
Do not be afraid to ask me.'
'Forgive me miss,' replied the bear,
'Would you like to have some tea?'

'Oh, yes, I would,' said Little Miss,
'I will have tea with you.'
The little bear began to smile,
He had found a friend so true.

They sat and ate and also drank
And soon became quite full,
The little bear looked to the sky,
The sky was now quite dull.

'Quick! . . . Little Miss, it's time to go,
The rain is on its way.
But thank you so much for having tea with me,
You made it such a lovely day.'

Sharon Reed

CAKES IN THE STAFFROOM!

There are cakes in the staffroom,
Or so I have been told.
They tell us to eat healthily,
How dare they be so bold!

There are cakes in the staffroom,
I'm going to take a peek,
I'm told that there are loads of them
And teachers eat them up all week!

There are cakes in the staffroom,
Fresh and sweet and yummy.
I'm going to go and pinch one
And hide it in my tummy!

Alison Deith

AS I LOOK UP AT THE SKY

I lie here looking up at the sky
As a river gently ripples by
I hear the sound of birds in trees
And the sound of buzzing bees

I feel the sun on my face
As I stare into space
The wind is blowing through my hair
As I lie here without a care

I smell the country all around
As I lie here on the ground
I think of all the things I've seen
And the places I have been

Cottages with golden thatched tops
And old-fashioned village shops
A quiet place with a scenic view
What a sight with the sunset too.

Alan Roberts

IT'S YOUR LIFE

Here, if you have just a few moments free
Stay for a moment and listen to me
I'm a very old lady, not long left to live
And now I have something precious to give

It's not jewels and riches, it's not property
They are not the important things in life you see
When you're old enough to look back on life
Through the good times or the trouble and strife
There are choices to make, so choose carefully
Your outlook on life is the person you'll be
Look for the bright side and it will help you
It will certainly influence all that you do

I hope this helps, it's true you see
So I hope you'll choose to listen to me
These words of wisdom were passed on to me
By a sweet old lady of 103

I was young at the time and just couldn't see
What she tried to convey to me
And now it's my turn to pass this to you
Please listen - for every word is true.

Sylvia J Clewer

GENERATION

G enerations, how many more will there be?
E nergy falling as fast as a cut tree
N o more laughter, no more play
E veryone's just taking this away
R ound and round the Earth it spins
A nd if people would just use the bins!
T ick-tock listen to the clock
I nnocent time is running amok
O pen air is running low
N ow please people, just say no!

Molly Austen

DUCKS

'Oh, Mr Duck, what's in your head,
To keep you in this riverbed?
It's cold and wet and murky black!
But happily you splash and quack.
There can't be fishies swimming round,
This river flows on stony ground.
So why do I still hear you laugh?
Are you happy in this murky bath?'
So said meddler to the drake,
Who sighed and quacked:

'For heaven's sake!
I do not know, oh, meddler man,
Why I like this muddy bank.
Or why I swim in grimy waters,
Thanks to your litter, flowing dank,
But Mother Nature says I should
It seems to work and it does me good
It seems it's just the way I'm made,
Like KittyKat who seeks the shade.'

So meddler man, he left the bank,
He thought that he had been outdone.
But secretly, old ducky knows,
He likes the muck because it's fun!

Vikkie Moule

WHAT ARE THEY?

I first noticed, as they appeared
That they weren't all the same.
Some were hidden and some were bold,
But all had a story to be told . . .

So I dressed them up with frills
And bows and sometimes a bit of bling,
And accepted them as a novelty
Which could teach my heart to sing.

Sometimes they got a little glance
From an appreciative passer-by,
Then I realised woo-hoo-hoo . . .
They could teach my heart to fly!

And this they did until the time
When they fed new life to grow,
And yes, their role had changed . . .
. . . Someone else had made it so.

Oh, then they became such wretched things
And nothing seemed to fit,
Until I discovered 'special effects',
To boost them up a bit.

One day I'll see they did their bit
As padding for a young heart,
And older and wiser I'll notice
A diminishing work of art.

No more glances and no more stares
But, still . . . sometimes a bit of lace.
Of course, then I'll know what they're for . . .
They'll have my life's story etched on their face!

Nikki Bednall

BECAUSE I LOVE YOU

Your weapons cut so deep
Because I love you
Your smile lights my world
Because I love you
I forgive you your sins
Because I love you
I want to be with you always
Because I love you
It pains me so

I carry your love
Your charms
Your friendship
Your pain
Your hate
Your beatings

Because I love you
I will be here always
Because I love you
I will let you take it out on me
Because I love you
I will die

Because you love me
You shower me with gifts
Because you love me
You tell me it all the time
Because you love me
You are sorry afterwards
Because you love me
I will die.

Lorna Smart

DUST, BUTTERFLIES, RAIN

Your first kiss had me dying
Your second kiss had me breathing
With your third kiss my walls fell down, all of me was shivering in tension
My veins felt like tightly wound violin strings
My heartbeats were an orchestra in my ears

You lay me down in your bed
I could feel where your body must have lain
There was still a soft embrace of warmth
The room was filled with your scent
It smelt like the fall of a rainstorm
I could smell the dust that is your daily companion

You lean down and kiss me tenderly
Your lips feel different now, like a butterfly's wings
They flutter across my face, closing my eyes
They feel like the dust of the earth, warm and alive
Everywhere your lips land a circle of warmth begins
Your lips leave soft tattoos of butterfly wings on my skin

The night is cold and dark outside
My skin is warm with your butterfly kisses
A heat starts searing through me, deep in me clouds are breaking
I feel like the scent of the rainstorm has entered my veins
The thunder of my heartbeat drowns out my thoughts
The lightning bolts flash through my flesh, I feel aflame

Your kisses are now too gentle
I arch my chest impatiently waiting for you to lift me
My heart beats out of me, wanting to pull your kisses within
You kiss my skin and I wonder why you don't burst in flame
I think the storm within is going to rip my body apart
I ache and everywhere hurts until your kisses become sharp and violent

Now your kisses become lightning bolts
Our bodies fuse into an ancient dance filled with the storm's rhythm
The clouds burst and my skin becomes liquid rain
The butterfly tattoos are drowned in the storm that pours through me
I cannot hold my body on the bed anymore, it aches to have you
Swirls of dust blind me and I enter the sun, purple clouds break within
My soul reaches paradise, my body is heavy lying in your embrace, the rain
quietens, I breathe.

Kim Koning

IN THE LIFE

In this life all of us go
Search for love, for sun, sometimes for snow
Whatever we find, we try to go
Further and further without law
Long time ago I was there
Taking my steps and going away
To find the truth in every way
Further and further by any way
But after such a long . . . long day
I cannot find my right way
This is life but anyway
At least I had a dream to keep away
Maybe one day I will find my way.

Tamer Mossud Mahmoud Abu-Amara

I WILL NEVER LEAVE YOU

As I sit here and watch as you grow
It hurts to think; one day soon I'll have to go
I won't be here, to hold your hand
Or to watch you build castles in the sands
But as I sit and watch you now
Just one word comes to mind, wow!
Such a wonderful little heavenly gift
Every day you make me smile and I feel my heart lift
So I'll be with you long after I'm gone
I'll be with you through all the rights and the wrongs
I'll journey with you, as you grow and as you learn
My spirit will be your guide, until the sun no longer burns
So I thank the Lord for all the days together we have had
I'll always be with you, love from your old grandad.

Karl Hunter

ADRIFT

I search so long, far and wide
I cruise the galaxies in my mind
What do I find?
What do I find?
Nothing?
Nothing . . .
Am I blind?

I listen to the stars and to the people
What am I searching for?
What use is a steeple?
The stories they tell
The things I've seen
They don't match at all
So what does this mean?

Perhaps I'm exploring a stranger's land
Maybe I wasn't put here by anyone's hand
To venture so long and discover I'm lost
When will I be found?
When?
What if no one knows I'm here?
What then?

Answers, answers, there must be answers
Sleep a little, wake some more
Find a link to open a door
A lunar beacon shines down on us
Think someone will see us soon?
Oh, I'm sorry, you don't know me
I must appear a buffoon

This curious mind beckons a familiar face
Yet none appear over here
All gone without a trace?
I'll seek on far and wide
Lit by moonlight, led by the tide
Perhaps the sea can calm a stormy mind
There be a friend offering wonders to find.

Sean Wylie

THE PEARL OF THE ORIENT

If you should ever visit China,
Many strange sights you'll see,
Take a slow boat to Canton,
Sail the China Sea.
There, people eat tortoises if you like the flavour,
Frogs' legs and snakes are something to savour!
Dogs are roasted as delicacy, deer are tied up with broken legs if that's what you
fancy!

Where street traders sell their goods on dusty roadsides,
As busy streets are full of cyclists trying not to collide!
The pollution is appalling, the smog is thick,
You can watch traders boil tiny birds, before skinning them alive, it's over pretty
quick!

Taoists practice Tai Chi in parks,
Whilst others take birds out in cages for larks!
Confuscian monks bow and worship their ancestors,
You can bet with hell money, play Chinese chequers.
The limestone formations in Yangshuo are a sight to see,
As you sail across the river Yangtse.
So why not visit the Pearl of the Orient?
It's certainly money well spent!

Colette Breeze

UNTITLED

We may not be able to see you
but we know you're all around
we may not be able to hear you
but you're in every sound
we will never forget you
which means you will live on
in our memories and our hearts
you therefore haven't gone
you're just a little out of reach
until we meet again
for now you just need to sleep
and are no longer in any pain.

Maggie Whitaker

MOON-TIDE TO TOES

In the calm ocean the waters swell
Strange forces shifting, like a magical spell
Oysters and urchins will feel again soon
This mystical message passed on from the moon.
Swell bursts forth and a white-capped crest
Charges in towards land like a bird to its nest
With spray and foam and a thunderous roar
Each wave collapses as each wave before
Crashing and washing all rocks within reach
The roar dies to a whisper approaching the beach
Then onto the shingle, like a roundelay song
Pebble to pebble, the word is passed on
And here, as I sit with my feet on the sand
I feel the translation and I understand
The moon is creating the tides as she goes
So there is a connection from the moon to my toes.

Bill Eden

FREEDOM AND CAPTIVITY

This prison is like a seashore,
This cell a tin can upon the beach,
Kicked into the sea, but
Carried back by the tide
To where it was before.
These bars are like the stanchions
Which support the breakwater
Against relentless waves.
The driftwood is the key which fitted perfect form.
These locked gates are the sand dunes
Created by the storm.

Robert Acland-Lamb

FOR THE ONLY TRUTH IN LIFE AND BEYOND IS LOVE

Dust and nothingness is this body,
which will deteriorate and crumble one day.
But the real we abide within.
We are all gifted and intelligent people of light
living in a temporary world of delusion and darkness
awaiting release into bliss and salvation in times to come
when we finally open our eyes and look into ourselves.
Beware of the fake gurus and saints who misguide us
when we are lost and seeking answers; they lead us astray.
Religion, politics and war are all manmade,
artificial creations which are ironically dividing mankind;
that's why I never believed in them and I never will.
We are all born equal and should respect one another,
living together side-by-side, in harmony, love and peace.
For the only truth in life and beyond is love.

Rajeev Bhargava

SPRINGTIME IN SUNSHINE

Purples, yellow, white and green
The prettiest carpet ever seen
Clumps of crocus in the park
Deep, some pale, some bright, and dark

Spring blossom next along the way
Cascades of pink near where I stay
Heaven may have sent me here
To marvel, write, rejoice and cheer

In nearby gardens I do declare
A mingled blend of heathers there
And daffodils along the path
A happy ever aftermath . . .

Norma Anne MacArthur

A GARDEN HOUSE

We walked towards the garden house
The walls a lilac hue
Wisteria curling up the walls
Disappearing out of view

Here the garden of my dreams
Starts its wending path
Around so many changing scenes
The eye to surely cast

Wander through the acers
In their different coloured robes
In graceful folds of shady leaves
They hang in silent mode

Azaleas in pink and gold
Heavy in scented bloom
Mixed with rhododendrons
Above your head they loom

You'll find a high-walled garden
With secrets to unfold
A summer house to rest awhile
It's thatch now grey and old

Sit awhile, your eyes half-closed
The birds you'll hear in song
The fragrance of the blossoms
Drifting past, then gone

So much to see, but time to go
From this garden house of dreams
Though in your mind you'll always keep
All wonders heard and seen.

Beryl Smyter

FRAGILITY

She shook tree
Pulled forth green tissue
Made a leaf
To blow in the wind

She shook breeze
Ruffling spirit of inspiration
Where reflections
Are never still

She touched a cloud
Caught the sunset
Created flower
Red poppy, wind dancer

She took feather
Flimsy, soft, blue
Made a bird
Flashing jewel-like in sun

She gathered petals
Water bloomed mauve
Wafting scent
Wisteria floating on breeze

She took fish
Poured into silken dress
Silver heads
Woven in morning's gold

She took fruit
Wove gold into flesh
Picked sweetness
Carried it in her mouth

She took water
Fleecy chaff against stone
Peace enfolded
Midnight stroked wetness

She took stars
Walked amongst crystal lights
Unwinding shade
Into miracle of life.

Teresa Webster

A WALK WITH MY DOG

I'll take you for a walk later,
As soon as I've finished this job,
He looked into her big brown eyes,
As she sat patiently, wagging her tail,
As he wielded his hammer and banged in the nail,
She watched, as he tidied his tools away,
Picked up his jacket and her lead and heard him say,
'Come on, girl, you'll enjoy your run,
Perhaps meet a chum and have some fun,
The wind is a bit chilly, but it won't worry you,
The grass is still wet, it was a heavy dew,
But the sun is coming out, it'll be a nice day,
There's sure to be others going our way,
We'll collect the newspaper to read back home,
Then you'll curl up and snooze until you need another run,
You're such a good girl and we all love you so,
When we take a walk, it's always go, go, go . . .'

Phyllis Wright

NIGHT STORM

Last night the moon
Shook her shadow
Over where
The darkness slept
In ghost clouds
Of unshaded time
Some moments awoke
The stirring
Of a tormented soul
And moonbeams touched
The threading of mind
Through broken skin.

Norman Royal

SWAN'S LAMENT

I closed my eyes with a tear
A noise I did not want to hear
The noise is so rare, don't you see
The swan song is not sung with glee

It must have been a sad day
As they were only hatched in May
Six little grey fledglings in the brood
I watched it all begin
The loving dance of grace so grand
Befitting for any ball before the king.

Oh, Sovereign Prince protect these
Webbed footed wonders of grace
What a gift to the park.

The heat of the summer filled the air with scent
The swan parade was so splendid
Each print echoed by the next one
Marching to follow the exact indentations

The frosty morn oh, so severe
The snow fell so thick and deep
Food so scarce, Mum began to weep
As her brood got weak

The pond shimmered like glass
As dark clouds filled the air
And Jack Frost said beware
As he covered the snow with a second
Coating of ice.

A song echoed in my ears and
Out wept in thousand tears
The swansong rang out minus two
To mark the winter they could not survive.

A Gilson

THE REAL WORLD

Contrasts of light, shade and green tones merging,
Like paint pigment on a water colour palette
Cool silver-blue to warm golden yellow
A bold splash of cascading petunia sprays
Majestic hostas with busy buzzing bees
Best dressed butterfly, so close you could touch
Lyrical chatter of songbirds in surround sound

Volumous sweet air you can almost taste
Senses stirring in summer-scented breeze
The dazzling radiance of solar star showpiece
Its penetrating rays warming pale, weak limbs
An infinite expanse of cotton-clouded sky
Ever-evolving, roofless and unrestricted
Bare feet in grass that tickles your toes

The real world, so long removed from
Daily existence turns imagination to reality
From summer meadow to sunset beaches
Frees a body confined from bed-boundaries
Where four walls envelop, encroach and invade
Here in my garden for the very first time
Strange it feels, the real world . . . like a dream.

Shirley Clayden

A CHILD'S WARTIME

What did the war years mean to me when
The heart-racing noise of the first air raid siren
Sounded one September Sunday morning
Without any frightening prior warning,
Sending us all fleeing, unaware
Of any tangible outcome for the stairs
To sit under the houses safest place?
Oh, God! What had happened to the human race?

Later the Battle of Britain going on overhead - bravery now retold
Of actions and men so brave and bold,
The tracery overhead in the skies
As allied airmen fought Germans for the ultimate prize,
The red glow as Portsmouth burned at night
Our firemen racing there to help at another dastardly sight.

A school friend's father taken prisoner of war
How long before my dad would be a soldier once more?
Eleven years on reserve finished six weeks before war began
Wouldn't be long before he would be a King's man,
The comforting sight of his double bass under my bed
As I knelt at the side and my nightly prayers said,
And then having to hand it back to the British Legion band
Meant that my dad was wearing khaki for his land.

Leaving my little bedroom for my mum's double one
Knowing that like me, her little world had broken down,
Saying my prayers with more feeling and fervour than before
'Please God, bless everyone and bring my dad back safely from war'
The evacuees sitting waiting in the railway station nearby
Then walking through the streets watched by not many a dry eye,
Some with their mothers and some all alone
'Any room in the Inn?' - wanting a home,
Made me feel guilty for feeling sad
Worrying about Mum and missing my dad.

Hit and run raiders as over the sea they hopped
The air raid siren often sounding as the bombs dropped,
Going to the Odeon to see Walt Disney's Pinocchio

A sign flashed on the screen - 'The siren has sounded, off home
you can go,'
'Look after your ticket, you can get back in,'
Running all the way home to the siren's wailing din.

Singing the Marseillaise and 'For Those In Peril On The Sea'
Also 'There'll Always Be An England' in school assembly,
Going to school, one week mornings, the next afternoons
That was looked on by the children as one of wartime's boons,
Finding out that it was difficult for Mum to pay her way
Trying to live on a serviceman's meagre army pay.

Then we had to sally forth
For Mum to do war work up North
Subletting our home to an airman's family
Leaving my school friends and grandparents dear to me,
Travelling on noisy steam trains to places new
And nearly always having a long wait at Crewe.

Standing or sitting in corridors of trains jam-packed
With all our bones feeling as if they were cracked,
To live in a strange Yorkshire town
For Mum to work at David Browns,
The only southerner at Berry Brow School
At just eleven years old trying to prove I wasn't a southern fool,
The headmaster by name, Hiram Whitwam
A rather gruff, but kindly, ex-naval man,
Told me to stand up for myself and fight back
Something that later I was glad I didn't lack.

Ashby-de-la-Zouche, Heckmondwyke, Thornton Moor,
numerous places
Dad stationed there, a weekend - more unknown faces,
Leaving Huddersfield on a Friday night
To travel back down south
Grandma's house, a lovely sight.

On Sunday night, back we would go
Making me feel very homesick and low,
Crossing London on the underground
People huddled on the platforms to escape the sound
Of the Blitz erupting overhead
Anywhere to lay down, making a bed.

forwardpress

A sleepless night travelling - Mum straight to work
Me off to school - wartime - we didn't shirk,
Then in August 1942, a lot of sorting-out to do
For the airman's family had left our home
We had to get it ready, to make someone else welcome.

On August 14th a Heinkel 111 flew low
With machine guns blazing made terror grow,
Talking to a lady in the back garden only fifteen minutes before
That German bomber making her another statistic of war
We had gone around the corner, into town
Went back to find it had all been bomb-blasted down,
No one present had seen us leave
The searchers cheered with relief.

It was all such a terrible sight
Flats, houses destroyed, by the bomb's might,
People looking dazed and scared
It was like a dreadful nightmare,
What was salvaged was put into store
Our home at 11 Lyon Street existed no more.

Tough little evacuees sent up to Yorkshire from Kent
Buzz bombs so deadly frightening - their lives were rent,
Southerners together we did unite
In the playground, the northerners to fight.

Dad stationed in Southampton in June 1944
Street after street packed with the vehicles of war,
GIs waiting to embark for they knew not where
Giving away 'Life Saver' sweets they had to spare,
After the weekend going back up north
Keeping quiet for all we were worth.

June 6th was the famous D-Day
Our men landing on beaches far away,
Our thoughts and hearts were with them all the time
Later I was worried about Dad's ship being struck by a mine,
He had told me to keep quiet and not tell anyone
That he was with the men going over to bring POWs back from Belgium
He said it was a terrible sight and the smell as well
The prisoners and the boats stank like Hell.

We travelled down to Southampton stayed right near the compound
A horrible, raw, snowy day with POWs all around,
A motley crowd as they marched through the gate
Children hurling snowballs at them in their hate.

Then in November, just after his 66th birthday
My dearest grandad in Chichester passed away,
We all gathered for the funeral at 204
Another episode of changing life touching that door,
The smell of chrysanthemums was pungent and pervading
A constant reminder of that day never fading.

Returning up north, Mum not feeling well
As it turned out, it was our last spell,
For Mum had a heart attack at the age of thirty-five
We had to return south for her to stay alive,
War work and rheumatic fever at twenty-one
Had left its mark and could not be undone,
So Grandma made us welcome once more
As we awaited that happy ending of the war.

Then, on that never-to-be-forgotten 8th May
We celebrated Victory in Europe day,
Gathering in Chichester's market place
Servicemen and civilians in one huge embrace,
Relief and thankfulness tinged with sadness
For widows and orphans not enjoying full gladness,
So we awaited the final day of war
When victory in Japan day arrived, we danced and prayed once more.

Then, after all the years Mum and I had had to roam
We had to hunt and hunt to try to find a home,
Eventually, we had a place requisitioned for us
After we had had to make a fuss,
Bombed out and nowhere to go
Why did we still have to fight so?

Dad was not demobbed straight away
We had to wait until late 1946 for that day,
Grey and white pinstripe suits galore
Thank God for the men and women safely home from war.

Sylvia Olliver

NIGHTFALL

Shutters close and barn owls call,
From ancient branches, long and wide;
To herald the coming of the night,
The blessed - sacred eventide.

Our kindly host, unseen and dear,
Projects his breath, so strong and whole.
It warms the chill that nightfall lends -
Bringing closure, to the weary soul.

The winking stars, so small and clear,
Are climbing near the heavenly throne.
Their bright glow, highlights angel forms,
Whose songs are heard by God alone.

A cheeky moon, bursts through the clouds
And smiles at everything in sight.
Approving of the harmony,
So obvious with the fall of night.

A whispering breeze, swirls round the nests,
Where tiny fledgelings softly doze.
And its draught, excludes all turbulence,
As through the night it gently blows.

A celestial bird, with feathers fanned,
Symbolizes peace and rest.
And this pastel creature, swooping low,
Is Heaven-sent, so we, are blessed.

Murmuring cattle, in the fields,
Are needful of this innate peace.
And the benediction of the night,
Will make their snoozing sounds increase.

A shaft of life, rests on the rock,
Where prayers are said - where folk unite.
And this ageing sanctum, draws the peace,
Which is more intense, throughout the night.

Creatures of the night, step forth,
From secret places, where they lie.
And they grasp the solace, nightfall gives,
Concealed by hedgerows standing by.

The magic fades, when dawn intrudes
And bids the world - awake and rise!
But the hours speed by and soon we find,
That nightfall, dominates the skies.

Patricia-Mary Gross

FLAMES

Patterns on pavement intertwining
Leaves all shapes and colours binding
Blending and lending a flame to the air -
Dying and drying and rustling there.

Leaves from the oak and the sycamore,
So beautiful, living and dead, even more
Looking so vibrant and glowing in flames
Laughing children scattering in their games.

The golds and reds, yellow and amber,
Memories of autumn for all to remember
Leaving bare branches for snow soon to cover
Warming the Earth, with love for the mother.

The mother who cherished the seed,
Blown by the wind, in the time of need
To the place where the roots could spread
Nourished with food from the bed.

The warmth in the earth and the rain
Swelling and filling the grain
Many years will worry by, till the
Leaves from that seed will fill the sky.

Falling again, as life's circle repeats,
Flames falling to Earth with the seed,
Will children still laugh and play -
In the future? I wonder! and wondering pray.

Peggy Morrill

CROP CIRCLES

Is there anyone out there
targeting our planet?
Why choose cornfields
to send coded messages,
or as landing pads
for alien spaceships under cover of darkness?
Never seen
except in the imagination.

Look again
at the wonderfully swirled patterns
geometrically designed;
not one blade is damaged
except by those
exploring their magic and mystery.
Even clever hoaxers
who attempt to imitate
have their limitations.

Nature herself
is more adept
at producing beautiful patterns.
Consider a snowflake,
a spider's web
sparkling in the dew,
Hoar-frost on the branches
of trees in winter.
Are there atmospheric conditions
we are not yet aware of?

The answer is out there!
Eye-witnesses have testified to a whirlwind,
a vortex of spinning air
electrically charged
imprinting symmetrical shapes
of dazzling perfection
on croplands and grasslands;
swirl patterns, starbursts,
some with spiked effects,
air-pressured tramway lines.

This is nature's response
to highly imaginative tales
of visitors from outer space!
The scientists, the meteorologists,
the true researchers,
let them have the last word.

Beryl Johnson

EDEN SARAH

Walk tonight's frosty starlit streets,
With still true, but broken peace
And still all to live for I see!
The target all the same,
A measure different from yours always,
So blinded by the lights,
So sucked in, how you bite,
Like this cold December night.
'This season's will be mine
For ways and beliefs - I stay true for my rights
This season's will be mine
For ways and beliefs - I stay true for my rights'.

So angel, pull away from the ring,
See how much more you'll sing
Eternal ways through these desperate cities,
This seasonal dreams can be crossed
So much more free.
Been so long, yet you I again see,
Since I met you, you always called me
Across decades and these frosty starlit streets,
Like this cold December night.

'This season's will be mine
For ways and beliefs - I stay true for my rights
This season's will be mine
For ways and beliefs - I stay true for my rights'.

There's still Heaven in my eyes.

Leigh Roberts

DARK ECHOES

When the moon is shining brightly
And the frost is ankle-deep
At the witching hour of midnight
It's as well to be asleep.

The sharp shadows look unnatural
And the light's a ghastly white
The hour and chill conditions
Lend the winds of fancy flight.

Is that knocking in the plumbing?
Yes, the seeds of doubt are sown
Now each creak becomes a footfall
And each breath of wind, a moan.

It's no common ghost that haunts though
Nor a burglar that you hear
It's Man's primeval legacy
Aeons of mystic fear.

Across the void of time and space
It seems past qualms are heard
That can affect the fretful mind
More than the written word.

Bolting doors and latching windows
Doesn't ensure peace of mind
Such malaise is intangible
To reason, deaf and blind.

If you'd rather not be witness
To night's dark oppressive powers
Take your nightcap prior to midnight
And bypass the troubled hours.

Robert Bowhill

PUBLIC NOTICE

Rats and pigeons spread diseases,
Usually, in their faeces,
We dare not risk taxoplasmosis,
Nor any type of tuberculosis.

Some would swim, oh, leptospirosis,
Or dabble with salmonellosis.
Others grapple with ornithosis,
Or fear pneumonia, that's psittacosis!

Beware, beware, the flea-borne typhus
And stay well away from dogs who'll bite us.
Rabies, not a very nice condition
Steer well clear - make this decision.

So feed no pigeons
Not one smidgen,
Lest our town become repellent -
Not one 'where time is pleasant'*.

*Christchurch motto, Dorset.

Laila Lacey

IT'S ONLY A DOG

It's only a dog with a leg at each corner,
It will fit in somewhere, it's only a stray
And that was the last word I had to say.
It's only a dog with a leg at each corner,
Soft, turned-down ears with long, pointed nose,
Bright brown eyes and very large teeth.

It's only a dog with a leg at each corner,
We'll give it a box in the kitchen,
But it lies on the sofa and watches TV.
It's only a dog with a leg at each corner,
It sleeps in the bedroom, on the bed, when I'm gone,
Only a dog with a leg at each corner,
Until the day he died,
Then I cried.

Peter E Smith

THE DAFFODIL

After the cold bleakness of winter who would think,
That with some food, some sun and a drink,
Something truly beautiful to behold
Could grow from a bulb that looked tired and old?
Stunning, vibrant colours of yellow and green,
Rise from the earth and in profusion are seen.
From under their blanket of cold, damp earth,
With amazing strength and timing, gives birth,
A breathtaking sight to brighten our day,
Heralding the fact, spring is on its way.
Blown and tossed by the wind above the ground,
Yet underneath, their roots are firm and sound.
They light the ground with a warm, golden glow
And bow their cheerful flowers in an effective show.
With their job finished, they shrivel and appear to be gone,
But their bulbs draw strength and continue on,
They'll burst forth again at the start of next spring,
Their colours outshining the crown of a king.
They bring a touch of majesty for everyone to share
And I, for one, am grateful that they're there.

Rosina L Gutcher

TO MY GRANDCHILDREN

Find happiness in simple things,
The joy that every sunrise brings,
View the world through different eyes,
The starry studded winter skies.
No diamond ever could replace
The smile upon a baby's face.
Try to see that every tree
Is fashioned for eternity.
The hum of bees,
The butterfly,
The blueness of a summer sky.
The rainbow after April rain,
The earth has been refreshed again.
The sweetest song you'll ever hear,
Is when a bird sings loud and clear.
If ever you have been denied,
Some peace of mind,
Then look outside
And you will see,
That all these things are yours,
For free . . .

Doreen P Damsell

THE MOUSE SAGA

It began with a scream from the kitchen
Then Mum ran in and jumped on a chair.
She cried that she'd just seen a monster
And there was no way she'd go back in there!
She said, 'Just get in there and kill it
Before my potatoes boil dry!'
And I knew that she really did mean it
Cos she had a strange glint in her eye.
So, there I was, armed with a slipper
As I peered through a gap in the door,
Scanning the room for a monster
Till I spotted it sat on the floor.
It wasn't a very large creature,
It fact, it resembled a mouse
And I hadn't the stomach to kill it
So I ordered it out of the house.
I fearlessly brandished the slipper
But the mouse still remained unimpressed.
Then he turned on his heels rather slowly
And wandered off back to his nest.

I tracked him to behind the freezer
And discovered a gap in the floor.
'Has it gone yet?' asked Mum, with a shake in her voice
As she peered through a gap in the door.
'It's gone into hiding,' I said with a grin.
'Thank goodness!' said Mum with a sigh
'But what's that strange smell?' she asked, venturing in.
'Flippin' heck! Look! My spuds have boiled dry!'

The next day she went to the market
And came home with a wooden mouse trap.
She baited it with some mature Cheddar cheese
And set it down next to the gap.
It was then that I started a-thinking,
Of the fate of that poor little mouse.
It wasn't as though he was harmful
And I didn't mind sharing the house.
So, that night, when I knew Mum was sleeping,

(I was certain, because of the snores)
I crept down the stairs very quietly
And silently opened the doors.

It didn't take long to set off the trap
So the mouse could now get at the cheese.
Oh, I knew very well that my mum would be cross
But I was sure that the mouse would be pleased.

And so it went on, night after night,
Mum said she was at her wit's end.
She really could not understand it
It was driving her right round the bend!
I saw the mouse several days later
He was looking decidedly fat.
In fact, if I didn't know better
I'd have taken the mouse for a rat!
I advised him to keep a low profile
And stay out from under Mum's feet.
And if he stayed under the floorboards,
I'd leave him some cake as a treat.

By now Mum was losing her temper
And she threw the trap out in the bin.
The mouse watched from under the table
And I'm certain that I saw him grin.
'It's time that we took desperate measures!'
Said Mum, as she pulled on her hat.
She was gone from the house for an hour
And then reappeared with a cat!
'The man at the shop,' she informed me,
'Said that mice didn't like a cat's smell
And the second the mouse caught a whiff of the cat
He'd be off like a bat out of Hell.'
She went in and sat by the fire
With a look on her face that was smug
And the cat went and sat down beside her
And curled up asleep on the rug.

On its face was a look of contentment
As it let out a satisfied purr
And the mouse, with a shrug of indifference,
Took a nap underneath my mum's chair.

Susan Robinson

THE TALE OF BETTY BUTTON

Little Betty Button was the maid for Madam Twee,
Madam Twee was spiteful and she bullied Betty B.
Not a pretty woman, thin lips, sharp pointed nose,
Whilst Betty's petite face was fair, a classic English rose.
Betty was from poor stock sent out to work at eight,
Straight from cot to scrubbing pots, such a wretched fate.
Betty had no choice in life, she was the first child born,
Her wage, you see, was sent to keep the other Buttons warm.
And so she did as she was bade, whatever Madam said,
She had to keep her job, because her siblings must be fed.
'Brush my hair you peasant, make my tresses into curls,
Pull my corset tighter, wench, hand me here my pearls.
Fasten up my bodice, my dress, my ermine coat,
Sit my bonnet tilted, no like this, you witless goat.'
Day in, day out, poor Betty B was constantly on call,
She got no thanks, no nods or smiles, no gratitude at all.
Now Madam Twee was married and William was his name,
Captain William actually, handsome, stout of frame.
He married her for money or so the gossips claim,
Well! When you looked at Madam Twee you had to think the same.
He had a wit about him that Betty found quite charming
And stirred a warmth inside her soul, the poor girl found alarming.
William had a butler, his name was Henry Bows,
He waited on the tables and sorted William's clothes,
He lit the fires, answered doors, he ran the household Twee
And also on his list of jobs was watching out for B.
Little Betty Button adored dear Henry too,
He'd guided her since she arrived and taught her what she knew.
They'd sit at night together, 'neath the stairs where servants stay
And sip their cocoa slowly and discuss each other's day.
'Twas much a night like this when Captain Twee called in . . . and said
'Just checking on you servants, making sure you're warm and fed,
Happy band of workers, happy house is what I say'
And looking oh! so striking, he winked and walked away.
Well! Betty Button felt the blood rush to her head and face,
Her hands began to tremble and heart began to race.

'Whatever is the matter?' old Henry looked aghast,
'It's nothing, honest,' Betty lied, 'just took my drink too fast.
I'll have an early night I think and that will surely do
And in the morning, Henry Bows, I'll be as good as new.'
The shame she felt consumed her, it swathed her like a shroud,

Nice servant girls don't feel such things, such passions aren't allowed.
But heavens! Worse as she lay there, it all fell into place,
The captain felt the same way too, she'd seen it in his face.
She must resign immediately. She'd tell madam first song,
But what reason for her leaving, what could she say was wrong?
She paced the room and scoured her mind all through that awful night,
For motives and excuses, but nothing sounded right.
I have no choice but fleeing, must leave without a trace,
And so with sorrow in her heart, she packed her tiny case,
Towards the door she headed, oh, so softly on her toes,
Just in case she made a noise and wakened Henry Bows.
But luck was not her ally, as through the door she stepped,
For in the yard was Butler Bows, who also hadn't slept.
'What has happened little maid? And why the tear-stained face?
And pray, where are you heading with your whole world in that case?'
'Oh, friend, do not think bad of me, for I am chaste and pure,
But things have changed within the house and I must leave for sure.'
'Beg tell your old friend Henry, what misfortune has occurred
And I will try to remedy your sadness . . . have my word.'
And so, with head hung meekly, she told him of her plight,
He frowned and then smiled strangely, as he said, 'I'll put it right
Between us girl, there is a chance, if you can hold your nerve,
To rid us of the Madam Twee . . . a chance we both deserve.'
He told her of his strategy and what she'd have to do,
'Well, are you going to help me, B? I'm doing this for you.'

And so, with hands a-tremble, she prepared the Madam's fare
And took it in for breakfast and set it down for her.
An hour later, Betty B and Henry, stood, heads bowed,
As undertakers came to put their mistress in her shroud.
That evening in the drawing room the Captain sat dry-eyed,
'Now, as you both will be aware, my dearest wife has died
And with that news comes changes, pray do not be offended,
But Betty Button sadly, your service here has ended.
My new love has no use for maids and so it is with woe,

I hand you here your reference and request that you should go.'
As waves of faintness captured her, she felt her legs grow weak,
She looked to Henry for support, but Henry didn't speak,
'Please help me, help me, oldest friend, halt this, my sad demise,'
But he was busy gazing into Captain William's eyes.
Poor Betty died of shock that day. Too late, but now she knows,
That the loving stares she took as hers, were meant for Henry Bows.

Susan M Fletcher

A RIDDLE OF EMOTIONS

Trapped in this dark night,
No allies in sight,
Time to pick up my sword and fight,
At the end of the tunnel is there no light?
Why are my enemies hidden?
Is everything 'above board' forbidden?
Where is the key that unlocks every door?
Who is it that is keeping score?
The wounds will heal,
The scares will fade,
In every era a devil is made,
My mental anguish holds me back,
Where is the conviction I lack?
Why am I on the receiving end of every attack?
Would I see the bigger picture if I step back?
A battle rages inside of me,
My heart against my mind,
Neither one of which I can bind,
Where are the missing clues I am trying to find,
Are you being cruel to be kind?
My heart concludes on personality,
While my mind bases decisions on rationality,
My heart chooses to give the benefit of the doubt,
My mind insists there is a rational way out,
How do I reconcile the two?
Which course of action do I pursue?
Why do your words not console me,
Neither do your threats scare me,
What is behind the façade I want to see?
Is it a way out?
Or something that will set me free?
Why am I trapped by my own desire to leave?
Am I expected to sit and grieve?
Who is it that manipulates my words?
Make yourself known,
I am the sovereign one that sits on the throne,
I rule the darkness,
I command the wind,
It is on one person your hope is pinned,
I control the rules,
Use your skills as tools,

I dominate the players,
I accept no pleas, or prayers,
I provide the glory and fame,
I am the game . . .

Farah Ali

CRETE

A magical wedding and honeymoon in Crete
Agios Nikolaos was where we stayed
A picturesque harbour behind which mountains meet
Lovely memories which never fade

An exquisite white dress with bow, sequins and lace
Excited, happy and in love
We pose for our photos together face to face
God watches down on us from above

The sun shines down onto the sparkling sea
With sky so clear and blue
With my handsome husband right beside me
From today our life starts anew

In the wedding limousine I feel like a queen
The Greek people smile and wave
In my beautiful dress I feel so serene
All these precious moments I shall save.

Lisa Pease

ANGELS DO HAVE WINGS!

Distant lovesick shores beckon wandering souls,
Open wounds need brief timeless goals,
Togetherness is a time wedged in motion,
Without a feeling of any past notion!

To dwell in the time you seek now,
Is to empty the rapture of an unconsumed how?
To sit alone is a pleasure in itself!
To love your own thoughts is true wealth!

Just to be and to allow thoughts to wander.
To open up new avenues, to liberally ponder!
It emerges in my thoughts and resides a while,
Opening up beliefs; spellbound within a memory file!

Hollowing out the deadlines that wedged around,
Weeding out the negative rocks that were ground.
Pressurizing deep, eating at my hopeless spirit!
Waiting for one of God's angels to naturally fit.

Angels do have wings, but they are spiritual!
Upon this Earth, they didn't land, they fell!
Fell into humanity, to open up goodness!
To seek out, the desired influential bliss!

The energy gained within begins to reach out
The hushed child, begins to laugh and shout!
Why are we given the quests we receive?
Is it to test what we actually believe?

Can we only be given problems we must solve?
Turning around in our minds, as thoughts dissolve!
Melting all the facts, to create a new substance,
Taking small directional steps and creating a dance!

We will consume whatever is warm when it is cold,
We will embark upon what we aspire when we are bold!
We will reach out to higher aims when we are inspired,
We will caringly rest when our searching souls are tired.

Caroline Champion

COOL

What is cool? Is it accepting fags off your mates?
Or going out on hundreds of dates?
Sniffing things that you shouldn't be
Looking in the mirror, only thinking, the state of me
Or is it knocking back ale, far more than you need
When some people think it's cool, really it's greed
What about popping Es in a nightclub, it's crammed
Pulling faces on the dance floor is not in popular demand
The next morning you're still awake but coming down
No one can look at each other, just staring at the ground
Slowly realising the people around you, you don't really know
Grabbing that tissue to give your nose a blow
Is it cool to smoke weed every day?
Skinning up on your weed tray
Puffing away, yeah man, you're getting high
Daydreaming a life that's passing you by
Is it cool to hang out with so-called people like this?
Leaving yourself hanging on by a thread
As your plans for your future start to shred
A new year approaches, you try your best to start right
With goals and resolutions, you vision your future looking bright
It's cool to do the right thing as your future is you
Instead of daydreaming, wake up, it's what you've got to do!
With no one standing in your way, except a conscience of being cool
 A small word that can direct a path in your life as being a fool
So, if you want to be somebody, if you want to go somewhere
Get up, get dressed and you go and get out there!

Kelly Marie Neal

TWO'S COMPANY

Two little bodies always together
Moving around, aware of each other
Fingers reaching, stretching, grasping
Touching gently, with love everlasting.
Two thick cords, coiled and distorted
Intertwined yet separately connected
Two plump placentas jostling for space
Bursting with nutrients, major and trace.
Turning face to face, with noses just meeting
Little Eskimo kisses, a positive greeting.
Thoughts gently passing between the two brains
Some are different, some are the same
A private, silent communication grows
An understanding of what each other knows.
A special language all of their own
Without the need for verb or noun.

One tiny child is larger and stronger
Its minute body, a little bit longer
While they both grow their separate parts
Fingers and toes, lungs and hearts
They move around and practice skills
In a watery dance of strength of wills
Arms and legs shoot random hits
Try out walking and grabbing bits.
With eyes unseeing, closed up tight
They cannot distinguish left from right
Immature ears hear muffled sounds
Of music and voices all around
Becoming familiar with mother's tone
They will distinguish her alone.
And so they grow to be together
United within the world forever.

Hazel Newman

THE REALM OF DARKNESS

Through the forests of invention
To a clearing in the soul
Where the weak cow tail in silence
And the strong score every goal
There's a heart so weakly beating
In its effort to be heard
And a sigh of whispered sorrows
Mutter willfully absurd
No one hears a call of anguish
No one shudders with belief
Every moment wrenched from sinking
Further down the dark beneath
Fingers groping for an answer
Eyes unable to perceive
Lost and lonely an existence
No pretender could believe
Hope, a word no longer witnessed
Love, a word much longer dead
Life, a sentence of revulsion
Starved of smiles and sickly fed
Drones the bell of retribution
Though it never peels in jest
For the lustful, hungry minions
Who will harvest all the best
And the one heart weakly beating
Fades into a silent hum
One more soul slips through unnoticed
But for beating on a drum
And the net casts out so easily
And captures one more heart
The suddenness surprises
And rewards with just a start
A mouth emits a silent scream
Two eyes spring open wide
As the demons in the doorway
Haul another life inside!

David Whitney

REFLECTION

(For Shannon, Georgia and Joel)

Through my children's eyes I see
So much love that's just for me
My only wish? That they remain
So innocent, untouched by pain

Through my children's lives, I guess
The way ahead, what's for the best
All my wrongs and as I blunder
They watch me close
Still full of wonder

And as they sleep so peacefully
Tousled hair, they fly so free
I feel such pride and love, you see
I am them
And they are me.

Shelly Hill

ONE MORE ANGEL IN HEAVEN

I miss my mum more than words can say
Since evil cancer took her away
Spreading itself through her body, stripping away her life
Like some horrible hunger that would never stop
She fought for years, not with weapons, but with something stronger
Her smile, her courage and her strength and her family
These weapons kept her fighting for six years
But her body just couldn't take it and she lost the fight
So now there is one more angel in Heaven
But that angel shines brighter than most, to guide her family
                              through their trouble
And waits outside the gates until her soulmate can join her

Mum, I really miss you and my heart aches every day
But you're always there to guide me
Like a lighthouse that guides a ship through the storm.

Stephen Black

RIGHT BESIDE YOU

Celebrate my life on Earth
Cherish all the good times I had with you
I haven't gone to some faraway place
My spirit is still right beside you
If you feel as though cobwebs
Are touching your face
Or you feel a gentle breeze
When wind there is none
I'll be standing right beside you
For my spirit continues to live on
If a song is played on the radio
That reminds you so much of me
Just send me your thoughts
To the spirit world above
And again, right beside you I will be
There are many ways I will try and make contact
Just trust and believe your thoughts, for it's true
Love is the link that forever binds us
And with my love, I'll watch over you
So the times when you really miss me
Send me your thoughts to the spirit world above
And I'll come and stand beside you
And enfold you with all of my love.

Lilian Pickford-Miller

TOMBSTONES IN A LEICESTERSHIRE CHURCHYARD

They lean like weary travellers, in faded dappled grey.
Born in some mason's workshop of feldspar, quartz and clay
enduring storm and tempest, reflecting moon and sun.
Telling their cheerless story, announcing every one,
the end of some cherished life.

Diverse of shape and outline, these objects soiled and worn
were made to guard the memory, of pilgrims long since gone
now some have fallen over and many broken down
having lost their remit, thus failing in that aim
to herald some special life.

'Sacred to Ellen Catherine,'
'In memory of Anne who died,'
'For Olivia, daughter of Olive and Thomas,'
how they tried
to keep their charges living within the minds of those
wandering this necropolis seeking some repose
reading of cherished lives.

One tells of 'Thomas dying in seventeen twenty-two'
that is the total story, the best his scribe could do.
But Harriet who went later, 'The treasured wife of John'
has listed in her orders, 'Father, thy Kingdom come'
reviving this cherished life?

Epitaphs shaped by poets,
tributes engraved in rhyme,
using the craft of the wordsmith to freeze a moment of time,
so 'John Jackson always kept his word as far as mortal could
to grieve for him would be absurd,
because his life was good.'
A perfect precious life?

Some have Belvoir, to watch them day and night,
still the stones are chipped and broken finding no respite
from the ravages of time and the planet's constant roll
their faith in the cherubim wasted, if this were point of it all.
To preserve these cherished lives.

They tilt like drunken soldiers, just clinging to their task,
decaying with their charges, their best years long since past
their splendour well diminished, by wind and sun and rain
and origins long forgotten, in the swirling mists of time
with those cherished lives.

Fulfilling yet their mission, these slabs of rock and stone
remind each generation, through life one thing alone
remains,
not fame nor failure, nor faith which mountains move
but what is left at the very end, is the love -
of cherished lives.

Ray Smart

LET IT FALL

The snow is falling as we speak,
The sky looks full and very bleak,
Cars are driving slowly past,
People are walking, not very fast.

Children playing on the sleigh,
Having such fun along the way,
Shouting, laughing, screaming too,
Such a good time, whatever they do.

Children excited as the schools are closed,
So they decide to get cold from head to toes,
How great it is to watch them play,
Wanting snow to continue falling all day.

Lots of snowmen being built everywhere,
Some with clothes and some just bare,
To see the smiles on the children's face,
Makes everything just fall in place!

Patricia Daly

DISPOSSESSED

It seems you've been abandoned
by those closest to you,
the very same who need to take
some time away from you -
not an easy choice to make.
The trouble is, that no one's told
you how all this has come about.
There's not one person bold
enough to take on such a task.

So here you find yourself,
set down amongst strangers,
dispossessed, anxious and alone,
pacing corridors and rooms,
while waiting for the telephone
to ring with vital news
of who you are and where you are
and, with luck, the name of who's
about to come and fetch you.

Whatever else, you are aware that
this is not your home;
they say you have a room here,
but you have no money on you
and, as it must be rather dear
you're feeling desperate - who's paying?
Where are all your clothes, your books
and how long are you staying?
All questions asked to no avail.

When you were just a tiny child,
loved and cosseted and cared for,
this would not have come about.
Cushioned through each stage of life,
of this there is no doubt,
no one would have snatched
you from your mother's side
and, without ceremony, dispatched
you to an unfamiliar place.

Now you're struggling to get around,
your uncoordinated limbs
beyond control, can seem so willful;

mobility you'd always take for granted
when once they were so skilful.
A toddler's staggering gait is charming,
whereas the slow and shuffling steps
of age are seldom so disarming.
Where is the outstretched, helping hand?

The optimism of the young can
banish obstacles at will;
when independence seems to beckon
ageing is a concept and no threat.
Very few of us will think about, or reckon
on being old and once more needing
much support and love and care -
perhaps a helping hand with feeding
in order to sustain our lives.

My prayer for you is that
you'll be allowed a resolution,
that in time you'll find the door
and will pass through it, quite unscathed,
to find the peace you knew before.
It is down to each of us to share
the blame for how your life has ended.
Our love and empathy could help you bear
the ignominy of becoming old.

Angela R Davies

PAUL THE METICULOUS FISHERMAN

'Pawlu is-Sajjied', as he was nicknamed was a quiet lad.
Every Sunday morning he would clad in a beige suit and tie,
shine his shoes with spit, like soldiers in the army.
He was neat, in fact, his other nickname, 'Pawlu Il-Fitt'.
So meticulous in his work, preached to all how life was so ridiculous.
His walk was a rhythmic sway, of self-confidence
stopping to observe the sea and the weather, like all good fishermen.
It only seems like yesterday,
Pawlu was shouting himself hoarse: 'Lampuki friski, hajjin hajjin',
I often wonder how on earth no one realised he was in deep crisis,
deeper than the sea from where he caught us fresh fish every day.
His luzzu, Santa Maria was berthed at Spinola Bay.
Now it's gone just like him leaving an empty space,
only a buoy to mark its place.
Now he no longer shouts, 'Friski, hajjin hajjin'.
The mornings are drear without his yellow smile.
When my dog ran out into the street last year
Pawlu gave chase and brought him back safe.
The Santa Maria was red, black and yellow
painted in honour of St Julian, the village patron saint.
It would chug out happily from the bay, sometimes with the moon rising
every evening for many summery decades, as many as I can recollect,
rippling through the reflected white light of a dimming sunset.
Then he would whistle an unknown tune,
until his silhouette became one with dusk.
He lived with his old widowed mother, Giuzeppa;
everyone knew she doted on him, her only son.
She came back from early morning Mass
one day and found him hanging from the neck.
The rope was tied by a fisherman's knot from the stairs' railings.
The doctor came first, then Dun Karm, the Parish priest.
Pawlu left us without a single word, his luzzu now only a ghostly memory,
as the moon now rises on an empty, quiet bay.

Pawlu is-sajjied il-fitt (Paul, the meticulous fisherman)
Pawlu il-fitt (Paul the meticulous man)
Luzzu (traditional colourful Maltese fishing boat)
Luzzu Santa Maria (the boat is named St Mary)

Lampuki friski, hajjin, hajjin (fresh dolphin, fish, alive, alive)
Friski, hajjin, hajjin (fresh, alive, alive)
Giuzeppa (Josephine)
Dun Karm (Fr Charles).

Raymond Fenech

TIME FOR TEA

Jack's our fat cat, he's fast asleep
(Mum says he can tell the time)
If it's three, then it's time for tea
But Mum's putting out crumbs for the 'cheeps'.
Dad's gone off to walk the dog
Our 'Hog', who's very hairy
So, I'm sat here, with Sally's Molly,
My sister's awful, silly dolly -
She's got big eyes that stare and stare
Until my sister combs her hair.
I 'spect she'd like to drink some tea
I'd make some for her, if I were three!
With choccie biscuits from the tin -
(It's got pictures of Mickey and Min).
My sister'll soon be back from school
To comb Moll's hair to make it curl
'We're off to Spaindot.com' said Dad
'Where one's sticky with the sunshine heat
Not cold and damp, like it is at home -
Where the sand's so hot, it burns your feet.'
Oh
Here's Mum, my mum, with her lovely smile,
'I'll lift you out, come here, my child'
And then she puts the kettle on
It must be three, as it's time for tea!

Veronica Bulmer

WALES AND THE WELSH

Wales' southern shores lashed by winter gales,
But her heart is warm so she keeps
A welcome on the hills and in the vales.
Hills well-rounded having beauty unbounded,
Until ravaged by coal mining, anthracite did
World industry excite, thus to
Earn a living inhabitants were resigning.
Beauty was born there, citizens heart-torn
At leaving there, to wander Lord knows where
When a living to earn they care.
A reputation for having learning since the time
Of admiring Romans, aggressive foemen,
The known world roaming,
For loot and advantage combing.
Recognizing the abiding talent of my
Countrymen, Celts once aggressively and
Possessive, by time tamed and by
Warfare lamed, invaded and jaded,
Weapons rusty and blunt-bladed
Content and bent on settling down
Happy to be bucolic and mayhap alcoholic!
Their homeland for foes a welcome land
Coveted as by inhabitants it was cosseted
But forced to bend the knee to Caesar,
Rendering him taxes when demanded and so
Commanded, Celtic slaves where once they
Were masters, since becoming peaceful
Procrastinators, of their times made prisoners.

Such be the history of the old homeland, which
Calls to me, tugs at my heart incessantly.
Down but never out as Richard the Lionheart
Observed in future times a United Kingdom
By them would be well served.
At Crecy, the Frenchmen defeated, put to rout
By stout, sturdy foemen, formidable Welsh longbow men.
Men although in past humbled, rose after
They had stumbled, still their spirit never ever crumbled.
At the centre of Welsh lands, people take the country
To their heart, so with great reluctance depart

From green soil, never mean soil on which
They gladly toil; folk sanguine, only loss of
Turf makes their blood boil.

Moving north, hear Welsh spoken with a different lilt,
Yet is patriotic to the hilt, emboldened to celebrate
Mount Snowden and a plentitude of slate,
Which was world prized as roofing material
For mansions and castles, as well as modest dwellings.
Vikings arriving were soon conniving to reap advantage,
On the ancient language, imprinting their stamp
To seal their devious ramp, so dimming the patriotic lamp.
Wales, a land of song and culture for eisteddfods and
Penillion fames; here harp plays one melody, whilst
A singer sings in counterpoint, like balm it does the soul
Anoint, to be a bard appointed be the ambition of
The poet who is not a musician, he is presented
With a carved, deserved chair on which
He takes his place with modest flair.
People in my time to art did incline,
Richard Burton would have preferred to
Have been a famous writer and to have
Represented Wales in its rugby fifteen.
No doubt but effective he would have been.
In lands Swiss, he did sorely his homeland miss
And when he took his final curtain,
Sally, his widow, discovered a sad little poem
Expressing that side of his misery.
The lament that to Wales he would never return,
No matter how much he did yearn.

'Thomas the Talk', Wynford Vaughan took a different route.
Famed as a war correspondent, then broadcaster
Of national events, a successful man represents.
Yet despite all his undoubted fame, never lost his
'Hiraeth'*, that extremely deep-seated angst for
His native heath, for he settled in Pembrokeshire,

A National Trust property, which to closely know
He did aspire. Swansea born, near the lovely
Gower, close to his heart, a peninsular of wondrous
Beauty, with heath and beaches that are
'Peaches and cream' and unbelievably clean.
Celebrated down through all time, this
Welshman is proud to belong to Wales, that land of mine.
Hiraeth* alive within me through all time.

*Hiraeth (He rae-th) a Welsh word almost untranslatable.
Nearest meaning - deep longing for one's homeland.*

Graham Watkins

MONEY

Paper, coins and plastic
In us these things shed fears
If not enough is had by us
We crumble into tears.
Paper, coins and plastic
Can be a pleasure too
When these things are abundant
Our happiness shines through.
Paper, coins and plastic
Makes the world go round
In banks and shops and stock markets
It never ceases to astound.
Paper, coins and plastic
Can be the ruin of us all
In the meantime, we toil to get it
A means to have a ball.
Paper, coins and plastic
Reason not why we are here
If only we could all spend love
As the money we all fear.

Ann Bridger

FROMAGE FRED

My name is Fromage Fred
I am a mouse extraordinaire
There is nothing I like better
Than nibbling Gruyere

I am a mouse of many talents
A cheesy connoisseur
And I can tell blindfold
'Twixt Brie and Camembert

They call for Fromage Fred
When recipes they fail
And I say croque monsieur!
With creamy Wensleydale

My knowledge knows no bounds
Cheeses, I know them all
Like Sherlock I am the best
Yes Watson, it's Emmental

Some, they are allergic
And for those, I do feel pity
For they will never taste
The exquisite texture of Caerphilly.

Katharine Kehoe

THE NIGHT, THE END

The night, the clothes, the hair, the preparation, the music,
the bling, the mirror,
the taxi, the bar, the friends, the laughter, the beer,
the music, the banter,
the courage, the contact, the eyes, the smile, the hair,
the drink, the music
the dance, the chemistry, the ambience, the touch,
the drinks, the toilet,
the lust, the proposal, the acceptance, the coats, the nod,
the taxi, the fumbling,
the stockings, the hands, the groping, the key, the house,
the vino, the stairs,
the dress, the undress, the bedroom, the nakedness,
the caress, the sighs,
the lips, the touch, the exploration, the animal, the breathlessness,
the longing,
the consumption, the exhaustion, the climax, the groans,
the contentment, the dawn.
The morning, the hangover, the sickness, the embarrassment,
the fumblings,
the exchange, the clothes, the farewell, the headache, the bed,
the day, the phone,
the ignorance, the call, the silence, the message, the nothingness,
the knock,
the words, the hurt, the distress, the getaway, the relief,
the girlfriend, the whispers,
the gossip, the truths, the lies, the whisper, the confrontation,
the deceit, the betrayal,
the upset, the parting, the pleading, the tears, the realization,
the calls, the knocks,
the silence, the week, the months, the phone, the other,
the unbelievable, the denial,
the test, the denial, the retest, the doctor, the confirmation, the disbelief,
the contraception, the deception, the recrimination, the drink, the tears,
the realization, the acceptance, the denial, the isolation,
the helplessness, the friends,

the reluctance, the parents, the lecture, the shock, the meeting,
the commitment,
the foetus, the heartbeat, the scan, the life, the trepidation,
the months, the sickness,
the bump, the fear, the pain, the discomfort, the tiredness,
the waters, the ambulance,
the hospital, the lights, the pain, the midwife, the fear, the agony,
the head, the nausea,
the body, the cord, the baby, the relief, the noise, the mother,
the ecstasy, the father,
the indifferent, the alien, the pub, the drinks, the baby, the toast,
the parties, the nappies,
the clubs, the drinks, the bottles, the depression, the chains,
the arguments, the money,
the jealousy, the anger, the lovelessness, the incompatibility,
the tears, the violence,
the resentment, the child, the bitterness, the realization,
the sadness, the alcohol,
the door, the finality, the end.

Michael Hartshorne

ON THE SANDS OF MORNING

(Dedicated to Jessica Mooney with love for her 21st birthday 24/7/2009)

Prayer in my short life of love,
Writing light, sacred poetry,
On the sands of morning:
Spain's Lloret de Mar,
Creating a wonder of simple
Prayer in my short life of love.

Edmund Saint George Mooney

A LETTER TO HER MAJESTY THE QUEEN

Her Majesty the Queen, answer me!
Tell me how can I get in touch with you?
I forgot to introduce myself
I'm that young of great promise
I've heard that your castle is the Heaven of peace
And your garden open to outsiders
I'm a bottle-fed child
I'm beginning to cut my teeth
I'm that orphan crying out in pain
Enough to wake the dead
I'm that boy in the street
I've no diploma hanging on the wall
But I've an answer to everything
You, mother of gloomy weather
Diamond of the first water
Tell me where are your good readers?
I'm that bartender, I'm that thinker
And my words burnt to cinder
Her Majesty the Queen, answer me!
I'm in a towering rage
I'm that writer and my paper's yellow with age
I'm that bird of good omen
Prisoner in my golden cage
And my innocence sold into slavery
I'm that busker, I'm always playing my own accompaniment
And the story of my life, is quiet romance
Her Majesty the Queen, believe me!
You can't see the wood for the trees
If you come to me, to see how the land lies
You, Her Majesty the Queen, in that island difficult to access
You're all sweetness, pureness and light
You are a woman whom I trust
You, who have a power to act
I'm in a Hell of a mess
Allow me to sing in your beautiful streets
To row round your green wood
That will do me a world of good
I'll swear, Her Majesty the Queen!
To sink in my second childhood

And to distinguish truth from falsehood
Her Majesty the Queen!
Forgive me my trespasses
And all my wishes for your happiness.

Hacene Rahmani

BEWARE, OH, TAKE CARE

Beware, oh, take care,
When crossing the road.
Beware, oh, take care,
When carrying a load.
Beware of the man,
He could catch you and then,
Who knows what trouble
You would be in.
Beware, oh, take care,
Of the things in the shadows,
Of the things that bring joy,
Or the things that bring sadness,
Like death in the night,
Or death in the day.
Death is the end,
Or the beginning, some say.
Beware, oh, take care . . .
But have a nice day!

John Murdoch

FULL CIRCLE

A 'bugger' of a lad is Kiernan Neath,
with nits in his hair and unbrushed teeth.

Mommy ushers Kiernan out
and packs him off to school.
But to educate requires intelligence
and that's the missing tool!

In class he's dreaming about a manor house
and of a Silver Phantom Rolls.
Yet he still wears his passed-down underpants,
with great big gaping holes.

Devoid of all etiquette and decent manners.
Teacher knows when he's guilty,
because he always stammers.

Mathematics to him, is like the Holy Grail,
put to the test, he will always fail.

Weekends find his daddy in the betting shop,
whilst Mommy's out at part-time work.
But all Kiernan Neath is interested in,
is watching Captain Kirk.

He arrived at his first interview,
in unwashed football kit.
Proudly displaying on his unshaven chin,
a pus-filled, un-squeezed zit!

He soon put his only one night stand,
Cecilia, up the spout.
All it took was one nervous wink
and a drunken saucy pout!

Mommy never gets involved
in any family matter.
She puffs hard on her ciggie
And has a good ol' natter.

Inherited his father's love
of gin-fuelled shakes.
And delights in extending
his employer's dinner breaks.

So, never get in the firing line
of his exhaled breath

you could end up intoxicated
or on the verge of death!

He boasted he'd soon be a manager,
when he first started work.
Five years later on
his title clearly stated
'Lowly Office Clerk'!

He developed a fetish
for office stationary,
then did a short spell in prison.
A timely reminder to us all,
to only take that which is given!

He went to support his local football team,
when the derby match was on.
A nose twitched, then someone shouted,
'Kiernan's here!' and everyone was gone!

Huge breakfasts are a testament
to his prominent belly rolls.
And he can never again stoop down low enough
to play his favourite game of bowls.

He worked for six months at the colliery,
where his attendance was the pits.
His last job was one week at the Indian,
where he gave everyone the s***s!

Now you'll find Kiernan, in the betting shop,
whilst his wife does part-time work.
With his kids sitting around the TV,
watching Captain Kirk . . .

David Paul Heath

PRE-SCHOOL PANIC

Mum! Have you seen my teddy?
I left him by the chair
He was sitting on the arm last night,
But now he's just not there.
Mum! I have to find him,
He always brings me luck.
You know I have a math test
And I'm sure to come unstuck.
Mum! I've lost my pencil case,
My favourite pen's inside.
It's definitely nowhere in the house,
I've searched for it far and wide.
Mum! My gym kit's also missing
And my lunch box has gone astray.
I can't have just misplaced them all,
I think there's been foul play.
Mum! It must be gremlins,
Maybe a poltergeist or fairy.
Something's moving all my things
And now it's getting scary.
Mum! My prefect badge has vanished,
I didn't leave it at school.
If I arrive without it,
Then I'm going to look a fool.
Mum! It's nearly 8am
And my cornflakes have gone soggy.
I think my only hairband
Has just been eaten by the doggy.
Mum! It's getting serious,
What am I going to do?
The school bus is coming round the bend
And I've only got one shoe!

OK, take a nice, deep breath,
Your shoe is under the bed.
Throw away the cornflakes
And eat my toast instead.
Your gym kit's freshly laundered,
Teddy's behind the settee.
Remember you lent your pencil case,
To nextdoor's Timothy.
Your prefect badge is on your shirt,

Just tie your hair up with some string.
I put your lunch box in the fridge,
I think we've covered everything.
See, no need to panic,
It's not a catastrophe.
Now I'll drive you straight to school,
Ummm - have you seen my car key?

Lynsey Yarnell

NEVER SURRENDER

Never surrender, nor raise in place of your standard -
A pristine, pure white flag.
Your standard may be torn and stained -
With your sweat and tears - let it remain -
The banner you carry with pride.
Be it faded, no more than a rag -
Hold it aloft - don't allow it to drag -
Or be dragged, nor trampled, underfoot.
Nor into a million ribbons cut.
For it tells the world about you -
Of your struggles throughout life.
The story of your courage in the face of strife.
Of the battles you have fought -
When you never quit - but, sought -
To see each skirmish to the end;
At times, without a single friend.
You stood alone - against all odds -
You stood alone - defying fate, defying gods.
You held your nerve, you kept your faith -
Your strength and wisdom kept you safe.
Never surrender! Keep the white flag locked away!
It was never yours to use - not even for a day!
Keep your standard close at hand - ready to command -
That all who see it fly - recognise the bearer.
Someone who has paid all dues - to whom respect is due -
A seed sown in the world - from which a giant grew.

Philip Mee

UNTITLED

When I looked up at the night sky tonight
I wondered if you were on that balcony in Spain, looking up
at the same sky
I thought, looking up, about how anything could have happened
to you in that operation room in those 30 minutes
And then I thought of all the things that could happen to you
every day
From crossing the street, to just being in the wrong place
at the wrong time
It suddenly seemed so awful, because I thought if anything
happened to you
On my birthday, when you were in hospital
I was worried
That you wouldn't be 100% sure that I was thinking of you.

Cos I never told you
How much your words mean to me
How deep they can touch me, when I let them
How I wanted to be holding your hand in the room and
How I want to always hold your hand.

(How I am scared and always have been, every time I felt
anything for you, to tell you
How I am perhaps coming up with bad things to make this all
not so great.)

I don't remember much of being gay and not knowing you
I don't remember what I used to do online before I met you
I don't remember what it was like - and has sometimes
been like - when you haven't been a part of my life
I don't want to remember.

I don't want to lose you in my life
In any part of it.

Chloe Smee

SWEET AS WINE

Drink to me only with thine eyes
Is something I'd never say.
It makes no sense to drink one's eyes
When they're needed every day.

I'll keep my eyes where they belong
Securely in my head.
They suit my face and furthermore
I'll need them when we wed.

Taking them out and drinking them
Is a drastic thing to do.
They look right where they are
And they're great for seeing too.

Drink to me only with thine eyes
Is the cruelest thing to say.
So why not toast your love and mine
In a perfectly normal way?

Just take a simple bottle
Pour the nectar in a glass.
Say a few words then drink it down
Let's show a bit of class.

And I really don't want folks to ask
What has happened to my eyes
'Oh, haven't you heard, I drank them'
No, that wouldn't be very wise.

Drink to me only with thine eyes
Is something Ben Jonson said.
He should have seen a doctor
But it's too late now - he's dead!

D M Griffiths

A NASTY NEED

It was ravenous times for the Flim Flam and he craved his
                                         dominion be more,
But before he addressed the army, he locked and bolted his door.
And deep, deep down in the Wild Wood, where the light fell weak and cold,
The elves were hiding in tunnels, but the trolls were becoming bold.
For the war was fast approaching with the time for sides long past
And down in the fiery dungeons the warwarks were unleashed at last.
The Flim Flam threw open a window sited above the horde below
And with eloquence and sincerity, implored them to crush their foe.
For he had mustered all the forces of that gullible, yet ruthless kind,
With promise of riches and power which is meat to the simple mind.
He claimed that Man was feeble and the time to strike was now,
His every waking moment to make the humans bow.
To him, the Master of the Magic, the Lord of the Darks Unease
And his mercenaries must go forward to satiate their needs.
His speech dragged on for ages under ever-darkening skies
And many truths were spoken but also many lies,
Then with valuable hours wasted to his rhetoric and his prose,
He felt his ego sated and cried, 'Death to all our foes!'
Mighty oaks then grew their foot roots, stirred by deliverance talk
And the signal to sally forward was raised by the gygan hawk.
The giant bird rose higher in an ever-lightening sky,
Its screeching cry the sire of the hordes that followed close by.
Out from the black woods' edges they poured with relentless pace,
The warks, the trolls, the faces of every ghastly race,
They rushed towards the horizon across the open ground,
With whispering, snarling, wailing, howling, chattering sound.
But lo, in the east, the saviour of humankind once more,
Sol Invicta raises its fiery, deadly glow,
The rays of light like arrows hit the ghoulish flank,
Causing every evil warrior to falter and break rank,
They fell in countless thousands with no shelter to be found
And dissolved like fading shadows on the warm and sun-kissed ground.
Bare six cohorts of the army struggled to the wood's embrace,
With minds set on the Flim Flam, the architect of their disgrace,
They stumbled to his dwelling and hissed to the creature inside,
To come and give them reason as to why their brothers had died.

But the Flim Flam was little bothered by the rag-tag down below,
He considered himself quite blameless in the building of their woe,
Though he flung the window open and addressed them once again,
For the test of a good orator is to take away all pain,
So, after hours of flowery discourse and with the sun fast on the wane,
He'd a promise the following Wednesday, they'd have a go again.

John Kevin Potter

THE UNDERGROUND

I love to be in the underground
Getting on the tube
Love the hustle and bustle
Escalators and food
People watching, people late
Hoping they will get cheap rate
The smoky smell, the closing doors
Criss-cross lines, uneven floors
Every race, colour and creed
Pungent smells, relating to weed
Pushing, shoving, sometimes a fight
Always busy, right into the night
Same procedure every day
I never get tired of watching the play
When my tube days are all over
I know exactly what to do
Go on the tube in Heaven
Run by me and you!

Elizabeth Corr

AROUND THE WORLD IN 24 HOURS!

They arrived silently in the dead of night into our street,
No warning, no alarms ringing. We awoke to the sounds of someone
Singing. A voice so melodic and sweet.
The words were strange!
Curtains were shiftily pulled back enabling us to see lots of children,
Toddlers, babes in arms, how many? Many, too many to count or see!
The once tidy garden, now strewn with pots and pans and a large zinc bath,
Whiter than white washing hung from the privet hedges and
                    the wispy poplar tree
She was plump and raven-haired, he was gaunt, sad-eyed and frail.
Dad said they looked a shifty lot. 'Bet he's just out o' jail!'
Our mum went to say hello. 'My name is Edna' and held out a warm hand.
She cried, 'Bella, Bella Donna!' but chatted on in words we
                    couldn't understand.
Mum reported, 'She's wanting Belladonna. She's going to poison
                    him, what shall we do?'
Dad said, 'Won't take much, he's so thin, leave it for a day or two.'
                    as usual.
She took no notice and gave Maria a clothes line and some pegs,
Homemade jam, a tin of Spam and freshly baked scones.
Father Riley said they were Italians seeking safety from the
                    ravages of war.
Dad found Monte Cassino in his atlas in a flash. 'Edna, you be
                    kind to them, there's a good lass!'
Father Riley assured us she didn't want 'deadly nightshade'
And 'Bella Donna' meant nice lady!
Within days children played, learning new words from each other
                    and yet they were still unsure,
Never strayed far from their mother, who smothered them with kisses.
Our street party was the best. The Zermanskys and O'Haras,
                    ate pasta from a huge, deep bowl.
Gefullte fish and matzo balls, soda farls piping hot,
We all ate the lot! Father Riley brought red wine.
Our beloved Leeds with its multicultural society had sown
            the seeds of friendship as we all touched hands.

'Hip, hip, hooray to Leeds. This wonderful city of mine!'
Shy Giovanni said, 'Hip, hip to the family Mascherini in Monte Cassino!'
Maria sang, 'Ave' and Mum cried real tears.
Would we ever meet in later years?
Who can know but when I think of that day so long ago
My old heart begins to glow.

Joyce Hefti-Whitney

REDUNDANT!

Lying on the ground like a bruised child,
it had been pronounced dead for a while.
Now, life had been completely ripped out.
Fierce winds had mutilated,
pushed and severed its roots.
Red dusty earth sprung from the ground
of which it had been part.
Persistent ivy clung to its trunk.
Honeysuckle stuck like lichen to its bark.
The washing line lay in the dew.
Redundant.
The still bright foliage remains,
nearer to the earth now than the sky,
providing a haven for wildlife.
Squirrels play hide-and-seek.
Birds hop and skip around its torso.
Soon, all this will cease.
The machines will arrive on Saturday
to chop and pulp it into sawdust.
Its life finished.
The wildlife's playground removed.
Just the memories of a tree remain!
Once healthy and indestructible.
A washing line forced into
Redundancy!

Lynn Craig

SATURDAY

It was a full fry Saturday when I got a mystic call
    I could see through the window, Dublin open up her stall
She beckoned me with promise, this sly and willful shrew
    I tried to subdue expectation, but alas, it slowly grew
So I reviewed my finances, checked on the piggy bank
    I rooted out a few quid from behind the old fish tank
Eureka! Things were looking up, found I was rather flush
    So I put on my best clobber and gave the coat a brush
Soon I was on her streets, wrapped in her magic shawl
    I left behind all worries, sure nothing bothered me at all
Ambled down Hanbury Lane, along its concrete valley
    Passed by the Little Flower, then through Engine Alley
Turned left down Vicker's Street to the builders' providers
    And the stream of dealers there, who welcome all outsiders
On down behind Johns Lane, on arriving at the Liffey
    Crossing then at Bridge Street, in the markets in a jiffy
I then slipped into Keatings pub as the tenth bell rings
    I called the barman over and asked him how are things?
Could I have a pint please? And sat up on a stool
    And what a pint he handed up, I had good cause to drool
Now I made myself comfortable, got my bum just right
    Took out the pack of fags and gave one of them a light
I had a long and lovely drag, I sipped upon the pint
    I looked at the same old faces; God I love this joint
I blew a smoke ring in the air and thought life is sublime
    Now could a man find a better way of how to pass the time
Then the peace was swiftly broken, with wild bawls and shouts
    As these hard-chaws entered (they are now called lager louts)
Then the mob got out of hand, so the barman marked their cards
    And as quick as they came in, the whole lot, they were barred
Yes, they got their comeuppance for their cruel intrusion
    I got my comeuppance too, I was barred in the confusion
There I was, in Chancery Street, with this mug-rough mob
    They called me to go with them, oh! sure, I love me job
So when they were not looking, up Greek Street I did dash
    Then around by Mary's Abbey was in Slattery's in a flash
So I called the barman over, asked him, 'How are things?
    Could I have a pint please?' And over one he brings
Then this guy comes over and he began to blow
    Saying he's just in to quench a thirst, oh, yeah! sure, I know
Then he introduced himself so we could have a chat

But all he wanted was an audience, my ears were sure of that
Yes, to him, I am just an audience for what he had to say
    You know, I am so agreeable I let him have his way.
He said he was a self-made man, well, that I sure can see
    Self-made men rarely finish the job it had occurred to me
He said he had a well-paid job, an office of his own
    Private toilet, a secretary, swinging balls and telephone
His son was going to Trinity, a doctorate is his concern
    Well, college is the best place, from his dad he will not learn.
This judgement was made in haste for each and all fall short
    So I dragged upon my cigarette, from my glass I had a snort
He regaled me of his varied life and booty he had bagged
    But when I ventured an opinion, his interest swiftly sagged
Yes, I was just an audience as he took centre stage
    Sitting in a dim-lit Slattery's, each of us showing our age
Then the talk turned to rugby and how he played the game
    How he knew Willie Duggan, a singular claim to fame?
Then he turned to religion, his dogma was sublime
    He said he prayed day and night and Judas was a swine
Then to crime and punishment with views not too far flung
    All rapists for castration, all murderers to be hung
Yet with his verbal onslaught, my mindset now was cast
    As he nattered to my, 'Yes! yes!' I dwelt amongst the past
I thought of when as a child with my brothers I would play
    Of slices of bread and butter and saucers full of tea
I thought of my good mother, of my father's smiling face
    How we walked up the park and down the hollow we would race
When times were getting better, we were taken to the zoo
    Then home through Parkgate Street and get an ice cream too
I thought of army lorries when the buses were on strike
    And how my father walked to work, he could not afford a bike
I thought of my school teacher, taught us everything he knew
    We stepped out into the wide, wide world without a flipping clue
So I sat with this fellow and as he played the host
    Little did this fellow know he was talking to a ghost
You see, my body was in situ, ie, listening to this sap
    My mind was forty years behind on my mother's lap
When the dream was over my glass had many rings
    I called the barman over and asked him, 'How are things?
Could I have a pint please?' I said in solemn tone
    And turned back to my friend and his constant drone
He harped on about politicians, how they destroyed the land
    How they played the poor mouth with a prominent back-hand.
Then he turned to literature, was there no end to his art?

Telling me Joyce was a chancer and Behan a sparra fart
We need more like J B Keane, Brendan Kennelly is just grand
    Yes, yes, I said sarcastically and ten more in the Artane band
He never got the inference, never copped my stoic rage
    He never listened to my words as he took centre stage
Yes, this man was all knowledge, had nothing more to learn
    Except in conversation when it was someone else's turn
His mouth was overactive, his ears almost defunct
    All this adds up to make a supercilious runt
I took a drag from my cigarette to make my mind more calm
    Sipped upon my pint and thought he means no harm
Then he went all maudlin, regretting all his sins
    No, he did not care who suffered as long as this boy wins
Now I'm not one for confessions, I find them rather dull
    There is nothing that I could hear that I did not try to pull
I played at his confessor, saying I know and all that crack
    But one thing's sure and certain, God will get us back
When I finished up my drink, I bid this chap adieu
    He was the class of sailor, with whom I would not crew
He was far too self-centred, far too ready with the boast
    Now he would make a politician or a television host
I left Slattery's behind me, I'm still without a care
    I skipped along Caple Street just like Fred Astaire
Saw my reflection in a window, my locks were looking grim
    So to the barbers in Dame Street to get myself a trim
Now this shop is not unisex, it was strictly for the blokes
    Well, I prefer men only, you get a better class of jokes
Arriving at the barbers, was welcomed with a grin
    Saying, 'So you want a haircut and will I shave the chin?'
I ran a hand across the smig, too true, the man was right
    I looked into his mirror, I was not a pretty sight
I said, 'Wrap the towel around me and soften up the chin
    Leather up the cut-throat and let the fun begin
And be careful with that swish blade, I'm not your Sunday roast'
    'Relax, you are in safe hands, sure I could shave a ghost'
The deed was done, he did his job, he left me nice and clean
    I was out there, smelling sweet, on my way to Stephens Green
Then Georges Street lured me and I was on the ball
    For me, only one choice the comfort of the Long Hall
I pushed the door open, as I heard Saint Patrick's ring
    I called the barman over and asked him, 'How are things?
I'd like to sample one of your pints that's known far and wide'
    'Of course and to those who say different, woe betide'

I finished my black magic, for which my belly did applaud
    I was on the street again, now feeling like a lord

I made my way down Wicklow Street, then I began to fret
    If I don't find somewhere soon, I will be somewhat wet
I made it to Grafton Street, was in Bewleys in a flash
    I fancied a cup of coffee and was dying for a rest
Oh, thank God for Bewleys, it is a Dublin institution
    It has no time for fancy pants or unnecessary evolution
Yes, the artisans of Dublin, see Bewleys as their Ritz
    The coffee is just excellent, the cake, well, you leave no bits
The oriental décor embraced the broad denizen array
    To with a boss-eyed cleric, a bag lady eating soufflé
An actor, full of acting, his script and neck wear tossed
    A housewife with a bag of wallpaper that's embossed
Two nuns in their civvies, gentleness you cannot hide
    A propensity to act normal, go flowing with the tide
A busker's jingling hoard computed on the counter top
    His guitar now playing tacid for this his coffee stop
The ambience of uniqueness, all colours, never grey
    As I sat there like an extra in this Dublin play
I rested my bones awhile, sat back and began to think
    Agreeing Bewleys was the best place, in-between a drink
Soon, past the Shelbourne Hotel, O'Donoghue's my destination
    For the ballads and the craic and some social recreation
I mingled with Americans, Swedes and English too
    I sat beside a German, who asked, 'Are you Ronnie Drew?'
I have nothing against Dubliners, but thought it very weird
    For me to look like Ronnie, when I haven't got a beard
I called the barman over and asked him, 'How are things?
    Could I have a pint please?' As the German loudly sings
'When Irish Eyes Are Smiling', at the top of his voice
    The American looked interested, they're polite, they have no choice

A Chinaman took pictures as the mass did heave
    With all the pushing and shoving, I got Guinness up me sleeve
I'm thankful for small mercies, but I won't get any here
    I decided it was time to go and lowered down me beer
The place was very congested, jammed out to the door
    When it comes to drinking, a little space I do implore
Peace now the objective, in some hallowed drinking den
    A quick check on my finances, I had a cock and hen
Walking through Stephens Green, stopped to feed a duck
    It was sad I hadn't got a crumb, so he was out of luck
It flopped up on the pathway and waddled as it knew

forwardpress

There was great mirth abound; for I was waddling too
The drink was getting to me, so I tried to straighten up
Disaster, I slipped and came eye to eye with a buttercup

Oh, leave me here a minute, leave me citizens, please
An auld one says, 'What are you doing?' on her flipping knees
She was full of kind concern, asking, 'Did you slip and fall?'
'Missus, this is the position I adopt, when out on a pub crawl'
'So that's the way it is,' says she, 'it's of the drink you're very fond
Well, there is plenty of it in there!' and rolled me in the pond
You sober up mighty quick when soaked through to the skin
With an exasperated park ranger asking, 'Why did you get in?'
Looking at him with defiance, saying, 'Do you think I am an ass?'
Triumphantly pointing to a sign stating 'Please keep off the grass'
'You see, I am an honest man and I do as I am told
Yet I have a small complaint to make, the water is very cold!'
It was then he got belligerent, he turned into a nark
He went and pulled full rank and barred me from the park
First the pub, now the park, it's bad luck I must concede
Worse yet was to come, I bumped into the yobbo breed
Intrinsic to all big cities, well known by certain traits
Graffiti that is misspelt and conversation that sedates
'Hey! Is that water wet?' a bleat from number one hood
'Well, thank you for telling me, I thought it was effin blood'
Sneering, making crass remarks, did I feel compromised?
No, I turned the tables fast, saying, 'I've just been baptized
Yes, I have found God my friends, I have been redeemed
And I was sent to redeem you too, so please do not demean
So let me share my faith lads,' I said, feeling bolder
As I grasped one very tight, a wet arm around the shoulder
Now I was dripping all over him, as he looked on in despair
He was now getting all wet and if was all so *savoir faire*
'Hey lads, this fella has gone nuts,' was his plaintive cry
'Let us get out of here, before I dye his eye'
They left me standing there and boy, did I feel good
If proves you think on your feet in my neighbourhood
Alas think again, I must to get my wet clothes dry
It's not just hot enough although it's mid-July
How I got soaking wet, I must have been a fool
So if that has been the case, let's go back to school
Trinity College came to mind, why, I just don't know
So, down along Dawson Street, my presence to bestow
I entered sly and quick and found a lecture hall
It amused me to think one more for roll call

For Trinity it now seems things are mighty slack
    A boy from Pim Street, the ultimate wet back
I got into the back row, took off all I had
    And wrung them thoroughly and put them on the rad

I gazed around, feeling sad at the learning I had missed
    Now eventually I am here in the nude and half-p****d
Door flung open, heads come in and I could not flee
    So, there I was, my friends, snagged by the university
Well, with me at the back, caught by the event
    They immersed in debate, philosophy was their bent
This young buck gets up, giving it chapter and verse
    He convinces all there, that we are very scarce
We were not there at all, was the basis of his thesis
    Which caused me to check all my bits and pieces
Then they got to nit-picking, began splitting the old hair
    The guy they were dissecting was a fella called Voltaire
Well, I got carried away with the subject matter
    I stood up and began to have a real good natter
Expressing my opinion, saying, 'Life is merely for fun'
    This one cried, 'Jesus Christ!' as if shot by a gun
'Why are you bedazzled? It's philosophy born of good health
    It exceeds all the others, notoriety, fame and wealth'
One said, 'You're entitled an opinion, it's written in our laws
    When it comes to legality, can you have one without drawers?'
'Oh, don't deny me on that basis, this I strenuously refute
    For Gandhi was no Beau Brummel and Homer was bereft
                              of a suit
Formal education missed me, secondary school: none at all
    College was non-existent, yet I read books, large and small
I'm fond of Damon Runyon, Sam Beckett gives me a thrill
    John Steinbeck is one I favour, I'm now into Nelson DeMille
So, please don't misunderstand me, I am not trying to be rude'
    It was then, it struck me, it's hard being intellectual in the nude
'Toss the dirty bounder out!' echoed through the halls
    As I did my level best to cover up my embarrassment
I said, 'You are a fine lot, wear clothes to great effect
    Me, I stand before you, exposing mere intellect'
So then there was a lull, some quiet, then long pause
    Then suddenly, this lot burst into loud applause
Now this verifies it for me, that academics are all bats
    You see, they were lauding a nude drunk, from the flats
I casually dressed myself with my now dry clothes
    And with a cool demeanor I regally arose

forwardpress

'So now my egghead friends, I must bid you adieu'
    And headed swiftly for the exit and out to get a brew
Then I was on the street again, where the crowd parades
    Before I knew where I was, I was standing in McDade's

So, I called the barman over and asked him, 'How are things?
    Could I have a pint please?' and over one he brings
So I scanned my port of call, an act that I find prudent
    What I had was a well-dressed sop, a slapper and a student
I'm keeping my trap shut, although talking, I am inclined
    This lot were all so dull like, now the pint, it was divine
Then the door swung open, a big man entered, cutting a dash
    How wore Crombie coat and soft hat, cavalry twills and a tash
He called the barman over and asked him, 'How are things?
    And slap up a pint there lad, before the fat lady sings.'
Well, this nice amiable fellow bought himself a drink
    Looked me in the eye, saying, 'Well, what do you think?'
So we got to talking, we got on mighty well
    He was such a charming man, had many tale to tell
He said his name was Anto, or Two Ton Tony Kelly
    And for the right price, he would get me a near-new telly
And did I know Slasher or Stitch-Them-Up McGurk?
    No, but I was familiar with John Joe, the West Meath Turk
I know all the Mulligans and the Currants in the flats
    I know the Punk and Fagan who's with your woman and her cats
I know the Potts and Baileys and the queer one in-between
    I even know the last verse of The Leaving Of Skibbereen
And well, I know Big Bella, she is so clean we hear
    The binmen make a collection for her each and every year
Well, that finally done it, it was when the penny dropped
    You see, it was in our school that Big Bella, the cleaner mopped
So there we were, the two of us, we were a School Street pair
    It was at that very moment, we decided to go on the tear
We drank beer by the bucket, yes, we went off the rail
    Then we hit the short ones to put the wind back in our sails
Then says he, 'Hang on a bit, you know I have a horse
    And I know for certain, that he can stay the course
So let's pool our money and put it on his back
    Honest to God, he's a sure thing and the jockey's name is Stack'
Then, over to the bookies we went and put on our poke
    The bookie looked and tittered, but we could not see the joke
Then, would you believe it, our horse, it won the race!
    And the stupid bookie's smile was on the other side of his face
Lady Luck smiled on us, gave us a great big grin

And now we are the nouveau riche, who said gambling was a sin?
Bellies started rumbling, we needed something to eat
    So up we went to Werburgh Street and Burdocks for a treat

There we ordered fish and chips and onion rings to go
    We sat outside, in Castle Street and ate them, nice and slow
We wondered about Burdocks, why they serve such a feast
    It was then we concluded it was how the fish was greased
Lord Edward stood on the corner, glowing friendly and warm
    'Do you fancy a drink Anto? Let's have a few ports in this storm'
We entered this establishment for the last of many flings
    I called the barman over and asked, 'How are things?
Could I have two pints please?' was my simple request
    'Of course you can, with pleasure, it will put hair on your chest'
As we stood in the corner, this lad bumps into my arm
    My pint goes skyward, hits a fellow, absent of charm
This chap lumbers over, saying, 'I think you have gone too far'
    Gives me an almighty wallop and I slide down the bar
Anto, well he took exception and gives your man a hefty dig
    To mine and Anto's surprise, he knocks off your man's wig
An old dear says, 'Look, a rat!' as she makes for the door
    As your man's Irish jig goes sliding across the floor
Then her drinking partner slowly goes into swoon
    Keels over onto this drunk that they call Muldoon
Muldoon wakes and shakes himself, saying, 'What is all this stink?
    I mean, God Almighty, can't a man have a quiet drink?'
Then baldy, he gets up and he's staggering more and more
    Saying to all and sundry, that he will even up the score
He set his sights on Anto, at him he goes and dives
    Just when the door opens and the publican arrives
Anto goes and steps aside, as baldy is in full leap
    He hits the publican head on and they end up in a heap
So baldy, he is in trouble, he destroyed your man's new suit
    And the publican kept repeating, 'It is like Beirut'
Baldy got his marching orders, yes, he had his last swig
    So that left me and Anto and a very mangy wig
The publican said, 'Gentlemen, you can stay till the last bell rings
    So tell me, any questions?' We said in unison,
                                'Yes, how are things?'
Tomorrow is another day!

E C Mulvaney

THE BUNNET

We all ken what a bunnet is -
The head gear for a male!
It comes in shapes and sizes,
Styles and colours make you smile.
But it's no laughing matter
To the mannie o' the hoose,
It's a very serious business
When you lose it to a moose!

This story gives us all a laugh
I'm sure you have a tale!
Of how a bunnet wasn't found
Oh, can you hear the wail?
They searched around, inside and out,
The bunnet was still lost,
But the answer came the next day
In a parcel in the post!

The use o' bunnets is quite large,
You wear them on yer heid!
You tak' them aff and use them
More to sit upon and read.
And if you find some mushrooms,
Then what's better than the hat?
It will keep them a' taegither
Till you put them in the fat!

Before this story ends itself,
I'd like you all to know
That we all tak' a pride to wear
A bunnet - just for show!
It's warm, it's auld and comfy
And I can vouch for that,
For you never can replace it
With any other hat!

Elizabeth M Sudder

FREDERICK WILD - A CAUTIONARY TALE

Frederick Wild, his sister's page
Took to drink at a tender age,
Her wedding breakfast, his downfall,
Drank red wine, champagne, port and all.
His father kept a public house,
Young Fred would creep down like a mouse
And help himself to wine and ale,
He learned to drink it by the pail.
Frederick Wild, precocious child
Drank pints and pints and pints of mild.
One night, he said, 'Well, just one more,'
Then slid unconscious to the floor.
His father, rising from his sleep
Went to the bar, his books to keep.
He stumbled over fallen boot,
Found Young Fred pickled as a newt.
His father never touched a drop,
Young Fred did not know when to stop.
Many times his father found him
Senseless; thought the drink had drowned him!
Couldn't break his son's obsession,
Thought he might yield to confession.
Next day Fred drank lots of brandy,
Father knew the priest was handy.
He went and fetched him from next door,
To save the boy upon the floor.
His father hurried in the priest,
Too late! The poor boy was deceased.

Roy Ramsay

A BALL OF NEEDLES

I was sleeping on the grass
Next to an old kettle made of brass
I was idling the warm afternoon away
Since the people who feed me went away.

I'm always busy come the night
Looking for food with all my might
Keeping the garden free from slugs and snails
Until the morning pales.

The children next door, they're really sweet
I can hear the pitter-patter of their feet
They play ball by the garden pond
And kick it in our abode beyond.

Yet the other afternoon as I had a nap
I was woken up quickly with a snap.
One of the boys picked me up
It wasn't my fault, he got the needles
They were given to me for self-defence!

He dropped me down upon my snout
He nearly knocked me right out.
He decided it wasn't enough
Kicked me again and started to laugh!

I thought I was a goner
I felt dizzy all around
Then heard his mother in the corner
Telling him to leave me on the ground.

I love people, I really do
Despite what a friend told me they do
They throw us hedgehogs on the road
Thinking we can leap to safety like a toad!

Raymond Spiteri (Havant)

MIDNIGHT ON THE RIVER

Moonlight spreading across the water
A small launch passes on its lonely way
The chugging of its engine sounds like soft laughter
Silent is the river disturbed only by the spray.
A peaceful picture, restful to the eye
Blackness broken by the moonlit sky
Depth and motion in black and white seen.
A loneliness, quietude, beauty all its own
Birds sleep, a different picture tomorrow will be shown
Small police launch on river this moonlit night
You make a serene and gentle sight
Surrounded by the water black as ink
Lovelier than an artist's brush could paint.
Only a camera a picture of you could take
To capture the movement you leave in your wake.
The dawn comes too soon with its cares of the day
And this picture so pleasing, will soon fade away.

Dorothy Leech

PAX PLUSCARDENSIS

Over Pluscarden the wind warps
Shadows across awned barley:
Yellow broom, tree-combed, heather weft,
Larksong waterfall, lambs' baaing.
A deer leaps forest fence:
Bell rings hollowed sky compline
Breaking the covenant of silence -
Sing, chant the vaulted centuries:
Rock, echoing rock.

Stuart Mortished

ROSY SKY

The passionately gracious grandeur, possessed within the sublime
tenderness of a divine rose.

Affectionately displays an amorous virtue, which only its
romantic trance delicately shows.

More poetically ardent than the amiable nostalgia, each subtle
petal's scenic verse enchantingly bestows,

Upon the opulent poise which a heart's zealous sentimentality,
so gregariously knows.

It shall have been affluently blessed, with such a serenity,
without the need for an arousing dream.

Superfluous to every audacious wish made by a child, or tiny
raindrop, within life's timeless stream.

For its compassionate subtlety weathers each day, to remain
Susceptible to the night's reflective moonbeam,

Allocating pensive desires to be aired, if merely by idle thoughts,
inspired by how we deem love to seem.

By its pure, radiant splendour, imploring emotions within the tender
grace placed upon each beating heart.

It motivates each eternal amen from a prayer, to seem provocatively
switched from the subtle end to the start.

Whilst emitting a desire to reveal that love's sheer empathy,
devotedly yearns to play romance's assiduous part,

Its sincerity creates the aptitude's emotions bare, like colours
displayed through a paintbrush's delectable art.

Submissively, suggesting that its affectionate romance, shall be
there for eternity and another day,

Radiating an intensive objective, sought by destiny, charming
an oblique fate to which one must obey.

How else might such a florescence portray in truth the beauty,
of the proposals which lovers may say,

Declaring to share, the love which they bare, with their hearts
and their souls, for eternity, within every way?

To emit such a precious empathy, to the emotional desires
when lovers must cry.

Refines compassion to never erode its composure, remaining
of its potent tact, so hypnotically high.

For its stem as it rises, appearing as its elegant complexion,
for all time which has gone by.

Allows nature to nurture its beautiful appeal, to all that which a
tender, divine rose presents in its presence . . .

. . . beneath the rosy sky.

Páraic Folan

ON BEAUTY

I have witnessed with my own eyes and can affirm that,
When the morning sun touches the snow fields of the high Alps,
The shades of mauve to pink light revealed to the climber,
Are of stunning beauty, as light transforms white.
I have witnessed with my own eyes and can affirm that
When spring touches the barren hills of Namaqualand,
The rainbow shades of the petals spilling across the veldt
Are of transporting joy, as flowers transform the desert.
I have witnessed with my own eyes and can affirm that,
When the racing green E-types snaked round the chicane at Goodwood,
In line astern, the thrill stirs the response from the onlookers
And as the heroes pass, gasping transforms to cheers.
I have witnessed with my own eyes and can affirm that,
The Berlin Wall fell, that Nelson Mandela walked free
And that our grandchild's first smile was for you
And that these were miracles all, as calm transforms to tears.
And yet the sight which is to me more beautiful,
That moves me most,
That fills me with wonder,
Is you, this morning, my love,
As, fresh from the shower,
You smiled for me.

David Lankshear

SEARCHING

Man's natural desire is to discover new things.
Discovery, a word of adventure,
Where seas rage in storms
And whales and dolphins surface to breathe the air.
Seagulls weave on the wind,
Ships ride on the waves,
Carrying cargoes to new places.
Where Captain Cook's vessel, named Discovery,
Sailed across the oceans
Carrying cargoes to new places.
Ships ride on the waves,
Seagulls weave on the wind
And whales and dolphins surface to breathe the air,
Where seas rage in storms.
Discovery, a word of adventure,
Man's natural desire is to discover new things.

Linda Knight

POETRY STEW

Take a cupful of words and simmer on a stove,
Add three pinches of Barnsley, Hereford and Hove.

Take a sentence, dice and chop,
Sprinkle in a comma and a full stop.

Take four capital letters and thinly slice,
Add to the words to make nice.

Stir in rhymes,
One or two
And you've made
Poetry stew.

Francis Page

THE THING

The whispers were so insistent,
you must go to Fletton Woods tonight.
I tried to push them from my mind,
useless. No more I tried the whispers to fight.

Reaching the woods it was so dark
why hadn't I thought to bring a torch?
Still something was luring me into those woods,
entering I found my skin beginning to scorch.

Suddenly, a hand tightly gripped my arm,
screaming, I tried in vain to break its hold.
The heat left me now, my skin felt icy.
Gibbering, I tried futively the hand to unfold.

Then a face appeared in front of me.
A face without a body, the hand on my arm ghastly.
My heart was beating so much, I felt it would burst,
such a horrible face, not human, but beastly.

Suddenly, the face started to kiss me, I gagged,
struggling madly, I managed to break the hand's hold.
Vomiting, I fled away from those hateful lips,
reaching home, surprisingly I was in bed, so cold.

Relief flooded my whole mind and body,
until, seeing on my arm a bruise like a devil's face would be.
My lips were burnt and painful as well,
if it were not a nightmare, what had happened to me?

I guess I will never know the answer,
never again will I listen to whispers specific.
No more visiting Fletton Woods ever again,
something nasty lingers there. Horrific.

Marjorie Busby

A WINTER FABLE

As I lay awake one winter's night
I lay there all stiff with fright
For sitting on the edge of my bed
Was a ghostly figure that had no head.
It spoke to me as I began to shake
And I pinched myself more wide awake,
'I'm sorry, sir,' this voice, it said,
'To startle you as you lie in your bed,
For I am in a quandary you see.
Please help to find my head for me,
For without my head I cannot rest
And keep wandering from chest to chest.
But once I know my head is found,
I may rest deep underground.'
'Fiddlesticks to you, dear sir,' I cried,
'You should have taken it with you the day you died!'
'Please, kind sir, do not shout,
Just lie there and hear me out.'
And as I lay there he told me this tale
That made me shudder and turn quite pale.
It wasn't until a long time after
That my body shook in silent laughter
As I thought of the tale he'd told me,
It filled my heart with a sense of glee
As he told me of a warrior bold,
One who'd been brave and true.
How he'd fought for his lady's love
And how he was made to rue.
'I'll tell you how my story began,
If you will hear me out.
And a stranger tale you will not hear
Of that there is no doubt.
It all began one summer's morn
As I strode along the road.
There, standing on a grassy sward,
Was a loathsome looking toad.
It fixed its bulging eyes on me
As it went hopping about, quite mad.
Such a horrible, loathsome thing
And yet, it made me feel quite sad.
It hopped along the grassy verge,

Matching me stride for stride.
I looked down at it, in pure disdain,
As it tried to catch my eye.
Suddenly, the toad spoke to me,
In a voice like gently falling rain,
'Kind sir. Dear sir. Please help me now,
As I am not what I appear to be.
I am not just a loathsome looking toad.
Will you listen to my plea?'
And as I looked at it in askance,
To my horror it began to dance.
Then it said, in a voice so clear,
'Do not worry, sir. Have no fear.
For a wicked witch cast a spell on me
And I am not what I appear to be.
Since I became a loathsome toad,
You are the first to travel this road.
Please help me, sir and do as I say,
Then you may leave to go on your way.
Pick me up and hold me close,
Then I shall tell you what to do.
Press me to your manly chest,
Hold me close to your breast.
From my bag take the bottle,
It's filled with wine, the very best.
Take a drink then kiss me twice.'
So spoke that loathsome toad.
I drank not once, not twice, but thrice.
As I stopped upon the road
I closed my eyes and then I kissed
That ugly old toad on the lips.
I felt it wiggle, I felt it surge.
I opened my eyes and there, on the verge,
Instead of a speckled, ugly toad,
A young maiden stood on the road
Naked as the day she was born.
She stood, so proud, so unashamed,
A beautiful picture to behold,
A picture that had never been framed.
I took off my cloak and covered
That beautiful damsel so fair.
Then I kissed her with a passion true
And caressed the gold of her hair.
I took her lovely white hand in mine

And said, 'Please tell me who are you?'
She answered, 'I am come from royal blood.
One who loves her father true.
I thank you for your cloak,
Which you have loaned to me.
Now I must go to my father's abode,
Where I'm sure he'll welcome me.
I know for me he will rejoice,
I am sure he will pay you well,
For you have brought me back to him,
From that wicked witch's spell.'
I thought, what else can befall me
Who'd performed such a heroic deed
As to kiss a loathsome toad on the lip,
Who had saved her from the abyss?
What more could that wicked witch do,
Who had cast her ancient spell,
To turn a maid into a toad,
Then cast it down a well?
What harm was there that could befall
Such a warrior, bold and true?
One who'd broken a witch's spell
I swear to you that's true,
Now, kind sir, hear me out,
As to you my tale I'll unfold.'
I lay back in my comfy bed,
Both hands placed beneath my head
And said, 'Carry on, please do.
Tell me what else happened to you.'
'I said to the maid, 'Please hurry along.
Quickly we must leave this place,
For I have no wish to meet this witch,
Or gaze upon her ugly face.'
Just then, an echoing, crackling laugh
Came racing across the sky.
'You are the one who broke my spell,
For that you must surely die.'
Lightning flashed, thunder crashed
And trees crashed to the ground.
I seized the maiden by the hand
And quickly did we bound
O'er fields, hedges, dykes and ditches,
Chased by warlocks and witches,
Voices ringing through the sky,

'Once we catch you, then you'll die.'
Tho' nearly spent, on we went,
With nerves all a-quiver.
Suddenly, through the trees, I saw
A wonderful flowing river.
'Quickly maiden, take my hand,
We must speedily cross the water.
We must go while it is still light
Or there will be blood and slaughter.'
Into that river we did leap
And swam for our very lives,
While witches, fiends and warlocks
Were left brandishing their knives.
And so, we swam, side by side,
Gone were our thoughts of slaughter.
For witches, fiends and warlocks
Cannot cross over running water.
As the witches, fiends and warlocks,
Screamed like banshees in the night,
We stood and embraced each other,
Then vanished into the night.
We laughed at them as we walked away,
Her hand was clasped in mine,
Tho' the night was as black as pitch,
For me, the sun, it seemed to shine.
We gathered leaves, grass and moss,
From which we made our bed,
Then side by side, we slept together,
Until the sun rose overhead.
Then waking from our sleep,
We rose and jumped to our feet.
Then as we stood and looked around,
We heard the most ferocious sound.
With beating hearts, we turned and saw
A most angry, fearsome-looking boar,
With wicked eyes, all rimmed with red,
It grunted, growled and dipped its head,
Then it came charging o'er the lea,
That put the fear of death in me.
I grabbed the maiden's hand and fled,
On feet that felt like lumps of lead.
With the maiden hanging onto my shoulder,
I dived behind a boulder
And the boar hit the rock with such a smack,

forwardpress

It broke the bones within its back.
There it lay, with its energy spent,
While we gazed at each other in sweet content.
I wiped the sweat from my brow
Then said, 'Fair maid, let us hurry now.
Let me take you by the hand
And lead you from this dangerous land
Through trees, scrub and prickly bramble.'
Hand in hand, we two did ramble,
Forgetting all about our hassle,
Until, through the trees, I saw a castle.
The bridge was up, the gates were closed
And a forlorn flag hung limply overhead.
'Oh, hurry kind sir, you must help me now,
For my father, he thinks I'm dead.
I know he will throw a feast for me
And pay you a ransom as well.
For you are the one who saved my life,
'Twas you that broke the witch's spell.'
As we approached the castle's walls,
A voice rang out from there.
'Who comes to see my lord?
Who is it that cometh there?'
I cried out, 'I am a warrior bold,
Accompanied by a maiden, pure and fair,
Who is your lord's long-lost daughter.'
'God's truth,' another voice cried, 'What do I see?
My favourite daughter has returned to me.'
Down came the bridge, the gates opened wide
And across he flew to our side.
A massive sword swung from his hand
And my feet turned to lead.
Shouting, ranting, cursing he came,
Swearing, 'You villainous, scurrilous hound,
You're the one who stole my girl,
I'll soon have you under the ground.'
He would not listen or take no heed,
His servants seized me in high dudgeon
And cast me into his dungeon.
There I lay throughout the night,
No one aware of my graceless plight.
There was no light for me to see
And only rats for company.
As I lay there, my heart was filled with despair

And I sometimes cursed that maiden fair.
Came the day they carried me out
And what I saw, filled me with doubt,
For gazing at me with an angry stare,
Was the father of the maiden fair.
I said, 'Please sir, don't blame me.
'Twas I that saved her from the slaughter.'
'I know, you rascal, what you did
And in return you ravished my dear daughter.'
What could I say, for it was true.
For on the night we crossed o'er the water
And slept on our bed of moss,
I took the love of his daughter.
As we lay with arms entwined,
She'd placed her lips upon mine
And we swore to love each other true.
That night for me the sun did shine.
Now I stood there like an abject wretch,
While his daughter made an urgent plea.
He just stood there, so grim of face,
Then I saw his eyes grow cold.
A trembling began within my knees,
I was no longer a warrior bold.
I said, 'Dear God, oh help me please.'
Then he spoke these words to me.
'Thou valet thou. Oh, thou scurrilous hound,
I'll soon have you under the ground.
Thou shalt not grow one day older.'
Then he struck my head clean off my shoulders.
It must have lain there, at my feet,
But this I could not tell,
For by that time, I knew for sure,
My soul was on its way to Hell.
They placed my body deep underground,
But my poor head couldn't be found.
I've searched the country, place by place,
But cannot find my head or face,
That's why you see me here,
Filling you with ghostly fear.
People ask, 'Why do you want your head?
No matter what you say or do,
You would still be lying dead.'
But that's not the point, you see,
For without my head, I cannot be me.

Each ghost who sees me, often asks, 'What is that without a head?'
Each one says he cannot tell,
So they don't know who is dead
And that is why I cannot rest,
Until my head is there, upon my chest.
Then all my friends will know it's me
And welcome me into eternity.
Satan took one look and said,
'You can't come in here without a head,
For who you are we cannot tell.
Was it you that broke the spell?'
I've been to the realms above,
Where I searched for my head.
They said, 'We don't know who you are.
We don't even know you're dead.'
So, all I'm asking, sir, from you,
Could you help me find my head?
And I can rest in eternal peace
Then all my wanderings will cease.'
I sat up straight within my bed
And to that ghostly figure said,
'Your head I cannot find, that's true,
But I have a photograph of you.
You must pin it on your tunic
Then all the angels will greet you
With their harps and music
And with the angels you may dwell
For you did break the witch's spell.
Then he said, 'Please, give it to me, sir
So I may pin it to my chest.
Thank you, dear sir, for all you have done,
Now I'm away to my eternal rest.'

The moral of this story is plain to see,
To those who lie dreaming, just like me.
Let your thoughts dwell in the land of fantasy,
I'm sure you'll enjoy it, the same as me.

Albert Gormley

NIGHTINGALE

Sing little nightingale
Your bitter-sweet serenade for me;
Lying awake on this moonlit night,
I'm snared somewhere between
Uncertainty and certain ecstasy -
A prisoner counting the chains,
My heart framed within that old refrain;
Robinson Crusoe, neither lost nor found
My emotions breezing on unchartered ground

Sing little nightingale
Your heart-thorned song for me;
Cupid's arrows,
So mean, so sharp, so narrow
Have me weeping like a willow tree -
Acting like a love-struck boy,
War-torn by the promise of so distant a joy;
Well-worn and smitten,
Bitten by the beauty of spirit
Of my loving vision

Sing little nightingale
Your melancholic muse for me;
Sing of wild child love
Roaming half-abandoned plains
Of Wildean pleasure;
My sweet salt tears
Corrode yearning inroads
To the heart of the lover
I would give my soul to discover -
Uptight and undercover

Sing little nightingale
Your bitter-sweet serenade for me;
As my love remains a shadow . . .
A tear misspent on an empty pillow.
Sing little nightingale
Your heart-thorned song for me
As my love remains a shadow . . .
A tear misspent on an empty pillow.

David Byrne

A LETTER TO MANKIND, FROM MOTHER EARTH

What anthem for my slow death?
Too late the anthem.
No need to compose a requiem, every
Living thing will have perished,
Because of your insatiable hunger and greed
You have, with your pollution, destroyed
The seasons, upset the balance of nature.
Before your interference nature was allowed
Time to heal the natural calamities, but
Then you, mankind, took on the duties of
A lesser god and in two giant steps went
From brilliancy to mediocrity, destroying not
Only your own habitat, but the habitat of
All living creatures.

I was, according to you, the most beautiful
Planet in all the universe, a jewelled orb.
From space I looked incredibly beautiful, nature
Arranged the seasons, every species had its
Compliment, then you came like an invading
Machine, that ever mobile being.
I have witnessed your Iliads and Odyssies
Throughout the ages of Man.
You have reached down into the very depths
Of the oceans where life-forms thought they
Were safe from your human pollution, my tears
Will never replenish those oceans.
Throughout the ages of man there have been
Prophets of doom, in bibles, holy books and
Among philosophers, they had no foresight into
The future, they had only to study mankind
And his follies to foretell your future.

Your greatest achievement has been the arrangement
Of war and your own destruction.
You do not need the nuclear bomb or
Indeed a nuclear accident to finally destroy
My beautiful planet, this jewelled orb, this
Incredibly beautiful; in your own words;
Mother Earth!
From my beginning I survived all the natural
Catastrophe's but this present unnatural catastrophe

I may not survive your final folly.
Perhaps in another time on another planet,
You, mankind, in your absence could be charged
With the crime of matricide.

I remain,
For the present,
Your Mother Earth.

Gerard Kenny

ACHIEVEMENT

Within this cultivated plot was beauty in profusion
No tangle weeds allowed to mix and mingle in confusion.
A wonderful oasis in the middle of the town
A credit to the owner, a lady of renown.

Her garden was a mass of blooms, a colourful array,
Of sweetly scented flowers, a grandiose display.
Green fingers worked their magic to produce this work of art
And every plant upon this stage played an important part.

Lupins in proportion, high stems in pride of place,
Whilst lobelia-aubretia and impatiens inter-lace.
The rose-filled arbour led onto a lawn of brilliant emerald-green
And in the rear a fountain played on this idyllic scene.

The lady, with her back to us, was down upon her knees,
A cameo in silhouette, completely at her ease.
Another tray of bedding plants was waiting patiently
To take their place, then amplify the beauty we could see.

Her smile reflected pleasure when she became aware
Of strangers at her garden gate who marveled at the care
Taken with every single task; that helped her to maintain
This perfect English garden in her very own domain.

Stan Taylor

THE LOTUS BLOSSOM

On the water
Is still
But the growth begins
And the water fills
The lotus blossom
Sweetly smells
The fragrance
Of Jesus foretells
The lotus blossom
Petals so wide
The beauty
No one can hide
From the roots
To the petals so bright
The water
The beauty cascading
So many to be seen
The lotus blossom
Beautiful, serene
Across the span
Of water fine
A beauty so refined
Across the banks
To the water's edge
Trails the lotus blossom
So beautiful leads
On and on it goes
The beauty
Of the lotus blossom
Slowly entwines
And grows.

Maureen Thornton

BY THE SEA

Sleep on the beach within the dunes
Watch the stars at night
Listen to the sea slap against rocks
Gather driftwood to light a fire.

Rise at dawn to see the fishing fleet come home
Buy fish from the boat on the quay
Eat sardines cooked on an open fire
Walk by the edge of the sea.

Make love in a beach house to a beautiful male
Two bodies as one surfing the waves
Smell seaweed on the breeze
Explore the bay to discover new caves.

Listen to gulls as they screech
On this empty, deserted winter beach
Try to paint the scene
In azure, ochre, brown and green.

Walk alone on the cliffs with the dog
Listen to the horn announce the fog
Feel the chill, make for home
Light the fire, cook a meal.

Kick the logs on the fire
Watch the embers spark
Put up my feet and go to sleep
It's dark.

Pamela Baily

SEASONS

Eternal light shines through the dullest day;
Though dark and dismal clouds, or mist, loom low;
Beyond this heavy greyness there is light,
This is as it should be, the seasons change.
The Earth needs cooling after heat-ray sun,
With wind and rain for nature to survive;
Likewise as humans, needing change of scene,
Each season guides us through this earthly scheme.

The winter's crisp and frosty air protects
The dampened soil, then snowy blankets fold.
Now nature sleeps its well-deservéd rest.
Below the ground, new roots begin to strive.
Soon spring returns and nature, now renewed,
Brings buds to life, then colours, softly hued.

June Cooper

HERE AND NOW

Amidst the economic strife,
The flowers bloom and come to life.

Amidst the anguish and the pain,
The country lanes thrive with rain.

Amidst the toil and careworn faces,
A smile and welcome still embraces.

Amidst the selfishness of Man,
Humanity will have also ran.

Amidst the uncaring massed around,
A small voice somewhere can be found.

Praising life with its ups and downs,
Thanking God for life which still abounds.

Rosemary Whatling

LAMENT FOR A FEATHERED FRIEND

She was walking along the garden path
Pretty and plump and brown
But death lay in the shadows
Ready to strike her down

Her mate sat on the old green seat
He loved to sit there and sing
But death was watching the little bird
Ready to clip her wing

I went in to put on the kettle
Too late, I heard her screams
For death had nabbed the little bird
And ended all their dreams

Her mate flew away
A bus passed; the telephone shrilled
Life just went on
On the day a little bird was killed.

Marjory Gordon

THE LEWKNOR CUCKOO

From a beech grove, catching fire
Of setting sun upon a pale
North-western Chiltern chalk-scarp hill-slope,
Which overlooked the gault clay vale
Near Lewknor in Oxfordshire,
A cuckoo called.

Did Leofeca, Middle Anglo-Saxon
Likewise listen here in hope,
Long ago hear her eventide dusk canon
Standing in his open wood - clearing at Leofecanoran,
Or did I, passing by, just catch
That ancient echo?

David Daymond

OUR WORLD

This is our world -
A farmer working in his fields,
Reaping what the good earth yields.
The seasons changing as he goes;
Hot in summer, then in winter it snows.

This is our world -
A factory worker in the mills,
A hiker plodding over the hills,
An aeroplane flying up on high,
Its vapour trailing across the sky.

This is our world -
A baby sleeping in its mother's arms,
Happy, contented, safe from all harms.
Golden sands and a calm blue sea,
Children playing and muffins for tea.

This is our world -
Bombs falling, shells exploding,
People running, screaming, hiding,
Earthquakes, famine, illness and death,
Funerals, tears and a last gasping breath.

This is our world -
Hot sun and deserts, cold winds and ice,
Riches and poverty, elephants and mice.
Black man or yellow man, red man or white,
Night-time there's darkness, daytime is light.

This is our world -
Beauty or ugliness, peace or war,
Cruelty or kindness and good deeds galore.
A sad old world, a brave new world,
With all its contrasts, this is our world.

Pauline Anderson

THE GIANT REDWOOD TREE

I started life as a seed
I soon outgrew every weed
I was reaching out for the sky
What I was thinking, was how high?

I sprouted branches here and there
Someday they will make a chair
Growing, growing every day
Grow some more that's what I say

I'm the tallest tree in the land
From top to the bottom I look rather grand

Standing tall in the wind and rain
Raindrops dropping down my grain
Sending messages back to my brain

My outer coat is turning dark red
I get my colour from what I'm fed
I grow many roots that travel underground
This way and that not making a sound

They would make lots of money if they cut me down
This kind of talk makes me frown
Our landscape wouldn't be the same
As people travelled by on the morning train

I hope I live to a ripe old age
Before they turn me into page after page.

Brian Botsford

THE SECRET

I am across a still, small brook
And a deer standing there beside it
I saw its eyes give a gentle look
Looking straight across at me.
It seemed surprised to see me there
For it suddenly turned around
It moved into the undergrowth
With a massive bound
I wondered whether to follow it
To see where it had gone
Just to see what mysteries lay there
Taking a walk and all alone
Further I walked into the forest
And came across a glade
I had never seen such beauty
With my standing in the shade.
Suddenly, the deer appeared
As if to say, 'You've found me'
There were animals of woodland kind
As happy as can be
I looked and nodded to the deer
Saying, 'The secret is yours and mine
For no one will come and bother you
Thank you for trusting me.
God has given you a little haven
So you can roam the forest free
The wonders that I've seen today
The secret will stay with me.

Jean Lloyd-Williams

THE FAIR MAIDEN OF SPRING

The sun is the gold of your hair,
The carpet of bluebells, your eyes.
The velvet of green grass, your dress,
Your brown shoes, the sparrow that flies.

Your hair is awake before me,
Filling the world with its gold,
Dancing around the daffodils,
Giving a new life to the old.

At your eyes, I stare with amazement,
The beautiful, cold, silent blue,
The air is heavy with perfume,
The promise of new life is true.

Sometimes, when I tread on your dress,
It feels like a cushion of air,
Giving the mountains their beauty,
Shaded sometimes by your hair.

Your shoes, they are my alarm clock,
Their song brings new life to the day,
In the woods, the parks and the gardens,
They always have so much to say.

Spring, you did not just happen,
No, you were a gift of love,
Thanks be to Him, who created you,
Thanks be to our God of love.

Sandra J Walker

THE YELLOW ROSE

Years ago a gift was given to me …
A yellow rose bush for an anniversary.
In my garden I planted it for all to see
For it held great sentiment for me.

It only flowered for two seasons or three
Even though I tended it religiously.
It looked so sad as the years went by
And eventually I felt that it had died.

I reluctantly removed it from the ground
As no sign of life was there to be found.
And sadly placed it on the compost heap
Praying that my rose would rest in peace.

No sleep did befall me that very night
As I felt I had robbed it of its life,
So early next morning, come the light of dawn,
I retrieved the rose bush, which looked so forlorn.

Stripped of its foliage, its roots exposed,
I carefully held my dear little rose.
Then, in my garden, a new location I found
And gently laid it in the ground.

But it looked so stark . . . no sign of life,
Its naked branches stretched up to the light.
I reassured it and tended it every day
In the hope that it would find its way.

It took some time but new growth could be seen
And shoots appeared where none had been.
And to my delight, I can honestly say,
It has flourished ever since that day.

From my kitchen window, it's in full view
For this dear little rose has a life anew.
I feel it is thanking me in a strange sort of way
For endeavouring to save its life that day.

I cannot believe the wonders I see,
Its recovery seems like a miracle to me.
Hence the power of prayer and its fight to survive,
I know that it's glad to be alive.

Thus, my dear yellow rose will always be
A very special rose to me.

Vivienne Vale

IT MAKES SENSE

With my eyes open, what can I hear?
Nothing.
With my ears pinned against the wall, what can I see?
Nothing.
If I hear nothing. See nothing. Ultimately I know nothing.
But by closing my eyes, so many distant sounds become clear.
Just by covering my ears, so many distant visions are now near.
All those sights to be seen. All that there is to be heard.
My eyes are firmly closed, but I still see more birds.
I recognise what is behind me, below me and above me
Although I face straight ahead.
Allowing my environment to speak to me
Becoming familiar with the language of nature.
Identifying with all that existed yesterday
Even though I only gained that knowledge today.
I watch. I observe. Slowly absorbing the sounds of the Earth's music
Listen carefully. Pay attention. So I can see how the Earth is dressed.
Because to hear, is to know.
To see, is to know.
And to know, is to want to know more.

Mark Cole

A VISION OF BEAUTY

As dawn greets the springtime rose
With its bright and silky glow
It fills my heart with such content
In a vibrant colour show

And as its petals come to life
Its perfume fills the air
Alive and swaying in the breeze
With beauty, style and flair

I stood back to admire
It took my breath away
Its sunshine lights a pathway
With its colours on display

I dare not try to stroke it
So fragile, soft and red
I merely wish to caress it
Alive in its flowerbed

But the gentle winds grow stronger
And its petals start to fly
A flaming silken beauty
Its ending made me cry.

Marilyn Davidson

OUR BEST FRIEND

He came to us a doggie stray,
The soldiers liked him right away.
Returning love and joy each day
No guns could drive our chum away.

Through many months of war and strife
He shared our fighting soldiers' life.
He raised our spirits with his joy
His comrades simply called him 'Boy'.

He lived on scraps and cadged our beer
Our soldier chum who had no fear.
With us on icy ground he'd sleep
But when we slept his watch he'd keep.

Then orders came to take a town
And we were told to, 'Put him down'.
In spite of pleas to let him live
The powers would be would never give.

They put a bullet through his brain
And no one spoke of him again.

Gordon Paul Charkin

WHY?

Why does it always seem to rain, on
    Weekends, or on a bank holiday?
Why does the bus I rush to catch,
    Not wait, but quickly pull away?
Why don't I look like Cindy Crawford,
    Even on a rare bad hair day?
Why can't I live the life of
    Riley in good old LA?
Why is there always so much
    Violence reported on the news every night?
Why can't we learn to live together in
    Peace, without the constant need to fight?
Why do we all rush around and
    Not take the time to see
The beauty of nature around us, the
    New buds on the blossoming magnolia tree?
Why did the three tiny baby robins
    In the nest in my garden, have to die?
Before they even got the chance to
    Spread their wings and fly?
I wish I could find the answers
    To all these questions racing round
      And round in my head,
Maybe then, I'd be able to relax
    More and enjoy my life instead!

Dot Ridings

IT'S COLD IN THE MIST ON DARTMOOR

It's cold in the mist on Dartmoor
and humans often lose their way
when everything is covered
in the damp, cold mist of grey.

In the damp, cold mist of Dartmoor
one is in the nether world
where the ghosts of human beings
wander uncurtailed.

They seek more souls to surrender
their claim to life on Earth
so the ghostly throngs of grey
float out to seek their human prey.

If you hear the banshee calling
you know you are going to die
in the damp, cold mist of Dartmoor
you will breathe your last sigh.

Then you will join the ghostly throng
that are the living dead
and you will help them to provide
the living humans, full of dread.

Your swirling coat will be as one
with the mist upon the moor
and you will come to float around
where you walked before.

Danny Pyle

I AM ... LIFE

Now with knarrelled bones I bend,
Once everyone's almighty friend.
A focal point, a calm retreat,
Where children would clamber to meet.
Born of root and sapling sprang,
A welcome shade for tired Man.
All caressing arms of me
To watch in witness as a tree,
Through the hours of darkened night,
The world's unending troubled plight.
I watch and stand and grow and sigh
At those who hurry quickly by
And birds their nest, each strand put straight.
From bush and flower and garden gate,
Have offspring, fragile, frail and weak,
Searching out with tiny beak,
For worm and berry, round and sweet,
To grow and fly beneath my feet.
While folk of busy nature rest
Awhile to catch their breath
Among the shade of branches wide
I hide them from those prying eyes,
To chat among the daisies small,
To tell of tales so long ago,
Fishermen, hard-working souls,
Who long for great things it's their goal.
While children hug and swing and sing
And dance in a happy ring.
But one among whose words did tell,
Of peace and joy and all is well,
His face, a beacon shining bright,
Throughout the day and through the night.
I stand and watch my fruit is ripe,
They pick to build up for the fight.
Their journey will be hard, I know,
Be on your guard as you go.
This one with peaceful thoughts and true
Is taken by a motley crew.
Tried for an outrageous crime
For loving his own fellow man.
For those who heard were full of hope,

With daily lives they now could cope
And those who were not there to hear
Prayed again for this inspiring cheer.
I stared in silence for you see,
I am the great, wise, olive tree.
I've grown old and I've grown free,
In the garden of Gesemany.

Sally Crook-Ford

BIRD OF PARADISE

Close my eyes
Searching for the page,
A silhouette dancing -
Phantom of the night.

No sound
To disembody
This silence - just
Savage moonlight.

And you - eternal
Bird of paradise

Drifting
In ageless flight -
Encased by
Lofty, ancient walls.

A seducing angel
To my sight.

I expire -
Beneath your
Robe of white.

Ken Price

IN A SPIN

He holds me captive, under
his control - life and soul

depend on what he gives.

He knows I'm scared of
dark and cold unknown, of
regions where I might be

cast adrift.

On a good day, I can truly
say, he lifts my spirits up

to where the stars run rings
round Saturn, Jupiter and

Mars.

Many times I've tried to
break away - independence

holds no sway with him.

So, his warmth and gravity
have won - as I, the Earth,

spin once more

      to the sun.

Jennifer Wootton

INNOCENTS

'Flowers in the garden' - the buzzing of the bees
A host of gentle butterflies dancing on the breeze
The birds above are gathering nests within the trees
But gloom the weather now does bring as the ground begins to freeze
I am concerned about this nature thing - here is the growing fear
As the birds no longer sing, perhaps the end is near?
I hurry to my garden shed to gather up some straw
As I dread there could be death for those I do adore
Some bedding for the woodland folk - the tortoise and the fox
I must provide some warmth for them within a cardboard box
Why, oh why this winter's deed - why such awful weather?
I hope that I will succeed to gather my friends together
The soil is cold and too uninviting - the plants begin to fade
I wish the sun was brightening with warmth within the glade
Save yourselves, you little ones, your Saviour is up there praying
This Hell on Earth is no way fun - that goes without the saying
When spring does come, I will look for you, to offer more of loving
Then when does come the warming sun, you will be back above in
'Flowers in my garden' have all now gone to sleep
My heart, it does now harden as I begin to weep
The birds, the bees, the butterflies - the others out there hidden
I pray that none of you had died as that by me is forbidden
'Flowers in the garden' the Earth about is warming
I'm glad that I did play my part in giving you that warning
Bless you all my dearest friends - I am your loyal 'brother'
My love to you this old one sends - God bless you nature's mother!

John Leonard Wright

GRAND BUTTERFLY

Butterfly you're so grand,
You flutter where spring and
Summer join hand in hand,
You flutter as the warm sun beams,
Where everywhere sparkles and gleams,
You flutter in the colourful
Gardens where secrets are well kept,
After winter has slept,
You flutter where the colourful flowers open,
Summer's love token,
You can hear the bluebells ring,
The birds sing, the woodlands call
Long after autumn fall,
You love to flutter in the meadow
Where the poppies are scarlet red
And the cornflowers are blue,
Yellow are the sheaves, as nature says hello
To the long summer eves,
You flutter near a trickling stream,
You then rest on a flower where you love to dream.

Joanna Maria John

WALLACE THE WORM

Wallace the worm decided one day
That he wanted to join the circus.
He was fed up of soil and his everyday toil
And he longed for excitement and trouble.

To the circus he went and he entered the tent
And he spoke to an elephant there.
He said, 'What can you do, it's got to be new?'
And Wallace, he just stood and stared.

He thought and he thought and he then did a turn
On the trapeze and he certainly looked funny.
Said the elephant, 'That's good and I think that you should
Make this circus a great deal of money.'

But as he swung high, there came a loud cry
From Wallace as he plunged to the ground.
He'd slipped off the swing with a strange sort of ping
And into the elephant's eye he did fly.

The elephant said, 'Wallace, just look what you'd done,
I can now only see with one eye.'
So a patch he now wore and of this I am sure,
The crowd they all shouted, 'Hi Eye.'

Is it a pirate or is it a clown?
An elephant with a patch on one eye.
He's got now top bill and that he is still
But to Wallace they shouted, 'Bye-bye!'

Amy Cornes-Torr

GLIDING WITH ANGELS

Sometimes I glimpse behind the door
of everyday reality to view
a rainbow stretching majestically across
a troubled sky watching with wonder
like a child upon virgin morning snow
but we are too engrossed with hectic lives
to admire the magic in front of our eyes.

Sometimes I glimpse behind the door
marvelling at mist floating over frost-filled fields
or a sunset turning clouds a flaming red,
like life transient before becoming grey again
gliding with angels in the awesome universe
and though I must enter the mad streets once more
I'm grateful to have glimpsed behind the door.

Guy Fletcher

AT DAYBREAK

Let us dance at daybreak
when fish spear the river
along sudden driftwood

Let us dance at daybreak
when fresh tears escape
from the gum trees

Let us dance at daybreak
when light begins to row in its canoe
and shadows hop on the ochre soil

Let us dance at daybreak
when the old woman counts shells
and shadows slither to the waterhole.

Mariana Zavati

FREE WITHOUT COMPETITIVE IN-FIGHTING

Of the sun, the moon is not a rival
For it isn't key to our survival.
But, as helper, it excels supremely.
Moonless, all nights would be dark extremely.

These top lights don't worship competition,
Like most humans, near to inanition.
Long-term, they both think co-operation,
Straining could upset the whole creation.

Thanks to both for their illumination
And contributing to Earth's salvation.
If we acted like a heav'nly body,
Our behaviour might not be so shoddy.

But, in noting this serene example,
We enrich our lives by just a sample.
Yes, the sun and moon are best at lighting -
Free without competitive in-fighting.

Allan Bula

THE CAT

Before the baby came the cat was king
Miraculously, a mother late in life, you still refuse to give up old loyalties
The cat knows this
Insolently smiling he curls under the baby's blanket
Suddenly, the baby cries to be fed
So you lift him from the cot to your breast
The cat becomes firmly entrenched
The cot is now definitely his domain
I can see by the way you turn to tease the cat
How the slowness of baby's feeding bores you
How different we are: maternal love consumed me when mine were babies
Or is that nostalgia? What about the fact that I do not like cats as kings?

Mónica Gurney

A STROLL ALONG THE MARMARA SEA

Into the Bosporus the sun dips . . .
Eastern gold bathes house-encrusted hills.
The Marmara gently shelters ships.
Familial fires stoke picnic grills.

Azure sea laps bolder-full beach,
And wind eases the heat-choked noon.
Silhouettes cast frugal lines, each
Rewarded - the calm an angler's boon.

A weathered man touts sweetcorn; all around
Tea brews in industrious kettles.
For once, happiness is the only sound -
All colour, joy and ripe red petals.

My youth is moored along this sacred soil,
This blessed, far off place without toil.

Thomas Humphrey

A SECRET YOU INSTIL?

I do believe I can receive the greatest gift of all
The only thing that matters is to listen when you call
You might be the spirit I might be a ghost
You might be the witness who brings the sacred host.

I might be the rainbow you might be the sun
Or maybe just an angel who knows the way it's done
In my heart I recognise that everything exists
But no one lives forever, only spirit can resist.

Call it love or call it truth, call it what you will,
An inner beat of mystery or a secret you instil?

Richard Spiers

WHEN AS A BOY

(And of a dunce)

When as a boy I stood alone in isolation's glare,
All humour vanished from my face, fain hidden in despair.
'O is this really happening, O am I so, so bad?'
I pinched myself and slyly glanced, O God, it must have had.

There's 'Peanut' Copperwood - the oaf, he's smirking ear to ear,
And Isobel - the vile hunchback, we call her 'Running Deer'.
Yet was it me, or one of them, mine innocence I sought,
It must have been most suredly, I was the one - was caught.

And so I stood, my face a mask, my mind blood-curdling shoots,
Whilst all around all carried on, they couldn't care two hoots.
Was I the leader of the gang - 'how now' mine erstwhile braves,
Each straining, wond'ring which is which - convex, perchance concaves.

At least I had not much to do there, standing in disgrace,
A pretty sight, a dunce's cap ill-fitting in its place.
And so the hours ticked away, I didn't have to learn -
Until some foolish fellow erred, and promptly took my turn.

In all I got quite used to it, the spiders clapped their hands -
As I approached the corner where they spun their mazy strands.
I used to marvel at their verve, their awesome industry,
Thence serendipity took stock, thereafter changing me.

And to this day, I take me to a corner of a room -
To think of all the positives whence privy to my doom.
For was it not the spider's zeal that showed me what to do,
And am I not the leader of a bigger gang than you?

Derek Haskett-Jones

A FRAGMENT OF THE COSMOS

No one can stay the leaves that fall in autumn
Or when night comes, still make the sun shine gold.
Our lives unfold within their preset purpose
So why should we have dread of growing old?
Is it false pride, or pain at ended yearnings?
Or envy of the young, their looks and friends?
Can it be doubt about a life hereafter?
Or thoughts of sordid rituals when life ends?

Yet death is just a word, a mental picture,
This built-up image creates all the fear.
No one in life is free from pain or sorrow
So why assume that death is worse than here?
Those fallen leaves, now dead, enrich the soil,
Their goodness brings the new growth in the spring.
Nature ensures that nothing old is wasted,
She will re-shape the poor man and the king.

Each day embraces morning, noon and sunset,
Each year plods relentless through four seasons.
All humans are mortal, and condemned to die
God has not thought to give us any reasons.
The mountains stood thousands of years before us
They will stand when we have gone from mind.
Perhaps when God surveyed all His creation
He took more pride in mountains than mankind.

How can one human be of great importance
Each one a speck on this large Earth of ours.
The Earth a fragment of one vast galaxy
Midst many other galaxies and stars?
Yesterday, death claimed a million people
They died of famine, pain, neglect and war.
Your gods glance down and see this every day
How can it really matter, one death more?

We must accept we are but transient guests
Upon this planet we call Mother Earth
Each of us a dust fragment of the cosmos
Awaiting death, and nature's own rebirth.
But when Mother Earth burns up and turns to dust
As all the stars and planets are bound to do.
Life on no other planet will mourn its loss
And none of your gods will remember you.

A E 'Mike' Turner

HAPPINESS

I have not reached the stars in all my days,
Nor scaled the mountain tops or trod the vales.
I have not sailed the mighty Maine,
Walked through forests green,
Or strayed upon a lonely plain.
I have not been in castles proud and strong,
In palaces or mansions grand.
Or seen the sunrise in the east
Or set beyond this wondrous land.
And yet, I've heard a newborn baby cry,
Held tiny hands, and wiped an eye.
Held larger hands and guided footsteps frail,
All with joy and happiness that did not fail.
And in this smaller world of mine
The clouds may form or sun may shine.
'Tis then perchance I stand and dream,
I'm such a small part of the planner's scheme.

Pat Adams

LEGACY

If the Earth was a close friend, you would listen
As she told you of her worries and her fears -
Of people making threats against her future.
You would hold her tightly, telling her
That you loved her and that it would be alright
Then she would be comforted and smile . . .

The sun would come out and the sky would be
As blue as the first cornflowers in summer.
White clouds playing hopscotch
Skimming across the pristine horizon.
You would hear the sweetest birdsong ever
Like straining your ears to catch the singing
From a distant abbey on a hilltop.

Grass would be oh so green underfoot
Like a velvet carpet. The perfume of a
Million flowers hanging heavy in the air

While the gentle humming of bees
Would play rag tag with shimmering butterflies
A soft fragrant breeze would gently rustle leaves
On trees - hanging like emerald dewdrops.
As you walked past the silver flowing river
You'd stop to drink from the pure, sweet water.

But . . . if you were the one causing all the worries and fears
You wouldn't care.
The sun would be trying to shine weakly
Through thick choking, swirling smog
The sky would be a sickly grey colour.
Pollution; you were warned
You did not care

The only noise you can hear now
Are the dying cries of the sick and hungry
As there is not enough food to eat
Water, that once was pure and sweet,
Is now undrinkable.
The green trees that willingly gave us life
Have now been sentenced to death
For what?
Just to satisfy Man's utter greed
'Birds, bees and butterflies, what are they?'

Our children will ask
Too soon we will forget

So, as the green earth, slowly turns brown
And we all gradually die
Pause for a moment in your ravaging of nature
- You may hear her sigh

Then as you continue to rape Gaia
For all she possesses
The last thing you will hear
. . . Is her silence.

Babsi Sherwin

STARLINGS

I was enthralled as I stood there
And watched the starlings in the air,
Sweeping and turning in unison,
Oh how! The dance went on and on.

Across the sky in rapid flight
Formation - manoeuvring a wondrous sight,
No stragglers there to spoil the dance
Or was this closeness just by chance.

'Twas like a ballet choreographed
By Nuryev or did they have
An inborn secret - that they alone
As starlings they have always known.

And as the darkness did descend
The birds' performance had to end,
And so they split away and veered
Towards their nests and disappeared.

John Dennison

A WEIGHT OFF MY MIND!

I'd like to be friends with the scales
You step on them cautiously, standing up straight
Eager and ready to check your weight
Breathe in calmly, silently pray, wondering what they'll reveal today
A certain shock - there's no disguise
For right before one's very eyes - it simply can't be true
The wretched things, they still display no change from ten stone two.

Despair. Sit in the chair. What is a girl to do?
I can't believe the scales say I'm still at ten stone two.

Feeling low, down and out
I'd like to throw the damned things out
Forget the diets, accept defeat, eat some chocolate, have a treat
From fat to thin or trim to slim
Which is it to be?
The scales they can never lie, nor be a friend to me.

Jules Leggett

PICKLE THE RESCUE CAT

As you sit on my lap and gaze into my eyes
I see love personified, a lady in disguise.
We love each other's company and really long to be
Together all the time - just you and me.
As I work at home you are always by my side
Waiting for a vacant lap, in blissful sleep to hide.
We communicate with knowing looks and body language so fine
That we know each other's needs, recognising every sign.
When you are fast asleep, I can't help but look at you,
Such feelings well up inside bringing a love so true.
Before you had little love but I can give you plenty
Now you've settled in and can take life very gently.
Before you came it was loneliness and emptiness and such
But now I feel fulfilled, that's why I love you so much.

Rita Hardiman

WHAT IS IT THOU HAST SEEN?
OR WHAT HAST HEARD?

Silent winged observance encircling the ancient oaks
To watch as horizons emerge, the unflinching disappear,
their scented fragrance on the air
Suspended for a voiceless moment to fall trembling in dignified elegance, leaving
an echoing thud on the earth
The repressive noise of buzz, stifling in the destruction
of the voiceless
Impatience, in their desiring to fell -
no observance to the first death, the dissolving of a life,
Man's intensity to abandon - to also fall
Death solitude, after 200 years of existing, 200 years of seeing, of hearing -
even the making of a spider's gossamer web
To have seen light in the darkness, as stars fall
and moonbeams dance on their branches
To have seen Man, bird, animal lovers, kiss under canopies of leaves
Bowing and dancing to the elements, but now motionless as metal grabs, grip
into your bark skin making you bleed
Leaving gashes as you are deposited onto a transporter
To be taken away from your birth - to be made into a second life by Man, until he
finally finishes with you and you die a final death
to be returned to the earth - uninvited into a permanent darkness
I have nested in your branches
I have felt you move to a soft summer's breeze
I encircle you in a final salute as you depart on motorway
with your sap tears falling - revealing the consciousness of being,
leaving a trail for someone to follow - farewell.

Hilary Jean Clark

SEAVIEWS

I fear winds that blow from west,
Kintyre and Arran veiled in mist
As cold descends like a shroud
Over distant lonely Ailsa proud.
All in grey as old Neptune rants
His rough an' cold hoary cantes.

Waves surge with shrieking tide
Across the stormy Firth of Clyde
Droplets vibrate again and again
As demons hammer on ev'ry pane.
Roof timbers loudly creak and cry
Like storm-tossed barks in agony.

Each wave a snorting wild-eyed steed
Foaming mane meshed in slimy weed
Churning maelstroms of shingly sand
In endless ranks storm waiting strand,
Assailing ancient foe of bloody yore
In timeless grinding of sea on shore.

Each raincloud like soggy balloon
Glidin' under pale an' sombre moon
Intent on casting off its watery coat
On poor sailor's storm-tossed boat,
Or on some soaked distant locality
Where folk do dwell, like you and me.

Lightning zig-zags from on high
From thunderous malevolent sky,
As dark peaks of Arran fluoresce
Momentarily in Thor's swift caress,
As eerie orange tinted, lighted sky
Glows as when sunrise's nigh.

Its gentle breezes from the West,
Summer's zephyrs are the best
As wavelets ripple at one's feet,
Amid the languid shimmering heat,
When tiny flecks of clouds fly high
In a heavenly calm of an azure sky.

I love to behold the red setting sun
As endless summer days are done,
Red, yellow, blue an' orange absorb

In flaming ambience o' blood-red orb,
Silhouetting isles in far distant view
In heavenly artist's, vivid sea millieu.

The open sea's a must for me,
None other place can ever be.
Sea's spirit never fails embue
Wraps my soul in rainbow hue,
Invigorating each languid part,
Recharging too tired old heart.

Ronald Deen

A NEW DAY

The stars are gone
And dawn's pink
Finger tip born,
Spreading across the sky.

The day awakes!
In the distance
The rattle of milk bottles
And the cry of a child

Birds are singing,
Then rise to the sky
Calling! Calling!
Floating on the wind

The sound of a radio,
And somewhere a
Car Starts up
Revving its engine

The roar of the sea
As it breaks on the shore,
And the love that I have
That is yours forever more.

Joan May Wills

THE LION IN WINTER

What does the lion in winter wear,
And who will be his dresser?
We questioned and then tried to probe
The brains of our professor.

>Who hum'd and ha'd and fell asleep,
>So independent we did meet,
>To plan outfits to warm our beast,
>Surviving far from torrid heat.

Downhearted trying to keep his pride,
In blizzards, sleet and snow,
His family growling bitterly,
Bemoaning fate, they'd sunk so low.

>By Internet around the world,
>Designers we did seek,
>To clothe and warm our lion king,
>In elegance so sleek.

Yves St Laurent and Zandra Rhodes,
Westwood, Lacroix, McCartney,
Dolce Gabana and Dior,
Gucci, Georgio Armani.

>Donna Karan, Ralph Lauren,
>Chanel, Alex McQueen,
>Designers vied to clothe in style,
>Our downcast lion, grown so lean.

Samples of high quality,
By airmail soon were sent,
Mohair, tweed and cashmere,
Only the best for his raiment.

>Eco colours naturally,
>No furry mink or sable,
>Perhaps some woolly-pullies knit
>In stocking-stitch and cable.

The Ladies Guilds then rallied round,
With crocheted scarves and hats,
Their colours dazzling to the eye,
Plus sturdy fleecy mats.

>Safari staff all ooh'd and ah'd,
>As outfits piled apace,

With fingers crossed we hoped to bring
The smile back to our lion's face.

But how to enter lion's den,
We huddled close and pondered,
And who would take the first brave step,
Across the snow we wondered.

Someone suggested melodies,
From classical to rock,
And heavy meals could tranquillise,
Our noble beast, we would not shock.

A stereo system soon installed
Poured music from all nations,
The lion replete had closed his eyes,
As we took up our stations.

But duffle coats would not protect,
Nor magic charms defy
Our lion's power, we would need
Some armour from the FBI.

The FBI disdainfully,
Our simple plea denied,
Berating us for wasting time,
With threats they let the matter slide.

So once again we met, discussed,
The problem's every angle,
A Superman or woman might,
Our tangled web, untangle.

A rustic meal with bread and wine,
Our spirits did restore,
Our old professor shared a glass,
First one, then two, then many more.

'Leave this to me,' he grandly said,
'Experience I have gained,
From circus folk in taming beasts,
Such knowledge I've retained.'

You'll see our lion smile again,
Clothed in designers' best,
His pride intact, his wife and cubs,
Preening in matching outfits rest.

What does the lion in winter wear?
    All ask our dear professor,
    Designers' best he firmly states,
    I'm his exclusive dresser.

L A Troop

THE HEART-SHAPED PEBBLE

Fingers stroke the pebble you place in my palm,
Heart-shaped, with a fossil embedded in time.
Bringing memories of turbulent seas now calm,
A beach chalet, our haven, yours and mine …

Gulls circling, above morning's soft haze,
Hunting with loud cries and inquisitive gaze.
Summer fun, children paddling, nana's showing their knees
Soaring kite-surfers, teased by boisterous breeze!

The thrill of air shows, Red Arrows over the sea,
Aerobatics, wing-walkers that waved to you and me!
Autumn sparrows, chattering among cliff-rooted trees,
Birds in migration, soaring over the Leas.

Shingle murmurs, sunset embraces undulating sea,
Reflecting still, on what used to be.
Content, aware of memories we share,
Evoked by the heart-shaped pebble, your gift to me . . .

Joanne Manning

UNTITLED

It's autumn now, and trees are shedding leaves,
As people shedding tears . . .
And streets are kissed by sun not in this place.
It's time for us to face our deepest fears,
Embrace the truth, and look into its face . . .

Oh God! My sufferings are endless . . .
Those people piercing me with their hollow eyes . . .
So lucky them, absorbed by their ignorance,
They are enjoying this exuberant charade.

Poor souls, they sing while making their chain,
Which binds them tight together with each other,
God, please forgive me, as I think they are insane,
It's not the way we were invented by the mother.

They eagerly took up a part in a masquerade,
Not questioning a purpose, what behind it . . .
But it's OK, there will be less to devastate
As all of them, for many years, will be silent.

Lena Benn

BATTERY HENS 1954

Young healthy pullets
Bright-eyed and combs of red
Feathers in place and smooth
Clean straight yellow leg

Oh poor bird, if you did but know
What short freedom you had is gone
Into a battery you must go
To stop there your life long

Not for you the open space
To scratch among the straw
But caged forever and a day
Behind a battery door.

Keith Coleman

THE COUNTRYSIDE

I'll take a walk in the English country,
Just imagine you're right there with me,
I'll start by the stile to the footpath,
And tell you some things I may see.

There's a field alongside the footpath,
All filled with long green grass,
If I stand very still and just watch it,
I may see a field mouse run past.

The bank and the hedge growth around it
Have some interesting things if I look,
I can't tell you all you may find there,
For this I would need a whole book.

There are primroses, daisies and violets,
And wild roses all rambling round,
Then hidden among the wild grasses,
Some rabbits and fox holes are found.

When the rabbits hear someone near them,
They run in their holes out of sight,
I'd be very lucky if I saw a fox,
For they mostly come out just at night.

There are birds' nests in the hedge growths,
The sparrows, blue tits, the thrush,
Sometimes I've seen their eggs laid there,
When patient and not in a rush.

The spiders have spun a most beautiful web,
They just wait there to bounce on a catch,
The sight of a cobweb all covered with dew,
Is a picture not much else can match.

Now a footpath that runs through a forest,
The ground is a carpet of blue,
And right in among those bluebells,
There'll be a tall foxglove there too.

Some pheasants stay still in the shadow,
Just waiting for me to go past,
But if I walk too close to them,
They take to the air very fast.

The male with its beautiful colours,
Make the female bird look very plain,
I'd see them sometimes on the roadway,
Or toddling along in the lane.

Now there is something quite near me,
Standing beside some tree,
I stand very still and look round me,
And see two eyes looking at me.

It's a stag with its wife and her fawn,
Watching me just like a guard,
As he stands with his antlers high in the air,
To keep still I find it quite hard.

But as soon as I make a slight movement,
He warns them and off they all run,
To walk and watch all those wonderful things,
Can really be such fun.

As I leave the forest trees,
And take a footpath up a grass hill,
I puff and I pant to walk to the top,
Where over villages I can see at will.

On that hillside sheep are grazing,
Enjoying that fresh green grass,
And down in the fields way below them,
A horse or a cow may just pass.

From up here the village looks tiny,
Way down in the valley below,
I can just see my cottage among it,
And now that is where I must go.

I'll run down the slope, jump over the stream,
As I now make my way to home,
If you like to take an interesting walk,
Then through England's countryside roam.

Walk quiet and slowly as you go along,
Then not much will miss a quick eye,
Our fine English country is everyone free,
It is something that no man can buy.

Just make sure you close gates behind you,
And stick to the paths all the way,
Then I'm sure you'll enjoy every minute,
And have a really nice day.

Nita Garlinge

THE CURE
(For my brother, Michael)

I felt a warmth and a magic in the air
As I dallied up the hill to the convent
Where I had been sent with a note
From my very sick mother
Who wanted prayers for a cure,
I picked a primrose here and there.

The portress said I was too late
The nuns were at midday prayer,
However, she took the note
And with another laysister conferred
Sotto voce as to the nature of the cure.
Then, seeming to concur
They said I'd have to wait,
But they'd show me how to bake.

I gave them the flowers,
They gave me tea and a scone;
Afterwards, in the sunny chapel, everyone
Sent up an earnest prayer.
At six, I had to leave
Without the cake I had helped to make.
Sister Rose brought me home
And what did I find there
But you, my dark-eyed brother.

Mary Frances Mooney

MOTHERS AND DAUGHTERS

Do you ever sit and wonder what you have lost?
A parent and loved one at what cost
Deep heartache - feeling guilty not getting to say
I pray my mum heard me as she passed away
In my heart all I feel is a loss and deep sorrow
My mum is not going to be here tomorrow
I have lost my soulmate, my best friend - my mum
We will meet again when my day comes
I know we were born to be taken away
Why was she taken from me today?
I face a life now without my mum - all alone
I feel cold, empty, fearful, angry and cold like stone
Mum, you are gone - you had a painful passing
Your life, your love for me, our past quickly flashing
Mum, when I think of you, my heart is glowing
Deep inside the tears are flowing
Mum, you were so brave till the end
I know my heart will never mend
We all have a mum so special to us
We love, care, confide in and trust
I sit and wait for my mum to phone
Feeling pain and all alone
I will never forget my special friend
I will remember my mum to the very end
I sit and feel and smell her all around me
To me my mum is always with me
As I sit here alone, I wonder why
My tears are flowing as I sit and cry
Mum, I miss your love so very much
Your gentle smile and gentile touch
Mum, your beautiful face I will always remember and always see
You, Mum, were so special and one in a million to me
I will never forget my special and loving mum
As I sit here and wait for my day to come.

Maureen Watt

MONTY . . . A LESSON IN LIFE

Monty likes to sleep all day,
I don't know why, he will not say.
On cushions soft or table hard,
On he sleeps, his dreams unheard.

Perhaps he dreams of mice and birds,
Comfy places night and day,
He quietly dreams his life away.

Monty has a lovely life of twitching naps
And stretched out flat by the fire,
His world so secret, so calm within,
I wish sometimes to be like him.

No troubles to worry,
No stresses or strife.
No deadlines to keep as in our busy lives.
Would I swap him? You bet!
And yet so lonely sometimes I think,
No friend or foe to keep him in the world we know.

Monty is a lucky cat.
With bowls of milk and food he loves we show our care
And though he has no voice to speak,
He shows his love with purrs and squeaks of pure contentment when we come.
Each day with woes and troubles bad,
He licks our hand and listens hard.

But there he is! He's gone again
Into the warmth of cosy dens and laundry nests
To dream of what I can but guess.

On he dreams. He hears no noise,
No telly, no toys, no naughty boys.
Until he's stroked by gentle hand,
'Come on Monty, dinner time.'

Monty never buys us things,
He cannot shop or talk to say how much he loves
But shows us with the softest rubs.
He warms our beds on winter nights
And knows just when we need a hug.
Christmas time he'd never miss, to help us wrap and sort out toys,
And creep upstairs to check for noise!

Through poorly nights and snowy days

We cuddle him and on he stays
Asleep with all his problems solved
By those he loves and trusts and knows.
Perhaps we all could learn from him
To live our dreams and enter into life with love and trust and care
And find another who can share
Times good or bad, happy or sad,
Valuing the time we have.
Ask nothing back but what we give.
We have only one life to live.

One day I know he will not wake.
On my lap with silky fur his paws entwined he'll be at peace in my warm arms.
No change in him I'll see at all!
His slumberings are undisturbed.
The sadness past, our lives go on filled with love and trust not hate.
No death to meet us soon it seems,
Just endless, peaceful happy dreams.

Caroline Cutmore

STEVE

A special person, a special place
A smile on one's face
You are still with us in your own special way

We are all gathered here to be with you today
When we think of you
We think of the one
And remember a special friend, brother, uncle and son

You are here and you are now
You rest peacefully as if sleeping
Thoughts of you always
And for every day ours for keeping.

Marina Reeves

COVETS

I walk the twilight lonning
Hearing the gravel scrunch beneath mine feet,
Whilst conceal'd within his covet
Crows the pheasant most discreet;

Somewhere out within the woodland
Where the leaves are yet to come,
Beyond the steady gaze of magpie
I hear the woodpecker's lonely drum;

To embrace the fields the ring doves fly
From bleak perch to meagre feeding ground,
Whilst the magpie listens unimpressed
To their taffy-tak' coo sound;

I process a little further
Thinking how easily such wond'rs are oft miss'd,
So contemptuous and unappreciat'd
As the sun peeps through the mist.

M Sam Dixon

BIRD SQUADRON

Geese, a feathered armada
Honking through pearl-grey light,
Set in sleek formation,
A superb and arrowed flight.

Following an age-old trail
To ribboned fields of grass,
Foraging with muted cackling,
Confident and bold as brass.

As one, the birds lift into the air.
Call to each other as they ascend.
A feathered band of nature
Against a sky that has no end.

Ellsie Russell

NATURE'S CHILD

In the dark the gremlins whisper,
Maisie the cat begins to quiver,
He vows he shouldn't have had that cheese
As he pulls the bedclothes around his knees.

The door that was left open a crack,
Silently, slowly, swings right back.
Something is standing there in the gloom,
Its pervading presence fills the room.

The bedspring creaks as a gnarled hand
Touches his arm like a hazel wand.
Leaving Maisie far behind,
He flies transported to another land

The storm that carried him to this shore
Finally abates and is no more.
A woman stands clinging upon the rocks,
Her beauty bewitching, although in shock.

Perilous the climb, he reaches her,
Closer to, some distant memory stirs.
Like injured animal she curses him
But so familiar, as if his twin.

Broken beside her he sees the cross,
Filling him with a dreadful sense of loss.
And in the flotsam of the sea,
What awful nightmare thing can be.

A newborn child from upon her breast,
Blue in the face but pale the rest.
Strangled not by any hand
But by the pollution of the land.

Chemicals sprayed far and wide,
Nature's harvest is like the tides,
Since ancient Stonehenge in the west,
People have prayed for a harvest blessed.

Acknowledge the hand that steers the ship,
Recognise the shoulder that carries the sheep.
Cherish the water that has been given,
Love the land as if it were Heaven.

Roy Baker

THE DOOR

The door was warped and rotten,
Our grandad's shed was dated,
Panes of glass were broken
It was so dilapidated

Grandad didn't use the shed
He'd died two years before,
We thought he wouldn't mind too much
If we opened up the door.

He'd always been a gardener
A very clever chappie,
The hours he'd spent in this old shed
Had kept him very happy.

The handle didn't turn too well
The screws were very rusty,
We pushed the door, it opened,
But everywhere was dusty.

The shed had really had its day,
It was a sorry mess,
What we would do with all the pots
Was anybody's guess.

We found a broom and made a start
By cleaning up the floor,
We coughed and choked with all the dust
Until our throats were sore.

Our clothes got very dirty
Our faces almost grey,
We hoped Mum wouldn't scold us
When she saw our disarray.

We'd had a really lovely day
Cleaning Grandad's shed,
The time had passed so quickly
And now was time for bed.

Of course we had to have a bath
To wash the grime away,
Mum wasn't too displeased with us
Just pleased that we'd enjoyed our day.

Anne Smith

LIFE?

I sat there, the world going by,
People moving so fast,
No matter how hard I try,
Can't stop thinking about the past.

The people I have met,
The places I have been,
My life seems to have set,
It all feels like a dream.

Going nowhere now,
It all just seems to stop,
Please someone tell me how
I'll ever reach the top.

Then my girls come to me,
The backbones of my life,
I don't know where I'd be,
If I didn't have their trouble and strife.

They are my reasons for living,
The only two in my world,
All my love I am giving,
They leave my life in a whirl!

But . . .
I wouldn't have it any other way.

E Raybould

THE TROMBONIST

I was thinking of learning to play the trombone . . .
In the book it looked easy as pie.
Though I knew it could take me three weeks or more,
I decided to give it a try.
I had visions of playing all over the land,
In concert halls, theatres . . . on boats . . .
As a soloist maybe, or part of a band,
From Lands End to John O'Groats.
Now a trumpet or clarinet wouldn't suit me,
My fingers would not move about
And press the right buttons, at the right time . . .
It seemed easier straight in and out.
So I jumped on the tube and went down the West End,
Where the music shops all ply their trade . . .
To Boosey and Hawkes, went in through the door,
Soon a trombone purchase I'd made.
A shiny trombone, in its new case,
Back on the tube, my steps to retrace.
'What's in his case, Mum?' a boy said out loud.
'Shush, he's a musician.' It made me feel proud.
I wasn't aware that the slide was so long,
With the bits joined up, I confess,
I knocked over my pot plant, broke open the pot
And I had to clear up the mess.
Then I lifted the trombone, small end to my lips
And I started to blow it like hell . . .
In theory, you vibrate the air in the tube
And the music comes out of the bell
I blew all day long, going red in the face,
But no sound seemed to come out at all . . .
'Til I noticed the mouthpiece was still in the case . . .
Believe me I did feel a fool.
At very long last, with a thunderous blast,
The note I played made rafters ring,
A picture of Grandad fell off the wall,
All the dogs in the street joined in.
I tried to play scales to strengthen my lip,
But it just didn't seem to come right,
The slide always seemed to be in the wrong place
Though I practised from morning till night.
Mr Grimshaw, next door, liked my playing, I think,

He beat time for me there on his wall.
The faster he beat, the faster I played,
We really did have a ball.
My neighbours on the other side,
I was sorry to see them go,
They said something about they could stand it no more,
But what 'it' was I really don't know.
I finally realised that it was no good,
A trombonist I'd never be,
For no matter how hard I tried to improve,
It just wasn't the thing for me.
My trombone is now hanging up on the wall,
But it doesn't make me feel too glum,
For you see I use it as a replacement pot,
To house my geranium.
Last night on telly, I saw the Scots Guards . . .
A fine body of men I must say . . .
They all blew the bagpipes as they marches around . . .
Now that's something I really could play.

David Kellard

ALL THAT WE HAVE

If all that we have is this moment
No chance of our rushing away
This fool mesmerised by your smile
Would decide he had something to say
I have loved from the first that I saw you
Light that brightens my room
If it's true music touches the soul
My heart wants to dance to your tune

When you speak, swear I hear angels singing
All the gods must look down with a tear
See a mortal as poor as myself
Filled with riches by having you near
If just for a while I could hold you
Feel the touch of your skin and your hair
This world it could end here and now
With your name being my final prayer.

Paul M Stone

SHOW DAY

I've had aphids in me tunnel,
And rabbits in me greens.
Blackbirds in me strawberries,
And blackfly on me beans.

Me tomatoes and me cucumbers
Are best you've ever seen.
I have some lovely pheasants
But they eat me lovely greens.

Me flower beds are a picture,
They have enjoyed the rain.
My currants and me gooseberries
Have flourished once again.

Me carrots (not me favourites)
Will not be fit to show.
But I am just the gardener,
Still, guess that I should know.

I've mown me lawns and pathways,
Placed me money box and chairs,
And I'll open up me garden
Cos it's just as good as theirs!

Hilda Hazlewood

DERRY CITY

Derry City, my favourite of all Irish towns
Its look and its setting is a joy to be found.

With its ancient inner walled city
A sight to be seen.

On a hill above the curving Foyle river
To me it's a dream.

Its people so warm, energetic and individual, buoyed with pride
In their town's distinguished history, they sighed.

Bloody though some may have been
Derry is different they claim - different it seems.

Today this indeed is a town reborn
Indeed an eye opener as visitors roam
Within this inner walled city
The streets now rebuilt.
To me it's still old Derry with its old Irish lilt.

Emma Hardwick

HEART ON THE LINE

This book of scribble is divine
Truthfully laying my heart on the line
Poets and songwriters do the same
Portraying life hoping for fame
We will not die, our photographs live high
Watching natural beauty of changing times
Laying one's heart on the line.

Laying one's heart on the line
Often too late in time
When a treasured one departs
It's too late to start
Remembering all you wished you had said
Along life's 'Windmill Tread'
So remember take time to
Lay your heart on the line.

Barbara Lockwood

MY JOURNEY

'Twas the twist of the knife which was my life
That forced me to the ground
My face, how it hurt as it scraped in the dirt
My sobs the only sound.
Just a shell that was me and I couldn't see
For the weight of my hurt kept me low
But I knew in my head though my heart was like lead
The path I would have to go.

So I started to crawl though I'd slip and fall
As I felt the lash of the rain
So cold and wet that I couldn't get
Up . . . all I felt was pain.
I had to go on though my reason was gone.
I had to be far away
From those demons who haunted, provoked me and taunted
Just one tiny step every day.

The bridge up ahead was what filled me with dread
It loomed so big and so long
But I'd chains which bound to the walls all around
And I knew I wasn't that strong.
I thought it was best that I stopped there to rest
To wait until I was well
But it took me one year to conquer my fear
Of the bridge on the road back from Hell.

I switched off my mind for I knew I would find
The love I still felt from my past
So no feelings, no pain, can't go through that again
'Til one day I was ready at last.

I saw them all there as I climbed up the stair
The people I met on my way
There were those who cared and those who just stared
And yet some who were with me each day.
Each time I would fall I'd remember them all
But I chose to be alone
There were those who just nodded yet those who prodded
When I tripped and fell on a stone.

Though that bridge was wide, I wouldn't look to the side
I walked that long straight track
For in every part of my aching heart
Were the strings which would pull me right back.

Then one day as I looked up to the sky
It seemed so bright and so blue
From behind the shroud of a fluffy white cloud
The sun came shining through
I couldn't wait to walk through the gate
As I gazed at the open door
I wondered why I could no longer cry
For that person who was before

I felt so free . . . this person was 'me'
Those chains were broken at last
I vowed there and then that never again
Would I live in the pain of my past.

And now two years on those feelings have gone
That bridge is so far away
But what pulled me through was the faith of the few
Those who walked beside me each day.

So I want you to know you're wherever I go
For you picked me up when I fell
You stayed by my side every time that I cried
On that bridge . . .

On that road . . . back from Hell.

H A Milton

FALLING LEAVES

(For Stanley)

My dearest friend
The news of your departing came to me this morning
The words tumbling through space, from satellite to satellite
Courtesy of digital sound: almost ironic isn't it friend
When remembering your regimental duties way back then
Exposed and alone, inching and feeling your way
Through the blackest of blackness and mind-numbing fear
Searching relentlessly, night after agonising night
For the break in the wire
Maintaining communications, from behind to the front
Until it almost destroyed you
You were such a gentle, simple, modest man
Full of grace and sensitivity
We shared so much - our town - our places - our people
But most of all, we shared the legacy of war
And paid the price - as did so many
I had new poems for you to read
But now instead . . .
I'll read them to myself - out loud
And hope that where you now reside
You'll hear them and they will make you smile

Jeanne Elizabeth Sagar

TUDOR REVELS

Oh 'twas a lovely autumn night
A warm, and star-filled, lovely sight.
Yon troup of minstrels gaily came
To dance, and thrill, and entertain.

For all the crowd was gathered there.
The lords and ladies, maidens fair.
They all had come from far and wide
To join with us, at eventide.

And hear a wondrous tale be told
By one Will Kemp, so brave and bold,
He told a tale of deeds so rare,
A morris dance, beyond compare.

A journey took from London Town,
O'er hills and dales for Norwich bound.
And he did take us on that road,
As his great story did unfold.

From time to time some others came,
To dance, play music, entertain,
A practised group they were indeed,
And through the steps of dance did lead.

With much laughter ladies learned
To 'spin', 'touch shoulders', when to turn.
Then gentlemen took their turn next,
While onlookers were quite perplexed.

A rest was called while all retired,
To sample *mead* was much desired.
A table of fine fayre was spread,
And all partook and were well fed.

And finally the night did close,
Fond memories of Will Kemp's prose.
Of morris dance and music fine.
Of sumptuous fayre, and *strong mead wine*.

Sheila Giles

ALPHABET OF HOPE

A is for *ambition*,
Which one needs for healthy mind;

B is for *behaving*,
As one should toward mankind;

C is for *contentment*
Of the mind that is within;

D is for the *daring*,
That we need for venturing;

E is for *enthusiasm*,
Vital for success;

F is for *good fortune,*
That we all hope to possess;

G is for the *grit*
We need when conquering a quest;

H does stand for *honour*
That maintains us at our best;

I is for the *ideals*
That we set along life's road;

J of course means *justice*,
That's the one and only code;

K is being *kind*
To next of kin and those we meet;

L means *loving*,
Being *loved*, this is what we seek;

M for *money*,
That for others, worldly riches meet;

N is for the *niceties*,
That help make life seem sweet;

O is for *optimist*
Who views life's every gain;

P means *persevering*
When life seems to be in vain;

Q is *quenching* each desire
Through weakness bringing pain;

R stands for *remembering*,
For value, not just gain;

S is *sharing* what we have
With those we hold most dear;

T is for *togetherness*,
Perhaps a laugh, or tear;

U means *unity* and peace,
For this we surely need;

V for *vandalism*,
Sheer destruction, ruin, greed;

W is *willpower*
That we need to keep in line;

X means *extra* blessings,
To which we're oft so blind;

Y is simply *yearning*
For each whim of heart and mind;

Z means *zest*
That we do feel, when health and wealth are kind.

Jennifer Hedges

KEEP GOING

Now I'm getting on a bit
I slumber in my chair
Listen to the birds chirp
As the sun shines right out there

I see skies of azure blue
The planes I once was on
To foreign parts I'd jaunt away
My heart did burst with song

The world it was my oyster
Boyfriends - many knew
Oh the dancing and the cuddling
But these days I will renew.

Mary Hudson

THE CORNERS

The corners of my life are square,
But I wish that they were round,
And my tree it has but seven leaves,
And six are on the ground.

And my bridge is by the water,
And my water by the bridge,
And I've climbed the highest mountain peaks,
But fell when on the ridge.

And I killed a king, who loved a queen,
A queen who loved a king,
And the music played the sweetest song,
Do you know how to sing?

And the sleep was in the moment,
And the moment in the sleep,
And the shallow waters soothe my soul,
But mostly they are deep.

And the ring was on the finger,
And the finger wore the ring,
And the choir sang with all their heart,
For they know how to sing.

And we can do all we can do,
To do all that we can,
The air was cooled in summertime,
For the lady used a fan.

And the fear was in the first month,
And the joy was in the last,
And my time was in the plenty,
But I was in the past.

And the race was for the winner,
And the winner won the race,
The inscription on the trophy read
Her name and then first place.

And we found the missing moment,
And the moment it was found,
We searched the world to find it,
And it was on the ground.

For the corners of my life are square,
But I'm wishing they were round,
My tree it had just seven leaves,
And all are on the ground.

Trevor Wiggan

ACCEPTANCE

I looked in the mirror and saw a face,
Old, wrinkled, quite out of place.
Who's that behind me making me start?
I turned round quickly, expecting to see
But no one was there, only me.

I looked back in the mirror,
The face was still there,
A little resemblance, no that's not fair.
The face was different years ago,
Who are you? Where did I go?

Eyes that are grey, were once very blue,
Now circled with lines, like feet of a crow.
The pink in the cheeks has faded away,
Hair soft as silk, now brittle and grey.
Where have I gone? This is not me.

Go away old woman, can't you see?
You're someone else, you're not me.
You're growing old she seemed to say,
You'd better get used to me every day.

Then someone called, 'It's time for tea,'
Come on old woman, you must be me.

Joann Littlehales

INVITATION TO WHITBURN

. . . Come walk by the sea with me in Whitburn near Sunderland
In the North East of England . . .

Come enjoy our bracing and refreshing air . . .
And tread on the sand, take my hand on the beach . . .
Feel the wind in your hair and be without care
Walk on pebbles, as the water you reach.

Watch the surfers in black, as the waves they attack
And their kites in the wind really blowing . . .
See the dogs chasing too, running fast towards you
As your face gets tanned and glowing.

Watch the boats with me, chugging out to the sea
As they head for some far foreign shores.
And the foghorns some days calling out in the haze
Makes you think *I'd be best off indoors.*

It can be quite hot, but sometimes it is not
As weather can change in a trice . . .
So never go to our beach without jacket in reach
For warm air soon blows cold like ice!

If a cliff walk you would like you can go for a hike
And a cliff path you will see straight ahead
With a stile to cross, high up from the beach
Marsden Lighthouse you can head for instead.

You will pass fields of green, best you have ever seen
As you gaze out to sea on your right . . .
Your legs may be tired and the wind may be brisk
And the path close at cliff's edge a real scary sight!

Soon Marsden Lighthouse is in view ahead of you
Making it enough for one day of fresh air . . .
So time for a rest, because you have seen all the best
Of our Whitburn sea breezes today!

Patricia Mary Saunders

THE SEA

I stand alone searching the sea,
Seagulls mocking overhead,
Blue clouds chasing across the sky;
Seeing the world so differently with new expression.

The rhythm of singing sea, flowing with smiling glances,
Makes lullaby wave lines
Breeze beauty bringing the pleasure of life,
Welcoming with summer horizon.

The boats move over the waves,
Far away from the shore,
Flickering in daylight motion,
Into some sea valley journey.

Rocks are sculpted into all shapes and sizes,
Surrounded by the echoing waves;
Watching the sun rise over rocks
Brings a cool, beautiful, salty appetite.

Heather Aspinall

THE DESTROYER

They thrust themselves upon the land,
With empty head and heavy hand,
To dig in deep to reach her soul,
Keeping their eyes tightly closed.

Bit by bit they tear apart
Mother Nature's broken heart.

She bleeds, she cries,
Yet still they stand with swords
Of death within their hands.

To break her down with no need,
To draw her slowly to her knees.

Suicidal men all are we,
For without her where will we be?

Kathleen Bruce

IN REVERIE

We woke each morn' without a care,
In those far-off summer days,
Our hearts were light,
Our troubles nought,
'Twas roses all the way,
And happy as the days were long,
We played our little games,
And life was good, and life was sweet,
In those far-off summer days.

In childhood friendship steadfastly,
We passed idyllic hours,
Went rambling, and caught tadpoles,
Picked blackberries and wild flowers,
And laden down with buttercups,
We'd wend our homeward way
As the gentle shades of evening fell
At the end of a summer day.

With simple pleasures, good and true,
We spent our childhood days,
And happy and content with life,
Secure in every way,
We never sought to change our lot,
Or pined for wealth or power,
Serene were we with what God sent,
And lived but for the hour.

Now oft I sit in reverie,
With tears upon my face,
As I think about those yesterdays,
And that magic childhood place,
I see their smiling faces,
Hear their laughing sounds of play,
And I would that I were a child again,
In a far-off summer day.

Dorothy Neil

THE SCENT OF BLUEBELLS

Beneath the morning's cloud-skimmed skies,
we walked and talked
of family and all the flowers of May we saw that day;
dandelion, red campion, bluebells.
We stooped to smell, remembering well,
fat bunches picked,
wilting, white-stemmed, sticky with sap,
heady with scent.

Each step a journey back,
we followed that deep, Somerset track
through high, green hedgerows,
listening to the robin sing
and wondering why,
of all the springs we'd seen when we were young,
we never guessed what paths our lives would take.
We stood and watched the cattle graze
lifting their heads to stare with steady eyes,
long-lashed, sweet-breathed.
What do they think as we pass by,
relive our past.
Their past is now, no future mapped.

Mary Bennett

THE AERODROME

One Christmas Day morning a few years past
The fog was quite thick, and was closing in fast
Took my dog Buster, a golden retriever, one of the best
To the old aerodrome a few miles west

Parked off the road, just by the gate
7am in the morning, did not want to be late
For the day's festivities, with the family and all
Hopefully a day full of merriment, have a real ball

So out of the car, and off we went
Striding out well, morning felt Heaven sent
Fog getting thicker and a real eerie feel
Wrapped up warm against the early morning chill

Walking on the runways now long past their prime
Out in the fog, it was like returning in time
You could feel the drone of the planes in their time
Feel the presence of the airmen all in their prime

Out of the gloom, a figure appeared
Dressed kind of funny, it really felt weird
In flying suit, helmet, large boots and a jacket
Out in the mist the planes were making a racket

Though startled for a moment, I swiftly said hello
He looked at me strangely, I thought he would go
But he smiled and said, 'Hi, my name is Joe
I am an American airman, but I guess that you know'

I nodded my approval, we shook hands and we talked
Said he came from Kansas, related more as we walked
Her piercing blue eyes lit up the gloom
His infectious smile would brighten any room

Said he was married, just wanted to be there
With his wife and children, sat in his old rocking chair
Though only twenty, he looked a lot older than that
I noticed the frown from under his helmet hat

The lines on his face truly said it all
How hard life was now trying to save us all
Suddenly I was startled by something he said
He missed them all greatly, now that he was dead

He looked at me caringly and just shook his head
Said sorry for disturbing me, it just filled me with dread
I looked straight ahead, dumbfounded at best
Thought I had better go home, I needed a rest

As I turned back to face him, he was no longer there
Just as he had come, he disappeared into thin air
I thought I was dreaming, just called Buster
Said nothing to no one, left the situation alone

My curiosity was raised by something he had said
About being in a churchyard and something I had read
About an American airman, killed in the war
Now I was intrigued, wanted to know more

So I went to the local library, dug out some books
There on a page, my airman's good looks
Staring up at me, I found it hard to believe
So more information I set out to retrieve

It seems he had died in his plane, that had been his plight
Flying over Southampton, one dark night in a dog-fight
His body was found and buried nearby
No one to mourn, no one to cry

Family so far away, lost forever it seems
Now he's just a memory, part of their dreams
I will always remember a chance meeting at best
With a poor soul we needed, now hopefully at rest.

Owen Cullimore

THE LEARNING CURVE

We formed the crew in Jerusalem in deepest Palestine,
Six of us including Tom who thought he had served his time.
For Tom had done two tours of Ops and fancied taking leave
Starting a third with a crew of sprogs he felt somewhat aggrieved.

His rank was Flying Officer so he wore a thin blue band,
We used to call him Skipper in the way of Coastal Command.
The rest of the crew were NCOs, Co-pilot Nav and three Wops.
The Skipper's task was to team us up then fly us all on Ops.

In the second's seat sat Paddy who sported an Irish brogue,
Bubbles the Nav, a Mersey lad and quite a likeable rogue.
Then three of us as Wop/A/gs; Eric, me and Skelly,
Destined to fly that fine machine we all knew as the Welly.

Our posting to an OTU was delayed by adverse weather.
Surrounded now by orange groves at last we reached Ein Shemer.
The coastal role required the Wops with ASV to wrestle,
An early radar system used to detect a surface vessel.

The Welly that we flew in was called the Stickleback
Spiked with aerials nose to fin, the enemy ships to track.
With these arrays for Search and Home we soon learnt the drill,
When the closing blip was central you were lined up for the kill.

Our training now intensified as we quartered the Eastern Med,
We practiced flying searches square and creep-in-line ahead
And homed on tiny fishing boats that gave a good return.
Occasionally doing a shoot up run to give us all a burn.

We'd never flown at night before and wondered how we'd fare,
Our skipper said, 'Don't worry lads, I know a special prayer.'
The Wops took turns at the radar, a change from dah dah ditting.
First watch for me was the radar, searching the Med for shipping.

I saw some blips on the radar scope still some distance away,
Selecting the aerials to Homing I switched on the Yagi array.
The blips now straddled the centre at thirty-five miles dead ahead
I passed on this gen to the skipper, 'Roger, keep looking,' he said.

In the rear turret was Skelly who asked permission to change,
We passed in the dark on the catwalk the ships now into range.
'The ships are below us,' said Skelly, updating the radar report.
Seated now behind the guns, *there's not much to look at* I thought.

But flashing past came tracers arcing through the night,
Not mentioned at our briefing this gave me quite a fright.
Switching the mike on quickly, 'I think we're being shot,' I said.
The skipper responded with, 'Roger, I think I'm allergic to lead.'

'Swing your turret around,' said the skipper, 'have a shufti about,
You're seeing sparks from an engine, if not then give me a shout.'
I did as the skipper requested and had to agree he was right.
It's quite unknown for an engine to shoot down an aircraft at night.

Landing I braced for the ribbing, the jokes I thought I deserved.
Just put it down to experience, a part of the steep learning curve.
I was saved by the bell in the morning, our *OTU* training complete.
The very next day we were posted to join 221 Squadron in Greece.

Ron C Houghton

AN EVENING CLIMB
IN THE MOURNE MOUNTAINS

Above our sleeping mountain's sculpted crest,
The curtains of the sky with pinks are blessed
And hang in shredded threads of majesty
On vaulted darkening dome from east to west.

The highest scuds of cloud are edged with rose,
Whilst topmost crag in fading sunlight glows.
Then all too quickly darkness takes control
And cooling summer breeze on Bearnagh blows.

A blackground, blue and puce falls round about
As Heaven's vanguard points of light shine out,
And ice-hot planets slice their orbits near
As we in sated awe give silent shout.

Descend we must and slip the snare of night
To reach the road by Spelga in twilight,
And when immersed in silent swirling ink
Head homewards to our haven's windows bright.

Alan Day

YOU AND ME

Thank you for your opinions,
For letting me know.
Who I should be,
And how my eyes should see.
I did try it for a while,
Over here and over there.
But with their eyes,
They chose to stare.
And look at me,
Like the misfit I am.
Well yes I am,
And look at me.
And then I met him,
He saw things so clearly.
He made life simple,
And yet he was risky.
But what else could he offer me?
I did have to wonder.
I gave him a go,
No great expectations.
It was not long,
Before I got slapped by realisation.
Support, attention,
Love and affection.
Stability, guidance,
His kidney.
And not forgetting,
He let me be me.
I've shown him my 1,000 faces,
He knows I'm no hero.
Yet his eyes still glint when he sees me,
There is no bigger hint.
He loves me,
He judges me not.
He loves me,
He judges me not.

Priti Meredith

LADLED OUT WITH LOVE

In those early post-war years
Our kitchen sported an original Belfast sink
The buffered brass tap gushed cold water
Freshly through our young spartan lives
Red and blue quarry tiles brought to
Carbolic perfection on Mondays
Mingled with the afterglow of copper stick
Boiling whites and the aroma of a pan of Irish stew.
On Fridays the fire blazed brightly
Dampers full out to heat the black and chrome oven
Butterfly buns, Bakewells, apple pies
Toddlers' podgy fingers helping to roll out the dough
Looking for Daddy's return and yelps of delight
As the headlights from his old Ford Thames van
Swept reassuringly across the yard.
Chuckling fun as we filled the tin bath
Banished the weariness as we wallowed
In the warm privacy of fireside bathing
Now decades of changes, revolutionary advances
Twenty-first century Man in his striped apron
Delving into cookery books
Gastronomic profusion from China, Italy, Greece.
And within the firm walls the family gather still
Held together by love, ladled out unstintingly.

Lyn Wilkinson

STRONG LOVE

Yes,
your eyes shone
like a burnished fire,
when we first touched
each other's path;
Yes,
I wore out
an old black vinyl
at 45rpm,
dreaming about
your tender impact
and no
the deep intuition
that men are not
supposed to have
never prepared me
for the way you
plugged a vast
mystical gap;
yet consider this:
O warm lover
that I've never deserved,
for I'm about to echo
a phrase
lest you ever forget
what time and kindness
has forged between us:
the thought touches
'the fear of mental loss'
for should age ever
creep upon us that
we forget who we are
then a strength
stronger than the darkest
ocean night
will gather around us,
a strange confidence
surround,

and though
we might employ
a guardian
to keep our minds,
one day,
unexpectedly,
we'll dig up
a treasure trove
of memory
and remember
that first walk together
by the pond
and me tearing my sleeve
in a flush of youthful love.

John Roe

POLWHEVERAL REACH

In such a place I could not speak,
Here moss and lichen clothed the ground,
Leaves sang in rich chromatic scales
And hung like fallen angels' veils.
My feet depressed the rain-soaked moss
And led me to the creek's tide line,
All motion stopped and with it, time.

Peaceful, serene, the creek still lies
Beneath the circle of the hills,
Dun coloured mud, October sky,
The haunt of teal and golden-eye.
Shy whimbrel to dog otter calls,
A speech I cannot comprehend
In this my heart's retreat - tide's end.

Frances M Searle

GLORIA

Gloria Vanderhoink went out to dine with the Trotters -
a family of grunters and devious plotters.
In her pink pigskin bodysuit she carefully dressed
that she may, of course, look her stunningly best - and - as well -
the family of trotters try to impress.
They supped of the hock joint well mixed with ham stock
though the gammon was too salty and as hard as a rock, but
Gloria engaged with the Trotters putting up with their swill -
until they decided it was time for the kill.

Poor Gloria became so snorted for she could not find a pen
to memo that never ever would she dine here again.
The Trotters were so devious they told her a porker,
knowing they planned to lead Gloria to slaughter;
no matter her squealing, nor how much she did cry,
they still led her to the cinder-trough in the old smelly sty:
where they anchored poor Gloria to a place on the spit
and revoltingly cooked her: as they turned her a bit!
They rotated and revolved her until she was looking quite thin
then they squeezed her and squashed her into a tight skin.

Oh, my dear! Oh my dear goodness! Oh - *what* a mezz
they transformed our poor Gloria into cooked sausages.

Well. What a pitifully hopeless sad piggin' tale -
now Gloria's displayed on a platter -
'Chipolatas For Sale'.

Diana Mudd

GATECRASHERS

We had breakfast on a sunny day last week
The smell of fresh brewed coffee filled the air
When all of a sudden
Two enquiring eyes appeared
Fixed on us with
An uncanny stare
Was not even invited
But undaunted there he stood
In a copper-coloured coat
And flash white socks
Then just as he appeared
That cheeky little fox returned to where he came
But something far more ominous was eyeing out the pool
From the top of the fir tree
A hostile hungry heron had a desire for the fish
For his succulent and satisfying tea
Then a squirrel got to work
Removing bulbs from around the rosebush
Amassing and discarding at record speed
By virtue of his small nose
A magpie appeared to alight on the lawn
On the very spot where my husband had stood
And even he is not a friend of ours
This dear black and white bird
Standing on the lawn
But we saluted him
As folklore says we should
Birds, bees, butterflies now come to visit
While we dine alfresco
On this, a peaceful Sunday morning.

Elsine Day

MAN

At dawn there's pain,
but slowly the sun rises and the mist begins to clear to blue skies
and a child begins his journey of life.
Into tomorrow, into today, into the unknown, into yesterday.
You walked on all fours but now you tumble and stagger
and soon as a youth you will swagger.

As spring and a new year gives way to summer,
those long days where the sun always shone at midday
and all your troubles seemed so far away.
A journey, yes a journey, into life, into the unknown

Soon the seed that was sown begins to bear fruit.
Good fruit from a good seed,
oaks, elms and lime trees.
See the forest at full bloom, the sun is high
but all too soon the clock face will show the afternoon.

And you are fading now all too soon.
Those long summer days fade and autumn comes with aches and pains
and a harvest moon.
For now the harvest is upon us
and the labours of our youth come to full bloom.

All is safely gathered in and not a moment too soon,
I don't move so swiftly now and there are grey skies in the air.
Soon winter will come and I will sit in front of the fire in my chair.

I recount the days, those heady days that were my life
and as the snow falls, the sun glows red on the horizon
and finally sets.
I now walk on three legs and must finally rest forever in the comfort
knowing that all is well and in time a new seed will rise.

Andrew Eddy

THE HIGHLANDS

Heather cushions creeping
up steep moss-covered banks
To meet green fir trees
precariously perched
    Where eagles fly
    in changing sky

Black, bare, jagged mountains
Rivers of shale falling
like warriors' wounds
Down their sparse vegetated face
    Where eagles fly
    in changing sky

Gently curving mountains
Heather and bracken strewn
Purple sheen in sunlight
Brown and green undertones
    Where eagles fly
    in changing sky

Grim, grey stoned cottages stand
guard, over crystal lochs
Stones steeped in history
recall long lost battles
    Where eagles fly
    in changing sky

Picturesque highland cows
An ancient hardy breed
Lifeblood of the crofters
in olden days gone by
    Where eagles fly
    in changing sky

Highlands, a way of life
Far removed from a clamour
Where nature reigns supreme
There's time to sit and dream
    Where eagles fly
    in changing sky.

Dora Watkins

THE RIVER

I was born in the hills from the chattering rills
    That spring from the melting of snow.
My companions, the sky and eagles that fly
    High over the valley below.
I bubble and babble to boulder and gravel
    In my lonely moorland glen,
Then join other streams that sparkle and gleam,
    Reflecting both sky and Ben.

I embrace the rocks with my white spume locks
    And plunge in a wild caprice
From ledge to ledge of my granite bed
    In a dance that can never cease.
Then, from the jag of a mountain crag,
    I leap, like a stag at bay,
With the thunderous call of my waterfall
    In a bow of coloured spray.

From the maelstrom below I gladly flow
    In a manner more sedate.
Now, deep and wide, I silently glide
    At a slow meandering rate,
Where fishes gleam in my silver stream,
    And moorhens build their nests
In the leaf-clad banks of my tree-lined flanks
    Where the otters play or rest.

Each night and morn my waters are born
    To the habitations of men,
For the gifts I yield for home and field
    Will nourish both meadow and fen.
When the sun rides on high in a hot summer sky,
    My waters are cool and calm,
Where children may play in the heat of the day
    In pools, and come to no harm.

But the call of the sea comes over to me
    As I feel the tug of the tide,
And I shall not sleep till the call of the deep
    Is answered, and not denied.
For its cresting foam is my natural home

And its waves now beckon to me,
So I gladly go with the tide outflow
    To the bosom of the sea.

John Wilson Smith MBE

MY CURTAINS SWAY SIDE TO SIDE

My curtains sway side to side
And I smile thinking that it could be you
You've come to wipe my tears away
And tell me that everything is going to be OK
I miss you more and more each day
So much to you I want to say

I wish I could tell you everything that has gone on
So much has happened since you've been gone
I've got a new man, new car and new life
Grown up so much I'm going to be a wife
Got myself a hobby like you always used to say
Running, gym and shopping on pay day!

I'm so happy Dad with all that I've got
But you do know that you will never ever be forgot
I love you so, so much
And living without you is still so tough
But it is getting easier like they all said
And some days it can be OK
So I promise that next time I lay watching my curtain sway
I'll begin to tell you everything that has happened that day.

Candice Toby

FALLEN LEAVES, FALLEN TEARS

Leaves of trees fall silently to the ground all around.
At the same time my tears fall, again so silently.
For mine are the tears of mental illness,
Seeking comfort as they drip from sad eyes.
Will the leaves join in and weep with me
And can I dare to hope?
Leaf and tear strangely uniting, at one for now.
Could this ever be reality, or a realm of fantasy?
These fallen leaves and fallen tears.

Garry Mitchell

THE STORM

The grim evening light
refuses to hide the tide descending my screen
like ocean waves, a powerful flow
the headlights of cars catch the raindrops
which flow like glass pearls
as the storm that bears them refused to go
people wear waterproofs
as howling gales shake branches of trees
like somebody performing a greeting
surface water begins to form
dry dirt has turned into mud
as the storm rages we take a beating
the gales bash against my car
as if trying to move a heavy load
clouds scurry guiltily in the sky
as if escaping from its naughty deeds
the rain lashes endlessly
as this severe storm refuses to die.

Trevor Vincent

MY DREAM

Last night I dreamt I was a tree, an oak long stood in majesty,
A salty wind with breath of sea with rough caress surrounded me.
My limbs for decades leafy dressed, were now with cup-filled acorns blessed.
And mistletoe twined round my crown, drank of my sap drawn from deep down.
Till Druids claimed the sacred bough, paid homage to their spirits now.
And I with them turned to the east, salute the rising sun, and feast
Upon the glory of the day and gaze upon its bright display.
Then in my dream I stood alone, 'twas winter cold and wind amoan,
My branches bare, my bark forlorn, my acorns squirreled away and gone
But when I thought all hope had sunk, a child ran up and hugged my trunk,
I woke with joy, no more a tree, my own dear child was hugging me.

Dorothy Beaumont

THE MYSTICAL DREAMER

To soar and glide along the winds, to ride the open sky,
Free to roam this heavenly plane, amongst the clouds so high.
I'd fly the bristling winds of chance, ascend this endless void,
Thrive within this exquisite domain that Man has not destroyed.
Through coral city, and sunken ship, beneath the shimmering sea,
Where dolphins dance and mermaids sing, that's where I want to be.
Ride the ancient currents, to where Atlantis used to stand,
I'd roam as one with all that dwell, within this watery land.
To languish upon white sanded beach, with palm trees hanging low,
Where baby turtles strive for home, to the frothy sea they go.
I'd let the sun wash over me, regenerate my soul,
On my Caribbean island is where I'd want to stroll.
Many ancient lands to live in, lots of fantastic places to see,
Nowhere is forbidden, for the mystical dreamer I be.

James Howden

SEPTEMBER SKIES

When I was young the snows that lay on Lochnagar
Seemed so distant, so far away,
As beneath the birch trees and the rowan
I spent my childhood in timeless play.

But I am older now and I have touched the snow,
The rock, black and wet, the cold, cold stone;
I feel the wind as never before
And sometimes I shiver to the bone.

By Dinnet and the Burn O'Vat I come,
With arum lilies, my shadows at my heels,
From a dappled sunlight of autumn gold -
Searching for the memories that time steals.

Let us pause to acknowledge the invited ghosts
We bring with us this day and every day:
In memory of those who still inhabit our lives
In the things we think and do and say.

A wedding is many things:
Part fairy tale, part romance,
Dressing up, playing parts, make-believe,
The colours, the flowers, the well-rehearsed dance.

But the flowers will quickly wither,
The whites and reds will fade to grey,
And you'll only have bits and pieces left
With which to remember this day.

The wedding dress will go in a cardboard box:
One day you may have a daughter who'll laugh at it;
You'll try it on again when you're forty or so
And try to tell yourself that it's still a good fit.

You'll look at the photographs years from now:
What on earth was that on my mother's head?
She fair thocht she was Airchie that day -
How long is it now that she's been dead?

All the expensive finery of this day,
Including this jacket which makes me look like a fop,
Will, on another day, gather dust on a hanger
On a back rail in an Oxfam shop.

Most of all, though, a wedding is a symbol of hope
And of promises to keep -
And I can only hope for you both
That your love will prove to be pure and deep.

May this day be validated by your lives together:
May you love each other so much
That you'll always be true one to the other -
And you'll always thrill to the other's touch.

I do know what I'm talking about
Because I've been lucky, whatever it seems,
For the woman who nags me every single day of my life
Is still the girl of my dreams.

May your love be like a snowdrop,
Withstanding the cold though bowed and slight,
Sparkling in the rain
In the pale winter light.

May your love be like an open fire,
Fiercely flaming in the dark,
All red hot embers and woody smoke
And showers of sparks.

May you often be together at sunset,
High up where the curlew cries,
Walking home, hand in hand,
Beneath endless September skies.

James McKay

LASTING IMPRESSIONS

You brought us through our childhood
And walked us up the aisle
You were always there to help
Dad that was just your style

You worked hard night and day
So as we'd receive the best
We were all well cared for
That's something no one can contest

You were always healthy
And never darkened a doctor's door
You seldom took a tablet
Or had a pain before

But then disaster struck
When stomach pains appeared
Tests were carried out
It was just as you feared

Cancer in the stomach
Reality comes to light
How would you cope with this?
How could you possibly fight?

An operation date was set
To have your stomach taken out
And hopefully remove the cancer
Without a single doubt

Still you kept on working
Right up until the date
Even on the night before
You worked till it was late

The morning of the op had come
And you were set to go
The family gave their hugs and kisses
Which was hard for you, we know

After five hours in theatre
You were in intensive care
We stood and watched you suffer
You hardly knew us there

Your arm was full of drips
There were wires everywhere
You were being ventilated
It really didn't seem fair

With five days in intensive care
You were back in ward 43
You suffered all the time
As far as we could see

Slowly you progressed
Still you suffered quite a bit
You couldn't lie in bed
On a soft chair you would sit

Two weeks had now passed
With progress very slow
Yet with all the drips removed
Homeward bound you could go

Day by day went past
Suffering did not cease
But still you kept on going
Hoping for some peace

Sometimes you'd get down
When you thought there was no cure
We'd always try to perk you up
But still you were unsure

People came to visit
All to wish you well
The pain you were suffering
No one else could tell

You suffered there in silence
By your side stood your wife
With activities cut short
You had poor quality of life

Your sickness still remained
More tests they had to do
Then you got a boost
When results came through

Doctors said the tests were clear
The best news you had got
Maybe it was time you'd won
The battle you had fought

Alas it was short lived
No victory in sight
Mistakes were made in tests
And still you had to fight

Another op was set
To have a look and see
What was causing sickness
Or what problems there could be

Five hours back in theatre
We hoped you'd be okay
Then doctors came to talk
And there was a price to pay

No good news was forthcoming
We knew the time was here
To stand up to reality
And face that awful fear

Just three-six months left
We'd have to let you go
Still you were unconscious
And you didn't know

We watched you lying there
Your body frail and thin
You had suffered oh so much
It was just a mortal sin

You had never right recovered
From your coma state
And you never spoke to us
Perhaps it was just fate

We were called in the morning
To watch your last few hours
With family by your bedside
God showed us all His powers

You took your final breath
No more suffering
No more pain and sorrow
For death had lost its sting

We know you are in Heaven now
Walking on the narrow way
Although we really miss you
We know you are at peace today

Dad we really love you so
We devote this poem to you
One who cannot be replaced
And ne'er will be forgotten too.

Heather Dickey

CORNFLOWER BLUE (SAILING SOLO)

A calmness, torn uneasy silence
arousing uncertainty
almost filling her sails with freedom
far away out of view
her varnished frame
manicured to perfection
today
winds blew and drew her far out from the protection
of the harbour
the ebb and flow
of sheltered waters
returning a final glance
the lifting, turning tide
closed nearer
the moment became more enticing
the empowering
prospect of a solo performance
made certain this would be the day
of courage
and seas of new situation
to find shores
brimming days of contentment
of excitement
and undiscovered serenity.

Debra Smith

I WATCH THE CANDLE BURN . . .

I see the candle glow; I watch its gentle dance,
Flickers of the flame, a pure hypnotic trance,
My mind at peace in nowhere land, a chance to reminisce
Of all the things life's given me and some of those it missed
I picture those who've touched my world and carved a poignant niche
And those who I let slip away, the ones just out of reach
Faces start to form in the shadows from the flame
A magic silhouette, each face a different name
The dancing flame continues, to rise then gently fall
Holds my gaze then beckons me, determined to enthral
The faces slowly disappear, never to return
Nostalgic memories as I watch the candle burn.

Diane Crouch

FROST

Jack comes through in the dead of night
The air chilly and white
When he breathes, he chills the night air
He creeps in when it's still dark
Nothing stirs, not even a lark
It chills me to the bone
I know with Jack I am not alone
The night breeze will freeze
The ground sparkles beneath my feet
The ground shimmers beneath my feet
The sun has a cooling glow, the frost refuses to go
When the air is cold and thin
Jack Frost has been
As evening calls, the evening frost falls
The ground is white below
Frost as cold as falling snow.

Samantha Groves

BROKEN ROSE

I look to see before me a crushed and broken rose;
But I know deep down inside that heart is a life
That longs for sweet repose.

If only they would listen, if only they could see
The life that I have to live and the pain that's hurting me.

Show me the love I long for, please don't turn your back on me.
Show me I can trust you.
Please don't raise your hand to me.

Nurture me until I blossom,
Teach me how to sing,
Take the winter of my life and turn it into spring.

Now see the fruits of your labours, as in love you did aspire;
For the rose that once was broken has responded to your touch;
Now there's a bond that remains unbroken,
And a love that means so much.

Robert Waggitt

SPRING IS COMING

Outside the window it is snowing
And the north wind is blowing
But down the dale the daffodils are growing
Spring is coming
And the birds are singing
Jack Frost is still about
And the snowdrops are coming out
The fruit buds are sprouting out
But down in the beck there is still snow about
In the garden the broad beans are growing
Which last October I was sowing.

Derek McNeil

LOOKING DOWN

I saw the daffodils from the top window
and looked around to tell you
about the yellow trumpets
and how amazing it was that everything came to life
even after that February snow.
Your mouth curved down to your chin
I knew then there was no good morning for me.
I clamped my enthusiasm
and stopped the words from gushing out.
I remembered who we were
why we were low
and rearranged the net curtain.
It was you who'd dug in the bulbs
whilst I mopped away the claggy mud
on the doorstep which separated house from farm.
It was you who'd limped to the greenhouse
and seeded just for me the coriander and
nurtured plants for the allotment
whilst I wanted to run and find another life.
I watched you from this same window
and did wonder how you held out
with pain spiking every joint
disfiguring each and every limb.
It got you. It grew. It rooted and sprouted
like the Mediterranean fig tree.
It harnessed itself to your muscle
twisting up and around, a leech
sucking every civil word away
nibbling at each fold of baby-powdered skin.
I hated the illness as it destroyed you
aggressively, ruthlessly.
There were leafbuds on the horse chestnut
and the cherry tree and fresh greenness
spreading on the damp old lawn.
There was a load dragging on my heart
and a battle in my thoughts.
With you I had become the woman
I never wanted to be.

Gillian Muir

THE BRIDGE OF LIFE

Their faces are an open book
For life has barely touched them yet.
The pages clean and waiting still,
The ink within the pot unspilt,
Hoping to capture what may come
As the road of life unbends
Eager to find the knowledge there
Changing paths and sometimes friends
While I, their grandmother, wait and watch
To see the pages fill and turn.
For only fools who cannot know
Would find a generation gap.
But those who really understand
Would see the bridge of hand-in-hand
For they are mine and I am theirs
And this can never be erased
As age means nothing in life's book
Chapters are merged where there is love.
Until my life comes to its end
They'll always have me as a friend.
And even when my book's forgotten
And left unread upon the shelf
Discoloured lines and gently faded
The words that represent myself
Of me a woman of their past
Who lived and loved as they will do
I'll be to them a moment's thought
A memory loved, and sometimes sought.
For still the link will always stay
To guide and help them on their way.

Vanda Gilbert

TRAPPED WITHIN EDUCATIONAL WALLS

The butterfly tentatively explored the grilled, gothic window
Searching for escape.
Outside the university the day beckoned;
Bustling, busy, beckoning life.
Through the dusty, dirty panes was love, freedom in the autumn hillsides,
Covered now with soft russets, pale dappled green and golds in a collage
Cascade of confusion.

Fragile, flimsy, foolish gossamer wings stretched, fluttered helplessly,
Then perplexed, relaxed.
Antennae defeated, despaired, debilitated, dormant.
Suddenly, frantic, furious, agitated beating,
The catalespy, cadavenous, carmine crimson capitulated, odds overwhelming.
To defeat the late autumn sunshine is an illusion.

Above the fireless enclave, in a tarnished frame, hung the no-name lady.
A mournful beauty, painted alone, inheriting the wrong genes or perhaps not?
Dark, sad eyes stared sorrowfully as the butterfly quietly waited,
Its soft, velvet wings shaming the dulled ruby dress in the silent portrait.
Where was the painted lady now and what had been her destiny?
Was my fate to join this imprisoned pair?

Quivering, exhausted on the lukewarm iron radiator, a drowsy slow death.
Leaving the security of a chrysalis existence to escape into the stormy world,
Torn asunder by class structure and status is an effort of will to survive.
The iron window latch was unyielding firm, like the bonds of family.
Still the butterfly struggled toward the window bolt, seeking the sweet
Fragrance of late October bounty blooms beyond the imprisoning, impregnable
glass.

Sadly, I cupped the crimson gold gossamer in my hands. Like a child.
Had I wasted my autumn sunshine staying in this place of lost learning?
Turning, I sought escape, perhaps a friend waited in the hillsides.
The gilded scarlet hovered avidly in space, revelling in her sudden freedom.
I knew then that I had reached an impasse of no release or even peace.

Jean Houghland

SHIP

I'm helpless and bobbing around in the sea
There's nothing and no one waiting for me
No sunrays hit my decks and warm my beams
This journey appears pointless and torn at its seams

No wind beneath my sails to take me on
To lands of warmth where the sun beats upon
And I harbour my soul to a quay with a view

I'm helpless and lost with a view I see through
A wide horizon and no one to talk to
The fear of loneliness is all too near
As this horizon is left all too clear

Dead calm shall it be before the storm
You know it's coming, air electric and warm
So what shall happen to my body of toil?
As I bob and I dip in this sea that's been so loyal

Should I look for a lifeline, that someone for care
The person who throws it you, now life to share
Take on the lashes of pain and torn body of wear
Pick up my pieces and handle with care

I entrust in you this duty
To take on this body who hurts with despair
You're my guardian, my life I shall share
For it's you who will sail me to shores of afar
With the love and devotion, you are my night's star.

Joanne Payne

WAR OF LIFE

Sat slouched among the rolling hills and valleys with the gentle groan of the farm and rustle of the trees. Nature as loud as an orchestra, silent as a hunter, singing joy and peace. The laughing of the animals and children, the elegant dances of the trees to the tune of the wind. Oh how the land cried and sang and danced in peace.

But how the silence of death has overthrown and enslaved this land. The whistle of the wind has become the scream of death due to the mind imploding horrors of shells. The elegant dance of the trees has been reduced to a depressant slouch. All is dead in this land, all physically alive, all spiritually and theoretically dead. Besides the blood, sweat and tears of the land. The lush grass decimated by overwhelming horrors.

The monotonous hum of the aircraft above, as if bees have populated the skies. The squeal of the juggernauts as if a thousand mice rang out their call. Oh how peculiar such noise, which would leave anything lifeless at its sound, to the silent whistling screams of the land can leave anything living haunted for all eternity. I raise my head above the line, only to be bombarded and suppressed by the crack and whizz of the golden wasps. Once again my dreams of peace and the lush land are drowned by the sorrowing images of mass murder and the destroying horrors it leaves behind.

Maybe just a dream, a dream, a figure of imagination, a bewildering thought. No. Too real, too bloody for the imagination of Man, more the imagination of the Devil, sheer evil. Then it came; it. That thing. I had been stung by those wasps. Suddenly I snapped into reality, shock and despair. Then I remembered the stag. Lying in the lush grass which had now become raspberry red with pools of blood. Immediately the ground lurched, throwing back the evil. A touch and the majestic stag was rejuvenated by the spirit of the land, yes, it was still alive, and the spirit of the farm which had been decimated by evil was repairable. But not here, the land is dead, no spirit here, no thought or feeling. Dead.

I wondered. Would I be rejuvenated, replenished with life by the spirit of the land in some distant place? From What I had seen, I now felt mind dead, only the memory of the spirit fuelling my fire, keeping me burning. I went, lost in a black void of despair. For now, all was lost . . .

Abruptly! I was reborn into life by the muzzled laugh of the forgotten land. The distant blur of the burnt cottage. I had returned, my destiny fulfilled by the shield of the land. My bare skin gliding through the soil of this place. As I hovered through this land I could feel the presence of the spirit. Unlike the horrors I had seen elsewhere they had not rubbed off on this place, a beacon for peace; it still had the might here for repair, rejuvenation. Mile after mile of lush meadow spanned and grew beneath me. Already the spirit immersed within me began to rejuvenate and spread life through the desolate farm.

And once again life was brimming on the beacon farm. And again I felt myself sat slouched among the rolling hills and valleys, laughing and singing with the children and animals. And dancing with the trees . . . to the soft gentle tune of the whistling wind.

Oliver Bird

FLOOD

Pitter-patter, pitter-patter
The raindrops splatter and shatter
They hit the concrete
Solid matter they cannot penetrate
They run off to ground
A symphony of sound
Slowly they gather
With purpose they come together
Making a deadly force
Creeping gradually under doors
The water level keeps rising
In a weather quite trying
Water rises to my waist
Making buoyant my weight
It seems life is at whist
Therefore, I cannot wait
Until every barrier is wreathe
I tell my body to be calm and breathe
As the escape boat is now ready
And hopefully sure and steady
No need to go out to sea
For only water now, I see
Nevertheless, carefully we row
All day long, till the morrow
Then finally, rescue we gain
Now we wait for the waters to drain.

Debra Ayis

FROM MORN TO MORN

Penetrating polar wind,
Your squalls bring snow,
Flying and skitting,
Settling on shrubs and roses -
A glimmering paradise,
Which in dawn's light,
Becomes an ice-blue moon,
Bereft of food for fox or fawn,
Above the earth - fires warm.

Frost - light,
Sun penetrates,
Brilliant haze
In the sky.

O, wondrous light
Of winter,
Of holly,
Vibrant sunset.

Inside, an ornament
Of pink shines
With its light
Across the room.

Shade -
Frost stays
'Til night -
Surrounds white.

Plain trees
Silhouetted
Into hoar frost -
Perfect crystal.
The snow was thick,
The air did freeze.
All the birds
Were huddled in trees,
When out the window
The cook did throw
Lots of tidbits down below.

In an instant,
The birds flew down
Had the greatest party
In the town.

Nola B Small

THE EMBRYO (MEANT TO BE)

I am given an existence, to elevate, even procreate
Another fish in the sea, I am meant to be
I can stretch, I can feel, not ready yet to breathe
I can hear, I can see, I am as safe as I am meant to be
A body, even a soul, I am part of life's goal
I have tears to cry, words to heal
Love to give for others to feel
There is pain to endure through a belief instilled
Times to feel good again after falling ill
There is time for food and time for thought
Chances to build and chances to be taught
Chances to teach others all I can learn
Chances to reach out, many stones to turn
I'll have stories to tell, tales to hear
I'll have joy to give and time to control fear
But there is a fate worse than being deported
My dreams all deserted the day I was aborted
I was given chances to add to Man's advances
Another fish in the sea
But someone else chose my life was not meant to be.

Paul Wightman

AUTUMN AMBIENCE

The scrunch of fallen leaves beneath my feet
And apple dumplings baking on the hob.
Grey mists that gather round the setting sun
Forewarn us that the curtain soon will close.
Gone is the fragrance of the woodbine, sweet
In its summer season. Solemn October
Breathes a cooler breath. The year has run
Its youthful course and Autumn shows
Her furrowed features. Once, across the land
A wide expanse of rippling golden corn
Revelled in radiance, 'ere a ripening hand
Caressed the slender stems; they might be shorn
To yield life-giving grain. Mid winter's thrall
May we give thanks for blessings of the fall.

Ida Goodall

SPRING LAMENT

Where, oh where, oh where is spring?
Nature's song of which poets sing.
It seems to have come then gone again,
The dank air filled with mist and rain.

When it comes, young men find love,
That's what young girls' dreams are of.
They spread their nets with winning guile,
Even old men can raise a smile.

For me I strain my ears to hear
The lark ascending tho' skies are drear.
The flowers bloom yet no birds sing,
Where, oh where, oh where is spring?

Ann Furley

A PERFECT DAY

The ripple of a stream,
A warble of the lark.
One can live a dream
In the beauty of the park.
Through the endless years,
Great oaks stand o so tall.
The murmur of the brook,
Leaves begin to fall.
Sunlight flickering through the trees,
A carpet of red and gold.
Wildlife scurries everywhere,
A breeze is taking hold.
Eventide is nigh,
Clouds roll by on high.
Shadows fall, end of a day,
Time to go to make our way.

E Champion

THE MOON

What colour is the moon?
I look up at the quarter moon

What colour is it?
How will I answer this question
From my little daughter?

I look up at the early evening
Winter sky

Dark, filmy, watery clouds
Drift across the moon hiding it for a moment

It's yellow I think
Yes, it's yellow.

Christine B M White

WINTER, SPRING TO SUMMER

Thou cold wind doth blow on my bare cheeks,
Through thou air streamlined vents of air blow.
Bitter my insides do feel so weak,
From head to toe though no flesh does show,
Thou heat of fire and smells of warmth I seek,
Thou cold wind gets where no man would go,
Close the door to that bitter cold and save heat,
Now the sun has upon us come, I shall seek
Glory, through thou sky doth it glow,
Piercing through our skin mild and meek,
Now my body uncover and off do show,
Oh what a glorious day, such a treat,
Now the cockles of my heart are warm,
Away from biting winds we are drawn.

Carol Paxton

WINGS OF SUMMER

Listen to that sound
Above our footsteps
Rising and falling on the breeze
In summer sun, near summer seas
The sound holds there
Shrill notes dance lightly in the summer air
Up from burling gap above the happy scene
White cliff tops dressed in Sussex green
We the audience enjoy nature's play
The skylark sings his part
And always has a lot to say
Nature's noisy messenger
Calls us to rejoice
Flying higher and higher
In everlasting voice.

Ken Johnston

A DOG'S BEST FRIEND

Hello! I'm Cash, a modest chap, tho handsome in my way,
I've lived in these parts all my life and I don't have plans to stray.
The laid back life just suits me fine, it's clear by my demeanour,
And you'll see me walking every day with my faithful pet Georgina.
There springs to mind one winter's day, quite frosty, I recall,
We went on the embankment for a game with Gina's ball.
The exercise is good, I find, it gives the legs a stretch,
And seems to please Georgina, yes! she loves a game of fetch.
But that day things were different, the ball bounced out of sight,
And when I bounded after it the brambles caught me tight.
Down, down I went twelve feet or more, straight into the canal,
I'm drowning was my only thought, then I spied my little pal.
Along the grassy bank she sped and jumped into the water,
Thinking back now, I must say it was just as well I'd brought her.
Moments later all was well, soon Gina had me free,
I could tell she was delighted by the way she looked at me.
I didn't bother swimming lest ungrateful it may seem,
But let her carry me ashore as I planned this little scheme.
A thorough shake to dry my coat, a scratch or two, and then
I'll find a stick to play with, and we'll do it all again.
Gina didn't seem too keen, she said, 'Once is enough,
I'm squelching in my wellies and I'm running out of puff.'
All this was witnessed by a man, but offer help? Not he,
His only comment as we passed was, 'What's her pedigree?'
Is that the time? I'll have to go, I'm ready for a snooze,
But first I must walk Gina and rush back to catch the news.
Of adventures in the future I'll be sure to let you know,
But in the meantime you take care, goodbye now, cheerio.

Beryl Thornbury

AFTERMATH OF A PROSTATECTOMY

Yard upon yard of clear plastic pipes,
Balloons and bags of different types,
Held together with plastic vices
And several other strange devices.
The stream will start from the bag at the top,
Down through the bladder and into the pot.
The idea is to control the flow
Which should be constant, measured and slow.
Problems arise if there's a blockage,
Caused by a clot and a painful stoppage!
This was the background to the cycle
When late one evening poor old Michael
Leapt out of his chair, writhing in pain,
The dreaded blockage had started again.
He pressed the bell, help came straight away.
'Sit down on the bed and do as I say,
Hold onto this tube, I'll pump full throttle,
I want to suck the clot in the bottle.'
Michael was brave, but clearly not happy.
'This is bad news so please make it snappy.'
At last the blood clot emerged from the tube
And Michael's language became far less rude.
What happened next were urethral spasms
Cascading over the tube in fathoms.
Onto the carpet, over the floor,
Almost out into the corridor.
Now what was needed was a bandage tight
To stop Michael leaking during the night.
This was achieved in a practical way
And his bed was bone dry at dawn next day.

Michael Carter

MOTORWAY MEALS

Where has the old dog gone
for we are alone
and I am a tired, hungry beast
who urgently needs to feast?
The cubs are asleep and smelly
against my warm belly.
I'll give them a lick and try to be quick
to find a fast snack, and then hasten back.

It took me a while to grab it -
that fast-moving rabbit.
Licking my lips and now yawning
I'll return to the lair before dawning,
under the old five-barred gate.
I must not be late,
though I think I should drink
from this rainwater puddle.
Now home for a cuddle
for the cubs have a need to snuggle and feed.

This traffic is busy and makes my head dizzy
as lorries roar past. I'll have to be fast
to cross to the ditch without any hitch.
What's this lump of fur by the verge?
My dog fox is dead! I feel my fears surge.
He did not make it! Weary and frazzled,
hurrying homeward, the lights must have dazzled.
I'll need to take care.
Run! Now! I'm nearly there -
I can hear the cubs crying.
Ouch! Through the air flying.

Sad though it seems, as everyone knows,
death to the foxes means food for the crows.

Doris R Townsend

DAWN CHORUS

Down the stairs quietly gliding
It's breaking light so early in the morning rising
I hear the dawn chorus busting
The singing of birds almost in unison
I pulled on my boots, slipping on my coat
Stepping out of the door, wandering down our lane
Breathing in the fresh air, wondering what's new again

Spring is coming from every place
The long tassels of catkins hang
Like elongated sunbeams shine
Sprigs of new blades of emerald grass appear
Bringing special messages of hope to wildlife here

The aromatic leaves and the first busting
Of pale green buds against the dark wood appear
In hedge groves birds in plenty abound.
Newts, frogs and hedgehogs are all here and welcome
Acorns have bust their sides, showing delicate white shoots

The wild creatures will have a great feast
Spring is surely here, the merlin loves to sing
And soar and dip on wing, then dive to catch its prey
While its mate gobbles the accustomed breakfast
So close, so near, just a bit from my feet.

M Richardson

THE TREE

It was an ancient.
It had stood upon the land as generations passed,
And it spread wide its arms to God's own will
With a green gladness every spring,
And it shed its browning coat upon the autumn chill.
It stood in the garden of the old house.
Sons climbed into its boughs
Whilst little sisters admired from below,
Mothers worried, fathers warned, knees were grazed,
But none were amazed,
It had always been so,
Until the year of the storm.
Then in a hurl and thrash of hurricane that no bough could sustain,
And no ancient roots tight hold against
It crashed, and all thought would never rise again.
And yet!
And yet a root held deep in the fertile ground,
And came the spring
Was wonder such as might seem unbelief,
A shoot was found, a shoot was found, a shoot was found,
And on that shoot,
A leaf.

Martin Harris Parry

CODY THE NAUGHTY GOLDEN RETRIEVER

Cody the naughty golden retriever,
Tried his best to do no wrong,
But his efforts all were thwarted,
For trouble found him before too long.
What at first seemed quite endearing,
Soon became an expensive game,
As Cody chewed up many an item,
Pants and socks were never the same!
How the children laughed and giggled,
As Cody dragged them across the lawn,
But their mother was not so happy,
When she found their clothes were torn.
Dad was also not too happy,
When Cody spied his unguarded coat . . .
It took him just seconds to find the money,
And even less time to eat the note!
Ethan tried to make excuses,
And with sister Robyn, he was not alone,
But their dad claimed naughty Cody,
Was eating them out of house and home.
Cody was sorry for being naughty,
And so decided to run away,
Because he thought that all the family,
No longer wanted him to stay.
So one morning whilst in the garden,
Cody jumped the five-bar gate,
And without a backward glance at Ethan,
Cody ran at an alarming rate.
Ethan and Robyn looked on in terror,
As Cody crossed a busy road,
Panting hard and dodging traffic,
As a lorry shed its heavy load.
Shocked and trembling the dog sought cover,
Somewhere to hide without a trace,
Then he spied a neighbour's hen house,
And knew he'd found the ideal place.
But the chickens all looked worried,
When Cody spied something beneath hen Meg.
Now he knew how to prove his value,
If only he could collect the new-laid egg.
So Cody grasped the fragile object,

As folk appeared from north and south.
All thought Cody would break the eggshell,
But Cody knew he had a gentle mouth.
Then one old man grabbed Cody's collar,
And made him drop the undamaged egg.
And while the folk all tried to catch it,
Cody slipped past the old man's legs.
Once out of town and onto farmland,
Cody now knew what he had to do . . .
Find a new job, new home and family,
So through a cornfield the retriever flew.
Then by chance he spied a spaniel,
Doing exactly what a spaniel does best.
Racing out to fetch the object,
His master had dropped in the lake with zest.
What better job for a dog like Cody!
For retrieving things was in his blood,
But at that moment a gun was fired,
And a poor little bird lay dead in the mud.
It took no time for Cody to scarper,
The scene before him was horrible to see.
He didn't like bangs and came to the conclusion . . .
'A gun dog's life was not for me!'
On he ran beyond the tree line,
And came across a field of sheep.
He watched the sheepdog run back and forward,
Which made him so tired he lay down to sleep.
When he woke he sat and pondered,
A sheepdog's life was not for him,
All that running around and chasing . . .
'I'm not a collie,' he said with a grin.
So on he walked and began a-thinking,
A country life was not much fun,
At least in town he had the children,
Who loved to take him out for a run.
Soon Cody came to a dangerous river,
A place where children should never play.
Cody sat down to watch the fishes,
And wished he had a place to stay.
Then something moved and caught his attention,
Far out near the other bank.
Two young children were on the jetty,
Running along the slippery planks.
Cody watched and suddenly realised,

The two small children belonged to him . . .
Robyn and Ethan were on the jetty,
And neither of them was able to swim!
At that moment he saw his Robyn,
Slip on the planks and then fall down,
Over the edge and into the water,
The river was deep; she was going to drown!
Without a thought or hesitation,
Cody jumped in to save the girl,
Then he noticed her brother Ethan,
Fall in too and be lost in the swirl.
Cody swam out to reach the children,
Grabbed Robyn's coat and held on tight.
Then to his relief he felt young Ethan,
Take hold of his collar with all of his might!
Wet and cold the retriever laboured,
To reach the shore before they sank.
His precious load to him was priceless,
And all he wanted was to reach the bank.
Finally he felt the bed of the river.
Under his paws as he reached the shore,
He sighed with relief, for the children he'd rescued,
He'd done his best; he could do no more.
Cody ignored the crowd that had gathered,
But then saw the children's mum and dad,
How he wished he'd been a better retriever,
And how he missed the home that he'd had.
Cody turned to leave the people,
With heavy heart and all alone,
But then he heard familiar voices . . .
'Come on Cody, let's go home?'
No longer, 'Cody the naughty retriever,'
No longer searching for family or job,
'You're our hero!' the family stated,
As Cody was hailed: 'The best guard dog!'

Trina Hulbert

THE WOODMAN'S CALL

'Walk in this wood, and then your clear eye sees
the leafy spires and strange green light that's made
from summer boughs of many brooding trees.
Your warm, alert flesh feels the cool, deep shade.

Softly the deer across your path will creep
dappled as sunlight through the trees revealed
and, as in fear, then suddenly she'll leap
- and in that dappled foliage be concealed.

Look up into the branches of that oak
and you will see the squirrel in her dray
- far off you scent the woodman's wafting smoke.
We twain must meet ere you pursue your way.

A small bird sings - a chime of elfin bells.
A golden stream meanders where you roam.
Follow these signs, and where the curlew tells
her plaintive song, there you will find my home.

You are a loner, curious of mind;
I am the vision of your bright-eyed youth.
You are a lover, passionate and kind.
You trust that all will listen to our truth.

But I know well, encircling us about
are spirits in the crevices of grey,
and some of them are evil to the root,
and some are fair - but snare us in our way.'

A river god, he called to me when young.
Softly I tread within the halls of men.
I've learnt about the world - less well than some.
Where are the thoughts that I was thinking then?

'Far more than this, you sought to tell and find;
I was the vision of your bright-eyed youth.
Many are lovers, curious and kind
- and out of dappled dreams shall shine the truth.'

Jacqueline Ives-Ward

TAPESTRY

Weave, oh sacred weaver, a tapestry to document
My passage from the cradle to my everlasting rest,
Spin a thread of living colour on a base of human frailty,
Show it all as plain as day, leave nothing to be guessed.

Start upon a silken cloth as pure and white as innocence,
And use a thread the colour of a newborn baby's soul:
Add the hue of pain that mothers gladly suffer during birth,
And then the shade of love and pride as first their child they hold.

Sew the colour of a smile as faltering first steps I take,
Of infantile frustration as I tumble to the floor,
Of grim determination in my childish clash with gravity,
Of triumph as I stagger from the fireplace to the door.

Would the colours stronger grow, as, learning to communicate,
The baby grunts and groans develop slowly into words?
What colour's curiosity, as, to the garden venturing,
My baby eyes discover plants and animals and birds?

Have you a thread, great weaver, which can show the colour of delight
As news to me is broken of a baby soon to share
My life? A baby brother or a sister who will play with me,
What colour is excitement, as I stand bewildered there?

Weave a thread of feeling of protectiveness instilled in me,
A buffer to protect my little brother from the world:
One arm to be a sword to fight to save him from adversity,
And one a shield, protecting him from every stone that's hurled.

Will your magic needle show the course of my development,
Progressing from the pencil to the realms of pen and ink?
Transition, will it show, from my infancy to childhood
As I look at things about me and begin to learn to think?

Thread the thread of impishness, of boyhood curiosity,
To show the tricks, unsavoury, that growing boys all try,
Discovering life's questions being answered by more questions still,
And suffering from pangs of guilt without realising why.

What colour would you use to sew my first romantic interlude?
What colour is a broken dream, when all does not go right?
Is there a thread that you can use to try to patch a broken heart?
Is there a thread to soothe the eyes that cry all through the night?

What shade is realisation that a lasting love has just arrived?
That she at whom I gaze is destined soon to be my bride?
What colour's trepidation, as I take her home to meet my folks?
Is there a thread so bright to show the passion and the pride?

Then in your sight, great weaver, as I plight my troth for evermore,
We stand as your apprentice binds us with a golden thong:
Use a double thread as you embroider our joint destiny,
To give us added strength to cope with things that may go wrong.

Sew a thread of fruitfulness and plant it deep within our loins
To show the deep fulfilment as our infant is conceived:
Show the cataclysm as the tiny bud bursts into bloom,
And colour in the joy of love both given and received.

What colour will you use to show the fusion of two separate people
As the child inherits parts of two to make a third?
The wisdom of her father, with her mother's beauty, soon combines
To make their future brighter as their past becomes more blurred.
Through babyhood and infancy, to childhood and puberty
The child seems to pass in but the blinking of an eye,
A person of her own upon the threshold of maturity
Whose parents look on mistily, with retrospective sigh.

My lover grows more elderly, as I do too: advancing years
Cause hair to grow more silvery, and joints to grow more stiff,
But feelings are much deeper as the autumn years progress along,
Love becomes a symphony, where once was just a riff.

The children of our child now give the pleasure in their growing up
That once our own child gave us in her childhood long ago.
What coloured threads do you intend to use to show the happiness
As we survey the paths we've trod, where they have yet to go?

Your tapestry is nearly woven, threads are coming to their end,
The picture that you sew now nears completion, I'll be bound,
The cloth on which you now embroider twilight, soon will have no room
For any further stitches as my ending comes around.

Just one request I'll ask, great weaver, let us both depart together,
Make me not to grieve for her, nor she to grieve for me:
Let us hand in hand continue into what you have in store
To never more be parted, now until eternity.

As we leave this world, great weaver, let our faces wear a smile
So those we leave behind us do not too much sadness feel:
Sew those final stitches with a thread the colour of contentment,
Let all our successors know our happiness was real.

Lay us side by side together, two as one in life and death,
As Mother Earth enfolds us in her final deep embrace,
And with your final golden thread, a stitch to join our souls together
Now and 'til forever, hand in hand and face to face.

Mick Nash

A DREAM OF 'WHEELS'

Oh for some 'wheels' - that I once more
might live my life as I did before.
Joining in - in the world out there,
not viewing it from my armchair.
But oh I've worn my poor legs out
and now I cannot get about.
My cats all think it's some new game
as I totter around on my walking frame.
Once I enjoyed my days indoors
even when just doing my chores.
Plus my painting or a crossword
for I'm really quite a home-bird.
Perversely now I just can't wait
to see the outside of my gate!
For after all these weeks inside
it's harder to keep occupied.
Some 'walking wheels' would do a treat
to help me get upon my feet.
First though, must get my legs stronger
then it won't be too much longer
before I can go and get my wheels
and oh, how wonderful that feels!
Then I'll be shouting - just like Toad,
'All aboard for the open road!'

Daphne Lodge

BLESSED REST

The world is sometimes at rest,
When the cloak of night falls,
Some say that it is at its best,
Because mankind forgets his chores.
Also the moon like a mantle on high,
Shines out from a starlit sky.

The world spins so silent around,
Always it seems at the same speed,
As dawn breaks lighting the ground,
This encourages life to tiny seed,
Soon crops will grow in the field,
And mankind hope for a good yield.

The growth of crops is often helped by breeze,
Nearby trees give complete shade,
With trunk, branches and many leaves.
Man is with many assets blessed,
Thankfully the world sometimes is at rest.

Ralph Stephens

DESERT DUSK

Night steals over the tawny desert and hides the chipmunk
                              that nobody fools.
The big red sun sinks into the Atlantic and the sky cools.
Cicadas chant Vespers in the still oleander,
While the fat, brown cockroach creeps out to wander.
'What was the meaning of today?' asks the white vulture.
'Hah!' laughs the lizard, 'another day to devour carrion in your culture.'
'I know night follows day,' says the white vulture, 'but I do not know why.'
'No more do I,' says the owl, 'no more do I.'

David J Ayres

RED KNIFE

There is a red knife in my chest.
And blood gently creeps
Out of the wound's delicate edges.
A pool of blood gathers on the stomach,
Then slowly drips down the side.
Sheets stained.
Ruined red.

Tick-tock. Tick-tock.

The sunrise is crimson, shading red into red,
Sticky liquid and incarnadine colour.
Light beams join the knife in violation.

Tick-tock. Tick-drop.

The day progresses without night's bloody victim.

Life and death enact their carefully rehearsed
Roles of pseudo innocence,
Their hearts equally dark.
A twilight world steeped in half-truths, half-lies;
Of shadows and nightmares incarnate.

Tick-drip. Tick-drop.

Christ has abandoned his sinner,
Left to die, blood slowly drying.
Red to black.

Drip-drop. Tick-tock.

A knife fast in the body,
A pinnacle of insult,
Insolence to creation,
A monument to death.

Night falls.

M S Lees

ORIANA'S VISION

In the violet twilight
The watching woodland
Is swathed in silence
And webbed with stillness.

There's a grey mist swirling
Round the phantom ramparts
In the dimming valley
A chasm below.

Feathered with dusk
An owl glides by,
An ivory blur
In the fir-dark shadows.

The roebucks pause
In the glimmering gloom:
There's a breath of unease
In the listening air.

Under arches of larches
And bowers of willow
Death is waiting
Pale as a star.

Oh, green as life
Are the leaves of the birch
And the talon'd briar:

Orion-gold
Are the shimmering blades
Of the three who lurk
In the fox-stirred fern:
But dragon-red
Will the blood be, shed
By the mirroring pool
In the tangled wood
On the haunted hill . . .

Eileen-Margaret Kidd

AWAKE WITH A VISION

Awake with a vision
My mind's eye can see
Not knowing will it understand me
Honesty, truth, passion a plea
Here it vision, have faith in me

This vision shows beauty
Fields of flowers and light
But a floating comfort
To wander alone at night

Visions are pictures of movement
Real, not frozen like a student
Young and innocent blood full-flowing
Visions can find a way unknowing

A vision of Hell
Hurt throws and thunder
Will Heaven's doors open
For love true wonder

But what of the future
Can visions help foretell
Will it end in a tear
Vision not you as well

Vision to vision catch the light
Study the video now in your sight
Don't hide in the background
Come forward and fight.

Mick Entwistle

THE SEASONS OF OUR LIVES

Our lives are like the seasons, young through to old,
From sunny springtime days to winter in the cold.
Every stage is different, like the seasons; sun and rain
Don't know what I mean? Well please let me explain!

The day that we are born, the springtime of our life,
The flowers are in bloom, the lambs are running rife,
So small and helpless, needing lots of love and care,
Dependant on our parents, so grateful they are there.

Summertime of our lives, school days are upon us,
Crops are growing high, the farmers make a fuss!
Holidays in the sun, out playing with our friends,
The best days of our lives, why do they have to end?

Growing up and getting married, with children of our own,
It's autumn in our lives, our bodies fully grown!
The trees are standing bare, leaves are blown away,
The dark nights soon begin, our days are fading away.

Soon the winter comes as we grow weak and old,
So vulnerable and frail, more open to the cold.
We'll sit and reminisce, remember seasons past,
Live life to the full and every day like it's your last!

Kelly Kinross

THE SEMI-AUTONOMOUS DUCHY OF MII-CHAN

(To I.V.E.)

Harken all ye Denizens of the Meep,
to the tale of Herb and a sorrow deep.

The agile young fox came down the wall
jumped over the cat curled up in a ball,
lustrous and red she most gorgeously leapt
her tail a white plume like a sail on a crest,
as the cow tossed her curds and hurdled the moon
unburdened of milk left to pool in a spoon,
and the spider slid down from the drainpipe a-glisten
spinning her filaments with perfect precision,
admired by all in the tenement toes
of the old woman's shoe and its sheltering sole,
where fear and dismay are kept well at bay
far from the fenceposts of Number 3A,
from where can be summoned by wing or by prayer
a dream or a miracle or a wish gone astray
or by the pestle of living just ground clear away.

For the Herm in the Garden of Herb is awake
- while at pause in their play, white rabbit and cat
in tortoiseshell cadence and bonhomie chat -
always awake and always at hand
whate'er it can do it will do for this band
whose sorrows are heavy, whose luck has run thin,
who long before Herb had chucked hope in the bin,

For here in the toes of the ivy-dressed shoe,
where once there was me and twice there was you
the words of the loved ones inhabit the night,
gone now the bright eyes, surprises, delights,
the purpose of waking to make sense of life:
you on the planet in the same place and time
- on even the same A-to-Zed page as mine -

oh fate laid the way for our days to entwine
then cut us apart with no warning sign
without any clue of its urgent design.

Herb gathers lone souls adrift in lost lands
surfing on atoms, just counting the sand,
sifting through minutes beyond our command
coasting on time both quotidian and bland,

And sometimes a loved one will reach down a hand
connecting the dots in the skies of a night
forming outlines of home
when we're whipped out of sight.

Denise Dresner

OAK

My name is Oak, I am a tree.
There isn't any tree more majestic or mightier than me.
Put your arms around my trunk,
I will give you some of my spirituality and energy.

Stand under my branches,
Take this advantage to oxygenate your blood and brain.
Let me take the strain.

Collect some of my acorns and plant them in a field by a babbling brook,
Where lots of insects and birds can nest
Including my friend, the rook.

I have had many folk sitting under me.
I seem to give them strength,
And this feeling of tranquillity.

I bask in the sun and moon blissfully free,
So that you may come and be comforted by me.

Sylvia Papier

DREAMING

As I sat today, looking out to sea,
a sinister dark blue sea, I watched it
roll back and forth till it met the sky;
then nothing more could I see
but the edge of the world:
Now I could see why they once believed,
that the world was flat; I stared and stared,
till on the horizon appeared a galleon
in full sail with a handsome captain at its helm,
his lady by his side; in the blink of an eye
it had gone and in its place a ship of the line,
one of the Queen's of course, and tomorrow,
my dream I would fulfil, to sail the seven seas.
Would I go round the world,
or over the edge - tomorrow I will see!

Audrey Allen

COLOURS

There's the red of the sunrise.
The grey of the sea.
The gold of the morning.
The green of the trees.

There's the white of the snowfall.
The blue of the sky.
The black of the smoke stack.
Royal purple, so high.

There's the crimson of blood flow.
The teal of the plants.
The orange of flowers.
The brown of the ants.

All colours God made them, for us to employ.
So, let us then love them, receive them with joy.

Peter John Morey

DEAR SILENCE

Dear Silence,
my part-time friend;
my sometimes ruthless nemesis.
Am I to dread this coming visit, even to fear it
or am I to embrace you as a long lost love?

I cannot say that I relished our last meeting.
Your friend's anguish and despair rallied against me
and your booming voice of nothingness
overwhelmed me and threw me to the floor.
You left me battered and broken,
fighting for my sanity.
How I have grown to hate you so.

My dear Silence,
what gifts shall you bear this time -
golden drops of peace and tranquillity;
the soothing balm of happiness
or are you to enchant me with your dark,
pervasive cloak of heaviness and loneliness?

I am waiting for you Silence.
I will not allow you to ensnare me with your charms
only to betray me once again.

Silence, come if you must
but you will not drown me out this time.

Susan Smith

CLEO

You looked at me with sun-filled, appealing eyes:
'Let's go!' Ears cocked to make your point
tail a question mark for my clouded brain
'Are you *here*? Let's go!'
quivering in anticipation

I took you - you took me ferretting along the summer fields
I sat on a stricken elm, let the tears flow,
you whined softly and nuzzled my hand
offering warmth
then, past human grief,
you masterminded trips through loveliest scents and sights
of hay, rabbits, chamomile, yarrow
with the deep grey sea below
'Are you there?' you barked, 'come on, let's go!'
tugging at the leash, taking me in tow

How I learned
the exquisite difference
as you chased ball or stick, cat or squirrel,
the peacock, flocks of seagulls over sodden sand
you sped back to me, panting:
'Once again, where were you? Did you mark how I nearly caught
its wing?'

We invented games of pulling-the-blanket to shreds
you growling, grunting, muttering excited little tunes,
glaring at me
your head rotating furiously to unscrew my wrist
to unlock the clasp, to outwit me
staking all your trust
on that vital inch between my fingers and your locked
crocodile jaw
revelling in muscle tension
arching so far back as to almost sit on your haunches
until the wild ripping apart
of fur or fabric
how you won!

Françoise de Pierpont

REJUVENATION

Across those endless voids of time and space
Orbits a barren planet which craves for salvation
A legacy of a species named the human race
Echoes from a lonely wanderer seeking rejuvenation

Lush verdant meadows and oceans now devoid of hope
Pointing to planetary decay and disintegration
Greed and avarice cascading down a slippery slope
Quiet whispers pleading with the wind for reunification

Tropical rainforests now devoid of their trees
All around vestiges of Man's thoughtless devastation
Sunlight now streams through lifeless canopies
What now are the chances of a new salvation

Lost the plaintiff cries of dolphins and whales
Echoes across the waters, calls of pitiful desperation
Trying to survive as that pale light fades
Attempting to relay a stop to senseless decimation

It could all be too late for a once living Earth
As mindless acts are perpetrated by each nation
Echoes in the wind cry for a desperate rebirth
Will mankind's time run out before a rejuvenation

As a pearl in the heavens no longer shines bright
Who will tell the children there is no unification
Will they ever know who killed off their birthright
Or could there still be time for a late rejuvenation.

Jim Wilson

THE CHILD SAID WHY?

Why is the ancient question that will never grow old
enquiring minds ask things like Dad why are fires not cold

Why is it Dad that the sky is so blue and with white clouds so high
when you put a seashell to your ear why can you hear the sea sigh

Why is it Dad that the birds sing songs throughout the whole day
Why do they sit in trees and have so many things to do and to say

Why is it Dad that dogs don't like and chase the pussy cats
and why do the cats stalk the birds, the mice and the rats

Why is it Dad you have hairs on your chin and up your nose
and why do I get my fingers pricked when I play with a rose

Why is it Dad when we all go out on a trip in our motorcar
everywhere we go is good fun but always so long and so far

Why is it Dad when we swim do you say the sea is so cold
when I think it's great, it's warm, is it because you're getting old

Why is it Dad now you're not here I'm unable to ask or to share
I miss you Dad and now only ask why in the form of a prayer.

Harry Noyes

TREASURE TROVE

A slender apple-sapling beckons me
And bids me pause close by a flowery moot
To marvel on, in deep humility
The efficacy of a tiny seed
Having enjoyed the sweetness of the fruit
The kernel's cast away with little heed.
We prize the flesh for its delicious taste;
The rest is refuse, destitute of care.
Yet a potential orchard dwells secure,
Encapsulated in the fragrant sphere.
That which we duly disregard in haste
May prove a thesaurus in miniature,
Riv'ling anon, in jewel-enclustered trees,
The fabled fame of the Hesperides.

Walter Blacklaw

SONNET EARTH

Our verdant Mother Earth,
once no one harmed your surface, just left it growing wild,
then, you produced Man, your errant child,
the day you gave us birth,
would start a chain reaction that was sometimes filled with mirth,
once only mist rolled down upon a field,
now, crops are forced to grow a massive yield,
but, now too many people still create a dearth.

Mines pock-mark your face,
things you had forged forever we displace,
your trees are all hewn down,
to make a belching smoke-filled town,
and round you out in time's dark womb,
our rubbish floats forever trapped and frozen in its tomb.

Jean Paisley

REFLECTIONS

I stare into the water, transparent, calm.
Fluffy white clouds dance across the clear
blue sky - reflecting a world I used to love.
I lift my face to the burning sun, its warmth
brings no comfort, not anymore.
The water looks cool, soothing, far below.
I lean forward catching a glimpse of the
person I have become.
I hear footsteps - anxious voices shouting,
disturbing my thoughts.
The water beckons, its depths inviting.
I must hurry - they mustn't stop me.
The water is getting closer, the images blurred,
then there is nothing, just the blackness and
cold, pulling me down, deeper and deeper.
It's finally over.

Susie Field

INSPIRED BY NATURE

You wake up in the morning
And what do you see?
The wonders of the world
And Mother Nature looking back at me.
You open your mind and take the fresh air in
Hark! You can even hear all the birds singing.
The heavenly blue skies above
Stretched out like a blue carpet
And the birds singing of love.

Sun rising up above
Just like a mother showing you her love,
Lighting your way and giving you strength
Showing you the light and the steps that you tread.
The rippling oceans and the babbling brooks
With the swaying of the trees,
The flowers, the butterflies, and the buzzing of the bees
The colours of the flowers in abundance to be seen.
The greenness of the grass
Like the windmills blowing around you as you walk past.
Close your eyes and I will take you to the ocean shores
The running of the oceans passing you by,
Look into your mind and you can see the azure sky.
White clouds above
Like angels playing their harps to the flowers below
Caressing their petals and taking away the rain and the snow.
What a wondrous sight, next comes the flowers in the fields
Their beauty astounds us; they tug at your heels,
Array of beautiful colours, so peaceful and surreal.

Buttercups all around
Hanging like trumpets making their sound.
Bluebells in abundance like a carpet thrown at your feet
Forget-me-nots are standing like a king upon his seat.
Daisies all around, peeking through the grass
Looks like they are saying,
Please look at me when you walk past!
The buds are bursting forth on the trees
Waiting to flower saying, 'Hurry up please!'
The sandy shores, pebbles all around
Waves a-crashing, you can even hear their sounds.
There's also peace and quiet, if you want to go there too

The quietness on the still waters just waiting there for you.
Frogs asleep on the waters that flow
Lily pads opening up and saying, 'Hello.'

This Mother Earth, is such an adventure,
That's why I'm so inspired
'Inspired by nature'.

Mary Woolvin

TEMPUS

It nibbles away, at each of our years;
ingesting our months one by one.
Our weeks are a part of its diet,
with days gobbled up as they run.

There is no way that we can control it,
to reduce, or increase its trend.
With none of us here when it started,
though each of us, will be at its end.

Some will accuse it of flying;
to suggest it stands still, is untrue.
The rate of its travel is constant;
it's a fable to say that it flew.

The effect on our lives is tremendous,
with its unidirectional trend:
a feature that stops it reversing,
keeping nature in step to the end.

It has a poor record for waiting,
as time cannot halt for a day.
Time helps the aged get older
for time's in control of . . . decay.

I'd love to reverse its direction,
for part of the past to regain;
to satisfy one of my wishes,
and make me a child once again.

Bill Austin

EARTHQUAKE

Run for the wind
Breathe for the hills
Beneath the grass, embers burn
A change in the air
The feeling has moved
The man in the moon is anxious
Nothing is here tonight

Aching, aching, pounding, breaking,
The leaves fall, as Nature dies
From gold to red the sky turns
The stars make their appearance
. . . We'll watch, wait for a time
Nothing will move
The night sky dances for no one but the pure souls
The Earth's core explodes
Human debris and ill-laid foundations spill
And we wonder why we're so disturbed

If skin colour didn't matter
If we were born colour-blind
Would it make a difference?
Would the angels still cry,
And the sun hide itself in shame
For bringing life into this world?
Would God still count his losses
And declare us his biggest mistake?
Like an orphan abandoned by its parents,
The Earth sings softly,
And rocks itself to sleep.
What happened to the saviours that came before us,
And the saviours yet to come?

They ran for the wind,
And breathed for the hills,
And watched the night sky dance
As embers burned,
Quietly through the night.

Emma Mackintosh

SUNSHINE

If the sun could he held in a bottle
Like the rain that seems always to be,
Would a little once taken at breakfast,
Keep us happy at least until tea?
If it came in a jar like the honey, all sweet like buttermilk spread.
So to eat it each day by the spoonful, or pour it on sweet warm new bread.
We all feel much better for sunshine, and a smile fits much better than frown,
Would depression no more be a problem, with the shadows dispersed from the
town?
Could we have it perhaps on prescription, and free to all people in need,
Would it finish maybe on the black market, making money for people with greed?
There's a price put on everything these days,
Even air that we warm sometimes cool,
So what's left with no tag is emotion,
Be it sadness or playing the fool.
If a smile helps you feel good each morning, and a scowl brings you lines later
on,
Take the sun with your toast,
If it's there, make the most,
Come tomorrow it all could be gone.

Doreen Foster

LIGHT ON THE WATER

Light on the water,
Splinters of fire
Pale as the starlight
Flash and expire,
Dark under shadows
Scatter like spray
Caught by the darkness,
Fragments of day.
Frost on the water
Light as the foam,
Wisps of quicksilver
Hurrying home,
Softer than snowflakes,
Slender as eels,
Dance in the ghostlight
Intricate reels.
Rising and falling
To music unheard,
Flashes of moonlight
Flit like a bird,
Flicker like laughter
Fading as soon;
Light on the water
Tears of the moon.

Michael Cotton

THE TSUNAMI

Once you were my friend and now you are my deadly foe,
Once you gave me life and now you snatch it from me.
The quiet lapping water's edge became an ugly deadly force
Destroying all that lay in its relentless driving path.

You left contorted and twisted the lives of gentle people
That had treated you as a friend and life giver.
The gentle balmy evenings we dreamily spent admiring you
Have turned into hellish nightmares in an instant.

How can we ever trust you again, you betrayed us,
Taking our loved ones, our friends and means of living.
We will find it hard to rebuild our lives and houses
But rebuild we must, we owe it to the past and the future.

Maggie Lawrance

THE TRAGEDY IN AUTUMN

The leaves of hues all so different
Drift gently from the trees to the ground
Covering the young girl's body
As it vanishes beneath shapeless mound

Autumn paints all nature's beauty
But hides tragedy that's best left unseen
For if found only grief will be on offer
For the loss of young life that might have been

Nature destroys so that it can rebuild
New life taking over from old
But mankind will destroy for its own selfish aims
That's why this young girl's body lies deserted and cold

Why was Man cursed with such evil genes
That makes him kill and destroy without qualm
And sadly the young ones will suffer the most
Are the innocents that would wish him no harm.

Don Woods

CULVER CLIFF TOP

Stark barbwire fences enclose the green;
A battered tightly belted scene.
A row of cottages defy the gale
And if they could speak could tell a tale.

The sheep make up a sorry band
Clumped together against wind and sand.
Their twisted horns plough furrows in the grass,
Grazing dutifully their time will pass.

The jackdaws and the seagulls talk
Of times gone by when puffins walked
Upon the cliff top that they love
And not to forget the culver dove.

Folk have leapt down past the chalky hues
In sad attempts to beat the blues.
And now the sorry scene allows
Peace amidst the dampened boughs,

Of trees stumped and bare on cliff's top edge
Where the peregrine nests her young to fledge.
Then soaring down from leaden skies
The raven seeks the rabbit's eyes.

The fingers of the hawthorn write
The story of the rabbit's plight.
And whilst the ramblers hurry on
Bent beneath the skylark's song.

Their footprints pin the poppy where
The rabbit no longer scents the air.
Mankind's cruel germ unleashed
Put paid to his life's natural feast.

Carol Lyon

AN ACORN LIES WITHIN THE SNOW

Beneath this oak with branches strong
Where birds once filled each morn with song,
Through winter, spring and summer, fall
Their graceful tunes did softly call,
We saw the buds and then the leaves
But now for us December grieves,
For love that died so long ago
An acorn lies within the snow.

Through summer in its restful shade
So many promises we made,
That we would stay forever one
But now all hope of joy has gone,
With passing days when skies so blue
When flowers bloomed for me and you,
But as the icy wind does blow
An acorn lies within the snow.

When autumn came this oak stood bare
No longer did we linger there,
The circle of our love complete
Had turned so sour, no longer sweet,
No feeling left within each heart
We sadly drifted far apart,
Now all alone as tears do flow
An acorn lies within the snow.

Andrew Blakemore

SEPTEMBER SUNDAY

Sunlit gardens, mowers busy on yielding lawns
Below a sea-blue sky the children laugh and play.
Chimney smoke spiralling upwards forming small clouds of vapour,
No other clouds in sight.
Welcoming smells of Sunday lunches
To whet a multitude of London appetites.

Let me guide you, stranger, unborn at this time:
I am memory, and now I carry you over suburban rooftops
Crowned with chimney pots.

Look down and see this peaceful city
Shining in September sun.
High above winding Thames, warehouses, jetties, docks,
Mooried ferries and pleasure boats,
Ships from many lands - all quiet now under the Sunday sky.
Keep close - let us descend into a watchful street
Far from small suburban pleasures.
Behind this ordinary door
The people here are sharing unspoken fears, prophetic glances,
Gathering with stifled breath outside the room of destiny.
Within an ashen-faced elderly man,
Frock coated, wing collared,
Sits at the long table before the black icon
Which waits to convey his message round the world.
A red light blinks, holds steady,
His thin hands strive to hold the paper
Which flutters like a dying heartbeat.
Then his words, 'I am speaking to you from the cabinet room of ten Downing
Street,' and so to, 'I have to tell you now that no such undertaking has been
received, and that consequently this country is at war with Germany'.
As the old man's words enter a million wireless sets
And pulsate into those peaceful homes
Someone, somewhere, sets off an air raid siren - a hellish wail of warning.
In Hendon a mother drops the Sunday lunch upon the living room carpet:
The country freezes, appalled: 'Dear God, has it begun so soon?'
No, a private plane, going cheerfully about its business
Picked up by secret radar panicked unthinking response.
Look, child of the future, do you see our fair island
Bestir itself to instant readiness - tell me what you see.
Yes - sunlit gardens, mowers busy, children laughing,
And the quiet calls to Sunday lunches, under a cloudless sky.

They have heard the accidental siren call of death
And on this perfect day dismiss its warning.

Not long to wait before its dreadful wail
Becomes a daily music - no accident now.
The children's laughter stops
Lawnmowers are silent,
And into our clear and peaceful skies
Intrude the crowds, the dark metallic clouds
Of unrelenting bombers.

Mike Shannon

SOUND

Shrieking like a kettle
the wind is burning cold
a night made for radiators
is coming to town.

My windows shake as if
the force of night
is crying for attention
on this howling evening.

Kissing and whispering
the hard rattling wind
brings voices on the air
sluggish trains and fast cars

echo on the breeze.
Then thunder cracks
the sky rolls heavy with rain
tapping on my window

like a pianist playing
some crazy abstract composition
which ends right in the middle
of a note.

Phil Knight

PERSONAL HARVEST

Clean crisp air filling my lungs
Fading warmth from the summer sun
Walking on frosty crunchy leaves
A stream of hot breath behind me
Berries that glisten and icy dew
Fluffed up birds rest in the trees
Walking in the woodland
Trees now lying dormant
Shedding their multicoloured leaves
A round white sun now fills the sky
Clear blue with wispy clouds
Picnic blankets and sticky lollies gone
Get ready to hibernate the animals cry
Gather the nuts and berries
Ready yourself for winter's approach
Autumn is a magical time
There really is no reason or rhyme
As the wheel of the year slowly turns
Each season brings with it, its own cheer
I really do wish you were here
Walking with me in this lovely place
Such a wonderful sight
And feeling of grace.

Jane Cooter

NATURE

How fresh the wind, in the open field,
Nature, her rich harvest will surely yield,
Tiny mice, scamper amidst the hay,
The hedgehog, scurries along his way,

Buttercups and daisies, together raise their heads,
The butterflies, flicker, through the garden beds,
Busy bees, buzz, through meadows of green,
How verdant, and rich, the rustic scene,

Reynard, the fox, chases after the hens,
But quickly they run, back to their pens,
Farmer Giles, raises his eyes to the sky,
The sweat on his brow, not yet dry,

How lovely the sky, sprinkled with stars,
Weary children go home, tadpoles in jars,
The cattle and sheep, settle down to sleep,
The beauty of nature, it goes so deep!

Ann Rowell

HENSHARD MY DONKEY

Henshard my love I've shed so many tears,
Since you were put down after 36 years,
The donkey sanctuary rang me today,
To tell me Henshard had passed away,
His liver had stopped working, he'd been given a pill
But nothing had stopped him being so ill,
They had to put him down last week,
Because the illness had made him shriek.
So special a donkey I hope he's in Heaven
His grave is now at Sidmouth, Devon,
I'm going soon to that special place
To see your body and hear your case,
I'll never forget you Henny dear
And as you're in Heaven I'll see you there.

Mary Rose

LOOK UP

I look towards a starry sky
The vessel of a million lights
And with my inner eye perceive
A multitude of silver threads

They join each diamond sparkling bright
In place on that black velvet cloth
And with a sudden trembling awe
I see the hand that set them all

How much like a jewel-encrusted sword
It would appear to those who saw
His needle stitch light to the stars
And hang this shroud above our fathers.

Frederic J Greenall

AUGURS OF EXPERIENCE

Silver whorls locked in future time,
Trace the tree of lilac-blossom ancestry;
Falling down the ages like quick lime,
Into a darkly pit of broken family.

Lost through time, apple-mead scents,
Burning narcissus, now black embers.
An iron grate, lost to sense,
Whitened soul, poison, remembers.

Break the willow, morning gardenia,
Sent to a green paradise, circled by stones.
Chestnut pink candles mirror verbena,
Reflecting lights of aged moans.

Moonchild brighter than spangled heaven,
Starry-night prism shatters,
Cradle's kernel is lucky seven,
A new light beckons, a demon scatters.

Hilary West

A HOUSEFLY'S LAMENT

My life as a housefly is often abused
For anything that's handy to swat me is used
Or when I am flying around in the room
You grab for the fly spray to hasten my doom

Oh, I don't know how my little body could
Grieve you so, for I just want to share your food
I'm the friendliest insect you'll ever see
I never sting, I'm not like a bee

I crawl all over you when I can
To worry you is not my plan
I only wish to share your life
I'm much more constant than a wife

So next time when, on you I land
Do not slap me with your hand
Or point the spray to do me down
Just stroke my little body brown

For your reward I'll do my best
To be your constant merry guest
And save you from a life of woe
For which you'll thank me ever so.

Royston E Herbert

TRAVELLING NORTH

There is no end to the white fog
and freezing mists of wintertime
which link the drifting snows and heavy skies
from late November until the middle of March.

Incredible incidents of nature
crack the ghostly shroud of frozen scenes
as a white hare struggles in slow loping movements
across our view, extending a mirage of action
in the eerily silent surroundings.

Storks' nests, abandoned temporarily,
survive the rigours of galeforce winds,
snowstorms and blizzards,
like sentries perched on high,
waiting for the end of bitter purgatory.

The dogs which guard the isolated houses
bark hoarse and feeble signals of our passing,
then muster up the strength to nourish their weak frames
with a few mouthfuls from their bowls of freezing scraps
before retreating to what comfort they can find
against the most sheltered gable wall.

The snowdrops of earlier years are distant memories
of new life which came and went, now lost in forgetfulness,
like lines of sparsely vegetated trees
pointing to dim and hazy paths,
leading uncertainly towards nothingness.

The long, slow coldness numbs body, mind and soul,
reflecting nature's rote in human pain.
Patiently we await the end of this unliving
until the world from which we came revives again.

But there is no certainty that it will ever come.
Expectation is absent and hope an alien thought
as in the mind there is no end
to the white fog and freezing mists of wintertime.

Gerry Miller

NATURE'S MUSIC

I sat and watched the ballet of the flowers:
Dancing to the music of a summer breeze,
Filling the air with perfumed showers.

Nature's music soothes the soul in troubled hours:
Aided by orchestrations of the birds and bees,
I sat and watched the ballet of the flowers.

This overture to life, a tribute to Earth's powers,
In tune with the sigh of leaves in the trees
Filling the air with perfumed showers.

These are the moments of the day to savour,
Listening to the rustling rhythm of the breeze,
I sat and watched the ballet of the flowers:

Butterflies float on air in this waving bower,
Wings beating to the tune, enter the honey bees
Filling the air with perfumed showers.

Webs of floating lace hang spun by the sower,
A petal falls and drifts as upon the open seas,
I sat and watched the ballet of the flowers:
Filling the air with perfumed showers.

J Clarke

REVIVAL OF A POET

Months and months without inking the pages,
My quill yearns to tango on blank pages
And the white papers long to shine in indigo joy.

The skies unfold their wings to embrace my new ghazals and haikus,
The silver clouds quickly return to read my new sonnets and free verses.
And the wrens hover in mid-air, waiting for poetry month, April.

The hissing river weaves happiness while the grass, a joyful rise.
Lilies and bluebells flare up like fireworks, tulips and roses sway in harmony.
Soon, a dead poet will revive to recite his poems to all.

Tri Tran

NEAR THE END OF LIFE

The man puffed the small cigar
Outside, the autumn leaves falling
Gold leaves covering the lawn
Reminding him winter was near.
He sat in his old rocking chair
Remembering his working life
Horses pulling, sunny days.
In his mind he could hear the hooves
Time dictated by seasons
Time for laughing, crying and smiling.
He remembered his long departed wife.
And as he enjoyed the memory
He died of cancer as expected.

Jenny Bosworth

SNOWING

For the two days snow
fell in faltering sprees
but managed to cover the Earth
like a vest settling on the ribbed body
spreading in its egg-whiteness
until the sun broke its shell
and gave way to the rind
Earth skinned back to new green blotches
and from resisting distance
and melted heaps -
looked like fins of a colossal fish -
hibernating over the Earth
every moment the broken accumulations
around the trees and paths
made crackling chinks
for eyes to peep
and the guesswork began
but the trees boasted white forked hands
stranded in their pensioned life
and wrapped protests
like islands colonised
but the snow kept the Earth
under its regimen.

Rizwan Akhtar

SPRING-HEELED JACK

In the city of London,
One dark and wintry night,
High upon its rooftops,
There stood a ghastly sight.

Clad in an old trench coat,
With grizzly, fingerless gloves,
His face is a haunting wreck
That would surely scare off the doves.

Climbing onto the window sill
Where his sleeping victim lay,
He knew what he was about to do,
That the voice would not stay.

Jumping onto the chimney top,
With the boy's voice in hand,
He slid it into a pocket jar
As if it were like sand.

He hurried back to his little cave,
That wretched mountain troll
And he placed the little wisp
Into a nice, warm hole.

So, listen up, you horrible lot
And heed my warning clear,
Behave yourselves and treasure
The voices you hold dear.
Mwahahahahahahahaha!

Christopher Leahy

THE VEIL

You are a veil, so red and painfully torn
Through battle thorns and emotions wild
Your mind cannot repair you, so deeply worn
You hide yourself away, blemished little child

Through battle thorns and emotions wild
Friend and foe, confused in your threads
You hide yourself away, blemished little child
You cannot hide, even thinking weighs as lead

Friend and foe, confused in your threads
Trust - a long lost myth, hope amiss
You cannot hide, even thinking weighs as lead
Hopeless you mend your threads and reminisce

Trust - a long lost myth, hope amiss
Anger rises, as tears solemnly fall
Hopeless you mend your threads and reminisce
Good times fade while threads disenthrall

Anger rises, as tears solemnly fall
Comforts fly as darkness laughs
Good times fade while threads disenthrall
Wounds expand, you're near in half

Comforts fly as darkness laughs
You question the light that loves you still
Wounds expand, you're near in half
Yet a light is growing and slowly fills

You question the light that loves you still
Your mind cannot repair you, so deeply worn
Yet a light is growing and slowly fills
You are a veil, so red and painfully torn.

Jeremy Paul

LIFE

Sleeping silhouette awash
With the lamplight's golden glimmer,
Haunting memories are flowing
Youthful days, soft beauty glowing,
Tassels white fluorescent shimmer
On silken dress and beaded cloche.

Recalling next your wedding day
The tall young groom so pale and nervous,
Happiness so sweet exuding
Soon through bliss a child including
Gone to war he fell in service
Your love remains in Normandy.

Sadness and pain, yet thankfully
Thoughts of joy and laughter brew,
Great-grandchild with *your* soldier's eyes
Awakens you with childhood cries,
Inherent blood from both of you
Giving life eternally.

Elizabeth Scharer

ME, JULIAN OF NORWICH AND HER CAT

'Only the cat can come and go at will
and the rats of course. She never goes out,
part of her job. I on the other hand
have to wait until the curtain opens,
until the queue works its way to myself
and I can ask her advice, her counsel,
about my mother-in-law, a woman with tongue
so sharp and viperous, even tame snakes
slither away to be out of harm's reach.
How can my wife, so docile, so loving
have been birthed from the groins of this Grendel?'

Julian looks at me with eyes of jade-green.
I think they change colour as needs present.
She just gazes, not a word forthcoming.
'All at once I see my wife's dear mother
bereft of her only daughter, the light
of her life giving all her precious love
to someone else, someone other than her,
and that someone is me. Oh Lardy-do.'

I thank Julian, doff my soft cap to her.
She still has not murmured a single word,
but I am at peace. The cat sidles up
as I leave, follows me to the side gate.
Near the latched door huddle seven kittens,
look-a-likes of their mother, all miaowing.
'Now one of these will sweeten the old crone,
let the milk of human kindness flow again.'

Away he walks with one under each arm.

Kaaren Whitney

THE FEAR OF LIFE

There's nothing to fear
But fear itself.
The fear of fearing it
Will tear you up so much
That the air you breathe
Will become contaminated.
Contaminated with emotions, sickness and confusion.
Why do we become afraid?
Why don't we just evolve and grow
And face these new challenges ahead of us?
I'll tell you why, because we are so scared
Of falling and messing up,
That we drown in our fears,
Letting it swallow us whole and spit us out,
With the remainders of guilt, sorrow and pain.
What goes up must come down they say.
But why do we acknowledge this saying
But still fight our way up there just to fall again?
The reason for this is we're scared
That in our lifetime we won't get that feeling of accomplishment.
So we go up, inevitably just to fall down.
All good things come to an end.
If this is true why do we even start
Trying to make all these great things in our lives
When we know sooner or later
It will be gone in a puff of smoke?
Probably just to *feel* something
Or probably just to *taste* happiness.
Who knows unless you have been in that position.
But all I am telling you is when you have something good
Hold on to it *tight*.
So tight that the feeling you have suffocates you with delight,
Because for all you know,
That could be your last shot at something good.
So don't fear what's round the corner
Stand up tall and conquer!

Sherelle Foreshaw

ELIZABETH

Down the road walks a girl
A ring on her finger, the stone is a pearl,
Head up, marching along,
Singing herself a small little song.
Wavy long hair loosely tied up,
It streams right behind her, a symbol of luck,
If it were untied it'd drop to her knees,
So golden it is - as golden as bees.
Beside her side walks her faithful dog
It is very strong - it could lift a log,
And the butterflies happily twirl
Beside the girl.
She brings happiness every step she takes,
As she passes by his window, the grumpy baker smiles as he bakes
But nobody knew her name or address -
So nobody could come to her house as a guest.
And nobody would ever know her name,
Some people said, 'She'll tell us when she's a dame,'
And others still wouldn't know because of the death
But you and I know - she's Elizabeth!

Olga Fenton

DISEASE

Bullets are firing,
Babies are crying.
Cannons are blasting,
People are not lasting.
A house burns down,
A man goes with it,
The death toll rises by another one.

Bombs crash down,
Devastating the whole town.
Soldiers run about,
They hear people scream and shout.
A man turns around,
Bang!
It's too late.
The death toll rises by another one.

Children can't go out to play,
Instead they're trapped inside to pray.
A plane flies overhead,
Then we realise another soldier is dead.
The death toll rises by another one.

War is a disease,
It's a major killer!
So let's join hands and work together,
To stop this number from rising,
Forever and ever.

Dilmeet Sangha

OUR TRAVELLING DAYS

Life is a journey we all make
Another travelling day when we awake
Onwards, onwards merrily we tread
Nothing that lies before us dread
Joys and sorrows will come our way
With faith and courage we'll win the day
Our way may be a smooth or stony path
Face each step with a song and a laugh
Life's journey begins at our birth
When we first entered this Earth
Childhood and our salad days
Then follows middle and old age
We will journey to places near and far
By plane, train, bus or car
Widening our knowledge of the history of Man
Experiences to see us through our life's span
Each day we gaily travel along
Leaving behind yesterday that's gone
We mustn't look back with a wishful eye
Because new adventures before us lie
Life is a journey indeed
Onwards, onwards, unto the end we proceed
Take the good with the bad
There's no time to remain sad
Each stage and chapter of life's highway
We explore and travel along it every day
For none of us can escape
The journey of life everyone must make.

Kathleen Fry

FORWARD PRESS INFORMATION

We hope you have enjoyed reading this book - and that you will continue to enjoy it in the coming years.

If you like reading and writing poetry drop us a line, or give us a call, and we'll send you a free information pack.

Alternatively if you would like to order further copies of this book or any of our other titles, then please give us a call or log onto our website at www.forwardpress.co.uk.

Forward Press Information
Remus House
Coltsfoot Drive
Peterborough
PE2 9JX
(01733) 890099